# THE DEGÜELLO

Scott A. Zastrow

# THE DEGÜELLO

ISBN:
ISBN-13: 978-1-977-04645-1

# DEDICATION

To Lizzie—

My greatest ally in this walk through life, who has always known the difference between the myth and the reality.

Roll on, Little Sister.

# ACKNOWLEDGMENTS

It is better to write for yourself and have no public than to write for the public and have no self.
—Cyril Connolly

This book is for the men of the Triple Nickel, ODA 555 (+). From start to finish, no one even came close.

There is such thing as a "natural soldier": the kind who derives his greatest satisfaction from male companionship, from excitement, and from the conquering of physical obstacles. He doesn't want to kill people as such, but he will have no objection if it occurs within a moral framework that gives him justification—like war—and if it is the price of gaining admission to the kind of environment he craves. Whether such men are born or made, I do not know, but most of them end up in armies. But armies are not full of such men. They are so rare that they form only a modest fraction even of small professional armies, mostly congregating in the commando-type Special Forces.

—Gwen Dyer
War

# Part I

# The Triple Nickel

CPT Luke Walen (Team Leader)

MSG Frank Galliano (Team Sergeant)

SFC Anthony DeNero (AST)

SSG Shane Speakman: 18B (Weapons)

SSG John "Rusty" Little: 18B (Weapons)

SSG Blaine Bastogne: 18C (Engineer)

SFC Steve Greenwell: 18D (Medic)

SFC Alan Scott: 18D (Medic)

SFC John "JT" Thompson: 18E (Commo)

TSG Calvin Michaels (Air Force CCT)

# CHAPTER 1

*Beware the fury of a patient man.*
-John Dryden
*Absalom and Achitophel* (1680)

## Eighty-three miles west of Juarez, Texas along the Mexico border

### September 2001

A 1984 Ford F-150 pickup truck accelerated down a desert road, leaving behind it a smoke screen of desert dust. Closely behind, a Border Patrol Blazer painted white with green accents, with police lights across the top, barreled through the thick cloud of dust weaving from side to side to get a glimpse of clear road ahead. The chase continued for several miles, over rolling terrain in the West Texas desert.

A Mexican man with long, unkempt hair held in place with an old red bandana stuck his head out of the passenger window of the pickup truck and fired a burst of bullets from an old, military-grade M-16 at the Border Patrol vehicle. Several rounds cracked the windshield; several more broke the red plastic cover of the police lights atop the pursuing vehicle. One of the Border

Patrol agents leaned out of the passenger window and returned fire with the same Colt .45 he'd used for seventeen years.

As the chase came around a large bend and through the mouth of two hills creating a pass in the mountainous desert, something pierced the hood of the lead vehicle, causing billowing smoke to erupt from the engine. Seconds later, another round penetrated the front grille, and the truck rolled to a stop. The two men in the truck threw open their doors and unleashed a barrage of automatic gunfire at the Border Patrol vehicle, causing its driver to lock its brakes and go into a side spin to the right. The driver's side of the vehicle was now in the direct line of sight of the two men in the pickup truck and exposed to their hail of bullets. The front tire of the Blazer exploded in a cloud of dust. Bullets peppered the engine compartment and moved rearward as the two Border Patrol agents hurriedly tried to exit the vehicle through the passenger door.

The driver was struck in the back as he slid across the seat, trying to escape the overwhelming fire superiority. His partner dragged him to safety behind the front tire and engine block of the Blazer, which were now totally riddled with bullet holes. He immediately returned fire with his Colt but emptied his magazine quickly and dropped down to one knee to reload. He glanced down at his partner, who was lying face down in the dust, blood coming from the back of his left shoulder. He was still conscious and writhing in pain.

The agent reached up to his left shoulder and squeezed the hand-mic on the radio attached to his uniform. "I need some help here!"

With the pause in gunfire, the smuggler saw his chance to attack. As he ran forward, suddenly his right shoulder exploded, sending blood and bone fragments forward several feet as a large-caliber round pierced his scapula. His right arm, still clutching its weapon, fell from his torso. Staring at own his missing limb, the stunned man fell slowly to the ground in complete shock and exsanguinated swiftly.

The passenger of the pickup truck slowly stood erect and stared bug-eyed at his fallen compadre.

Meanwhile, several more Chevy Blazers marked with Border Patrol emblems on their sides, and with police lights flashing, came in from both directions on the road, sliding to a halt in a cloud of dust. Within seconds, a dozen uniformed agents, armed with automatic weapons, surrounded the perpetrator, yelling commands in Spanish for him to drop his weapon. The man, still visibly in shock, continued to stare at his limbless partner on the ground in front of their vehicle. The Border Patrol agents quickly surrounded the bewildered man, took his weapon, and placed him in handcuffs.

A medic wearing full tactical gear tore through the wounded agent's shirt, exposing his gunshot wound. He pulled a roll of gauze from a chest pouch and wiped the blood away from the wound to get a better view of the damage. The medic quickly dressed the wound. He continued to perform his primary survey on the wounded officer, checking for any other potentially life-threatening wounds. Satisfied, he set up a sodium chloride IV as the shadow of a helicopter covered the two men for a single second, breaking the scorching sun's rays. Most of the Border Patrol agents on the ground looked up and followed the sound of the helicopter but looked directly into the sunlight. The glare caused some of them to put their hands up to their eyes.

\* \* \*

"Coyote two-three, this is Tumbleweed five-five, ready for extraction."

"Roger, Tumbleweed, en route to your location. Two Mikes."

On a hillside plateau, a mile away from the scene below, Sergeant John "Rusty" Little, a sniper from ODA 555 emerged from under the desert camouflage netting covering his riflescope and stood erect. He was wearing a ghillie suit fitted with fake weeds and sticks identical to the surrounding terrain, making him almost invisible from the ground below or the air above. He had different shades of tan camouflage paint on his face in a pattern completely random but with a hint of organized application. There was a coiled earpiece in his left ear, attached to the AN PRC-148 radio on his chest.

Sweat poured down his face and neck. He'd been out in the sun for hours, waiting for his moment. He pulled a small water bottle from his cargo pocket and took a long-needed drink. He'd replaced the water bottle in his pocket and reached down to pick up his Barett Model 82A1 .50 caliber sniper rifle by the carrying handle when the familiar helicopter shadow overflew his position.

"Tumbleweed five-five, this is Coyote two-three. We have visual of your beacon. Prepare for extraction," called the pilot of an EH-6B Little Bird from the 160th Special Operations Aviation Regiment (SOAR).

Seconds later, the small, single-engine helicopter with a clear "bubble" cockpit landed within feet of Rusty on the plateau. He approached the helicopter from the pilot side, placed his rifle in the storage area inside the Bird, and sat on the exterior troop seat. The Little Bird's engine whined high, and the copter lifted off as quickly as it landed, flying off into the horizon.

* * *

"Chaos five-five, this is Coyote two-three. We have picked up the package and are returning to base," called the pilot.

"Roger, Coyote. Tango Mike. Chaos out," returned the call from Sergeant Shane Speakman, the senior weapons sergeant of the Triple Nickel.

Sergeant Speakman was wearing civilian clothes and looked innocuous among the Border Patrol agents. With the classic civilian garb of tan cargo pants, hiking boots, Oakley sunglasses, and tan shirt with photographer's vest, Shane blended in well in the desert environment—except for his tan hat with the Combat Diver logo on the front and "Triple Nickel" embroidered across the top.

"Mr. Speakman," the Border Patrol agent said, gesturing for Shane to join him by the pickup truck.

"What do you got, Nate?" Shane replied.

The agent used his eyes and a slight head nod in the direction of the canvas tarp in the back of the old truck. He reached down to his cargo pocket, pulled out a pocketknife, and cut the twine that was holding down the tarp. Once he cut through several small strands of twine, he pulled back the tarp, exposing a sizable pile of M-16 rifles. There were also several boxes of 5.56mm ammunition and a large trash bag with M-16 magazines in them.

The two men looked at each other and began to grin. Speakman walked two steps forward to get within arm's reach of the agent and reached out to him with his fist. The agent responded in kind with a teenager-like fist bump.

"Great job, Nate. You guys should be proud. How's Fernando?" Speakman inquired, referring to the wounded officer.

"Medic says he's going to be just fine. He's on his way to the hospital now. We appreciate everything, Shane."

"We got lucky that truck stalled," Shane said as he walked away from the pickup.

"Yeah. Lucky," the agent replied sarcastically. "Stalled, my ass," he said under his breath as he walked to the front of the vehicle and looked at the massive hole in the hood, still leaking steam from the busted hoses. He reached up with his right hand and placed his index finger into the hole created by the .50-caliber round, and then he turned toward the general area from which Rusty had made the shot. He held up his right hand to block the sun but saw nothing but

hills in the desert. The agent put on his mirrored sunglasses, cracked a smirk, and walked back to his bullet-ridden vehicle.

Sergeant Speakman got in his unmarked patrol car, a white Chevrolet Caprice. He turned the vehicle around and drove away from the scene, with a long trail of desert dust billowing behind his vehicle. He looked up into his rear-view mirror and caught a glimpse of the agent

watching him. He was surrounded by half a dozen Border Patrol vehicles with their lights flashing and a dozen or so uniformed men taking pictures, placing flares in the road outside the scene, and writing in their tablets the circumstances of today's events. Of course, there would be no mention of the rounds to the vehicle's hood, how the Mexican culprit lost his arm, or the helicopter that no one actually saw. Speakman was acting in an advisory role and had no part in the apprehension of the suspects or discovery of the weapons.

This was the just the way these men liked it.

The only attention they would get from this incident would be in the form of questions about why it took Rusty two shots to stop the truck.

# CHAPTER 2

*Freedom itself was attacked this morning by a faceless coward, and freedom will be defended ... The resolve of our great nation is being tested. Make no mistake: we will show the world that we will pass this test.*

-George W. Bush
Barksdale Air Force Base, Louisiana

## September 11, 2001

"Enter the water," echoed a voice from a handheld megaphone pointed at the twenty-four men standing on the gunnel of the pool. Seconds later, there was a large splash in the deep end as the candidates took one large step forward.

Gardner Pool in Fort Campbell, Kentucky, was a newer pool with a mechanical retractable roof that was pulled back on sunny days to let in the fresh air and sunshine. On this cool September morning, there was a nice layer of steam rising from the warmed pool water.

Poolside, Special Forces Operational Detachment Alpha (ODA) 555, AKA the "Triple Nickel," was training twenty-four fellow Green Berets for success in scuba school. Although the candidates were all fellow Special Forces soldiers and friends, the atmosphere was that of drill sergeant and basic trainee. This relationship was imperative because of the dangerous training taking place.

Without the control over every aspect of training, serious, life-threatening accidents could happen.

Five of the scuba team members, dressed in UDT shorts, silky black T-shirts with a shark logo on the left breast, and soft-soled dive booties, were standing on the deck of the pool, yelling instructions to the students in the water. The candidates were repeatedly entering and exiting the pool, wearing full dive gear consisting of twin 80cc tanks, an eighteen-pound weight belt, buoyancy compensation devices, mask, booties, and fins. This exercise continued until they worked as a team and splashed all together as one unit.

This skill, although seemingly simplistic, is extremely difficult to master at first. If one person is early or late, he might fall on—or be fallen on by—a fellow diver wearing upwards of one hundred pounds of dive gear, which could result in a fatality.

Some of the ODA members were acting as safety swimmers in the water, swimming around with fins, masks, and snorkels and observing the tasks from an underwater perspective. They relayed to the cadre on the deck what they observed below the surface, and who needed extra attention.

There were also several civilian lifeguards working at the pool who usually tried not to interfere with the training, even though it went against everything they were taught to do. Men on the verge of drowning—flailing around in the deep end, coughing up water—and shallow water blackouts were daily occurrences in Pre-Scuba. It was enough to give any normal lifeguard a stroke. Usually, they gathered in their office and listened to the radio or watched television. There they talked about how easy the training would be for them, had they been given the opportunity to try it.

On the first attempt at entering the water with all twelve students, one of the candidates was a second slower than his peers and landed right on top of the man to his left, catching the J-valve of that man's tank right into his left cheek. One of the safety swimmers on a breath hold at the bottom of the deep end noticed blood starting to flow freely from the man's face. Knowing that blood in the community pool could end training for the day, he quickly finned over to the student who was bleeding, grabbed the front of his buoyancy compensator, and pulled him to the surface.

He signaled two of the instructors on the pool deck, and they reached down and quickly removed the soldier from the pool, in a fashion that showed they had done this hundreds of times before. One of the men in black peeled the man's hand away from his face to see where the blood was coming from and to gauge the extent of the damage. He stood and signaled another cadre member across the pool.

"Steve! We got one for you!" the man yelled.

Sergeant First Class Steve Greenwell was thirty-three years old and a ten-year veteran of Special Forces. He was a short, thick man, standing five-feet nine and coming in at two hundred pounds, hard as a rock. With sandy blond hair and a chiseled jaw line, he was considered a handsome man by many an admirer. Always the class clown, he would never let an opportunity go by to make someone smile, and he was always ready with a laugh at the slightest hint of something jovial. His zest for life and fun had gotten him into trouble more times than he could remember, but to him, it was all worth it: Life is short; have a ball.

"Get his gear off," Steve dictated to the other men in black who were standing on the pool deck.

The cadre followed his direction and systematically removed the soldier's gear, piece by piece, until he was left with nothing but UDT shorts and a brown T-shirt with the name JONES in one-inch black stencil across the front of it. Jones was assisted to a white plastic lawn chair that was against the glass wall of the pool house.

"You're done for the day, Mr. Jones. Take him back to the team room and get him stitched up," Steve directed as he walked away, removing his purple exam gloves.

He returned to his perch atop the diving board, where he had a good view of the students who were still in the pool. He was responsible for the overall safety of the entire training program, and a small laceration to the cheek paled in comparison to other accidents that could happen with all that gear on.

The head lifeguard at Gardner Pool grabbed another doughnut from a box on the desk, filled his coffee cup, and sat in his captain's chair in front of the thirteen-inch television in his office. He was a retired Army man, in his sixties, who had been running the indoor pool at Fort Campbell for many years. He had white hair in a standard, thin comb-over and a rather large midsection—not from overeating, but from ascites, a condition in which fluid is retained in the abdomen but nowhere else in the body.

He worked hand in hand with the SCUBA teams when they ran their pre-scubas to coordinate and schedule the pool hours around the water aerobics and lap swims. He never let an opportunity pass to tell one of the young Green

Berets how easy this training would be for him if he were forty years younger. He had seen many of these courses, and he was always there with a helpful word for the troops, giving them tips and tricks to help them make it through the series of events. Some were helpful; others, not so much.

He was watching CNN when the headline BREAKING NEWS flashed across the screen. As he watched in disbelief, he saw the news that a commercial airliner had struck the World Trade Center in New York City. He stared at the TV in awe, unable to move.

"Oh, my god," he said aloud to the other lifeguards gathered around in the office. He jumped from his desk, went out to the pool deck, and approached Steve, who was encouraging a student to continue his training.

"Let go of the fucking wall!" Steve shouted.

He leaned forward, reached down, and grabbed the man's hands, peeling them off the gunnel of the pool and releasing him back into the deep end. Steve watched him merge back into the traffic of the twenty-three other students, who were swimming in a large circle and wearing eighteen-pound weight belts. Every so often, a tired soldier would make his way to the gunnel and grab a hold of it for dear life. This was followed shortly thereafter by an instructor coming over to offer some words of encouragement, and a helping hand when needed.

"Hey, Steve, you've got to come see this!" the lifeguard yelled as he motioned toward the office.

"What is it?" Steve responded.

"There's been an accident in New York. A plane crashed into the city."

"Really? Wow," Steve responded as he quickly followed the guard back to the office.

They watched in a trance-like state as footage of a burning American landmark was shown from every angle. By now there were about ten people gathered in the office, looking helplessly at the screen.

After about ten minutes, Sergeant First Class John Thompson came into the office, looking slightly angry. "Uh, Steve, are we going to work today?"

John, or JT, was the communications sergeant of the Triple Nickel and was one of the newest men on the detachment. He stood at five-feet ten and weighed 215 pounds, with jet-black hair that was never without a handful of styling gel. He was extremely strong and very confident, but he also had a very calm and cool demeanor. JT was considered one of the most intelligent men in the entire group. Before coming to Special Forces, he worked as a radio repairman, which was an enormous advantage for a communications sergeant. He had the ability to fix nearly anything electronic with a soldering iron and a pocketknife. The only negative thing about this ability was that he was always tinkering with electronics. The Triple Nickel's team room was always cluttered with electronic circuit boards, motherboards from broken computers, video game pieces, and dozens of small pieces of cut wire. If it was electronic, JT could fix it, even if it didn't need fixing.

"Man, this is unbelievable," Steve said as he turned to walk from the office.

Steve followed JT out the door to the pool deck. The students were gathered in the pool with their left arms on the gunnel, preparing to begin their next set of laps around the deep end.

Blaine Bastogne, the Special Forces engineer sergeant on Triple Nickel, was giving the students some constructive criticism on their performance up to this point.

Blaine, thirty, was six-feet two and 225 pounds, with blond hair and blue eyes. He was a big country boy from Kiln, Mississippi, who stereotypically drove a four-wheel-drive truck fit with hunting stickers, gun rack, and Mossy Oak seat covers.

Blaine was the most recent graduate of scuba school, and this was his first pre-scuba as cadre. He had taken a little while to adapt, because of the pain and trouble he'd endured while completing pre-scuba himself several months earlier, which was a common fault among recent graduates. Either they were compassionate, because they knew how hard it was and didn't want to see their friends have to endure such pain; or, because of how difficult it had been for them, they turned up the heat, so everyone felt the pain they had gone through. Blaine was both firm and fair, but he also enjoyed his job.

"You men make me sick," he scolded. "You haven't listened to a word I've said. You can't fight your way through the water. Use your brains, and swim smarter, not harder. You're flailing around like a bunch of wounded geese, with no technique whatsoever. The water is the great equalizer—the harder you work, the less you get. Well, there is no easy way to impart this knowledge. Release the gunnel and start swimming."

The men stared at him with a blank expression, as if to say, you're kidding, right?

"You heard me! Let go of my fucking wall!" he yelled.

Slowly the men released the gunnel, and they began to swim clockwise around the deep end of the pool as the other cadre members smiled at the out-of-character anger Blaine displayed.

Each man in the pool was wearing his weight belt—eighteen pounds of lead weights on a nylon belt—a mask, and fins. Swimming like this was an extremely difficult task to accomplish, even for the most advanced swimmer, as that much weight caused a person to sink quickly. Some would try to kick feverishly to maintain forward momentum, but they only tired out quickly. Others swam slow, almost to a complete stop, and slowly sank toward the bottom of the pool, using every ounce of energy to push to the surface for just an ounce of air. The key was to stay relaxed and keep moving. This event would test everyone and push most to their breaking points.

The other instructors gathered by the diving board to point out the students they were sure would go under and need to be rescued. Steve and JT were discussing the news they had just seen on CNN when the guard again yelled from the doorway of the office, "Hey, Steve, there's been another crash!"

This time Steve, JT, and two other men ran into the office and saw glimpses of both towers ablaze. Fire and smoke were billowing out of them, with debris falling to the street below.

"That is no accident," Steve said aloud to no one in particular.

It would be the only words spoken over the next thirty minutes, as instructors and students alike gathered in the office and watched the TV helplessly as images of death and destruction were flashed continuously across the screen. The banner at the bottom of the broadcast displayed a continuous stream of information such as flight numbers, suspected death toll, and dollar cost of damage so far. No one could believe what they were witnessing.

JT made the call to stop pool training for the rest of the morning and head back to the team room. The students were told to pick up their equipment and load the bus headed back to the classroom, where they would receive classes on such things as diving injuries, dive physics, and nutrition.

Blaine maintained control of the students and got them loaded onto the bus. Some engaged in discussion of the attacks, while others sat stoically in their seats. Each man had his own way of dealing with the tragic news he had just witnessed.

JT and Steve were still glued to the TV in the lifeguard office when another cadre member came in to let them know that the students were on the bus and headed back, and that the pool area was clean.

"All right, let's get out of here," JT said to Steve.

As they began to leave the office, yet another breaking news story came over the airways. A plane had crashed into the Pentagon in Washington DC. Dozens more had been killed, with hundreds wounded. The Green Berets glanced around the room at each other in silence; the expression they wore was a familiar one.

Counter-terrorism was one of the main missions of Special Forces. These men had been involved in combating terrorism in many countries around the world. They had seen it up close and knew its signature—only this time, the terrorists had brought the war to the United States.

They knew that what they were watching was history in the making, but what they didn't know was how the events in New York City would soon alter their lives forever.

# CHAPTER 3

*In every real man a child is hidden that wants to play.*
-Nietzsche

Tink. The familiar sound of a titanium-head Callaway Great Big Bertha driver striking a golf ball echoed on a clear Tuesday morning. The ball sailed long and straight down the fairway, bounced several times, and rolled to a stop some three hundred yards from where it had originated.

The dew was still fresh on the morning grass of Cole Park Golf Course, the only course on Fort Campbell, Kentucky. Sergeant First Class Alan Scott and Master Sergeant Frank Galliano were teeing off on their regular Tuesday morning round.

"Nice ball," Frank muttered almost angrily as he approached the tee box to set up his own ball for a drive.

The pair have been playing golf together for many years. Frank grew up in Long Island, New York, and was a caddie at Shinnecock Hills Golf Club in Southampton, New York, as a teenager. There he saw many great players and became familiar with the secrets of a good golf swing. At forty-two years old, he was the oldest member of the Triple Nickel. He had a break in service several years earlier because he was injured on a dive in Okinawa, Japan, and didn't feel he could contribute what he needed to the team he was on at the time.

He had gone to Texas to be a civilian dive engineer for an oil company, working on their drilling rigs in the Gulf. There he met other former military divers who would sit around and talk about how hard they used to be while in the service. It occurred to Frank that he was not a has-been just yet, and that he could still perform better than most of his peers. With the encouragement of his family, he reenlisted in Special Forces, and he was sent to the 5th Group, where he soon made team sergeant.

Frank was five-feet ten and 215 pounds, with black hair and a thick mustache. His New York Italian-Catholic heritage showed predominantly in the way he looked and talked. Sounding like he came straight from an episode of The Sopranos, he constantly referred to the Triple Nickel as his "family," as he found many similarities between an SF team and a Mafia family. And he ran his team accordingly. He was in charge, and everyone knew it. He was very direct and very clear with his instructions and standards. He held his men accountable to the responsibilities that came with being in the top 1 percent of their profession. His detachment set the highest standard as their minimum standard, and he counseled his men regularly on areas that needed improvement. Much like a parent of teenagers, Frank had made the decision to be a leader, and he did not let friendship get in the way of his ability to command.

Alan, thirty-one, was six-feet tall and 165 pounds, with dark hair, dark eyes, and a deep tan from many hours spent on the golf course. He was the second medical sergeant on the Triple Nickel and a ten-year veteran of Special Forces. Known for his loud voice and arrogant swagger, he was a constant antagonist to the status quo. His overtly aggressive nature and tactless mouth sometimes got him into trouble, both personal and professional.

He was a classic underachiever, with above-average intelligence, who would rather be the class clown than valedictorian. Due to his smaller-than-average physique, he pushed himself harder to prove he belonged in such an elite peer group. He did not believe in the myth surrounding Special Forces, and he knew that just being in the unit was not enough. He strived to be the best at everything he did and considered life a competition. Right now, golf was his passion, because it was a game that could not be beat, and for a perfectionist, that was a hard pill to swallow. Even though he maintained a single-digit handicap while in a profession with such a high operational tempo, he was always working on his game, because there would always be those that were better.

The two have been playing golf almost every Tuesday morning since their introduction, and today would be no different. As Frank stepped up to his ball in the fairway, he was aiming down a much different line than Alan had.

"You'll never bend it around those trees," Alan said as he stared down the line Frank was aiming.

"I'm not going around those trees. I'm going over those trees, with a little draw," Frank responded, with a hand motion to describe the flight his ball would travel.

"Tin Cup, Kevin Costner," Alan came back with a smile.

"Right on," Frank replied, acknowledging Alan's familiarity with golf movies.

It was a common practice in the military to speak in movie quotes. These men spent months on end in foreign countries with no access to television except one local channel and, if they were lucky, CNN World. To make up for it, most deployed A-teams had a morale box with a TV and VCR or DVD player and an extensive video collection. When they watched the same movies over and over on a deployment, they tended to use the best lines in the movie as quotes in their daily conversations with each other. It was a game they played to name the movie once the line was spoken, and if no one could name it, the narrator would state the movie with a condescending tone, as if to say what an easy catch it should have been.

Alan and Frank were no different; in fact, they were very good at it. It was just another way they could show dominance over each other, by knowing obscure quotes from obscure movies the other couldn't recognize.

After Frank hit his ball perfectly down the fairway, he returned to the golf cart with a smile and replaced his club in the bag on the back. The two men drove to their balls in the fairway and grabbed the necessary clubs from their cart. Alan approached his ball and began his

pre-shot routine but paused his setup when he heard approaching sirens in the distance. These were police sirens: a sound much different from that of an ambulance or a fire truck. He heard another, more distinctive, siren from a different direction, causing him to back away from his shot. A Fort Campbell Military Police car raced by on the street to the south. To the west, just outside the fence surrounding the installation, three Clarksville City Police cars went screaming by.

"What the hell's going on?" Frank wondered as he looked around.

"Could they turn those damn things off? I'm trying to concentrate here," Alan responded. "These people have no respect for the game."

He addressed his ball and prepared to make his swing, but the familiar sound of a Palm Treo 600 cell phone echoed from Frank's belt.

"Don't these people know today is my golf day?" Frank said, looking at the number.

"Oh, hell no! Don't you even think about answering that call," Alan complained. "You're not walking away two-up on me."

Frank held the phone up to his ear and walked away from Alan to answer it. He used his other hand to motion for Alan to go ahead and make his shot.

Alan addressed the ball and stared down the green like it was a familiar foe. He pulled the trigger on his swing, sending a perfectly struck ball whistling high over the trees toward the right side of the green and landing softly just forty feet from the pin. He was home in two and looking at eagle.

He glanced back at Frank and saw him staring down at his feet with the cell phone still to his ear. "I suppose you didn't even see that," Alan said, pointing in the direction of the green.

Frank holstered his phone to his belt and looked up at Alan with a look of bewilderment, one Alan had never seen.

"My god, we've been attacked," he said matter-of-factly.

"You got that right," Alan retorted. "You just got attacked by a phenomenal 3 iron that sets me up for an eagle."

"No, really, we're seriously being attacked," Frank answered firmly. "We've got to go."

"What the hell do you mean, we're being attacked? We're on a fucking golf course," Alan replied, gesturing with his hands and arms and looking around the fairway.

"The country, man. Two planes just hit the World Trade Center in New York, and another crashed into the Pentagon." Frank got behind the wheel of the cart. "I can't believe this. The round's over."

"Bullshit," was Alan's immediate response. "You're just trying to get out while you're ahead. You always pull this shit!"

Suddenly, two military police cars came screaming up to the fort's entrance gate, just east of the tee box behind them. The two cars pulled in nose to nose, blocking the entrance, and several MPs jumped out and ran up to the large chain-link gate to pull it closed. They were all wearing full kit: black BDUs, body armor, Kevlar helmets, and load-bearing equipment full of ammo. They carried M-4 carbines with all the bells and whistles: PEQ-2 laser sights, ACOG scopes, forehand grips, Surefire lights, the works.

Seconds later, a Clarksville police car pulled up to the city side of the gate, and two comparably dressed SWAT officers exited their vehicle and approached the gate to talk with the MPs.

"Well, that can't be good," Alan commented sarcastically, looking back at Frank.

"Come on, man, let's go find out what the hell is happening," Frank directed.

The two jumped in their buggy and began the long drive back to the clubhouse. They cut through trees and across several fairways to utilize the shortest route possible.

"Man, that was a good 3 iron," Alan said. He lit a cigarette and then threw his lighter into the storage area of the cart in anger.

"Let it go, man, let it go," Frank replied.

# CHAPTER 4

*A person often meets his destiny on the road he took to avoid it.*
-Jean de La Fontaine

The 5th Special Forces Group Isolation Facility, or ISOFAC, was located far away from any populated or frequently traveled area on Fort Campbell. Within a ten-foot-high security fence topped with triple-strand razor wire, the two-story, rather bland-looking brick structure served as a facility for Special Forces A-teams to isolate themselves from the outside world when planning missions. The building housed two large conference rooms, a chow hall, a gym, several large planning bays, and the main purpose of the structure: the isolation rooms themselves.

Each bay was totally self-contained, with a large open room on the first floor fitted with tables, chairs, dry-erase boards, and corkboards on every wall for maps and charts. The second floor held a sleeping area with bunk beds and a shower room with lockers. Each team was issued its own ISO bay, where they were completely shut off from the outside world.

Their only link to the outside world was the area support team, or AST. This was not a team, but rather an individual Special Forces soldier who was assigned to a specific isolated ODA to be their eyes and ears and was their go-between to the command group. He was the person who brought questions and answers into and out of the ISO bay, and who set up ranges, transportation, ammunition, and delivery of equipment and, of course, pizza and beer.

Teams were isolated before each real-world mission to keep others from knowing their plans and to keep them from knowing what else was going on in the bigger picture. If their mission were to be compromised, or a member captured and interrogated, they would not have any information to divulge that might affect what another team was doing. They simply would not know. The only one's privy to this information were the AST, the command planning cell, and the group commander himself.

The AST played another extremely important role, and that was to backfill the team should a member be unable to complete the trip for any reason, or to replace a team member should something stop him from continuing the mission, such as sickness, injury, or death.

The men of ODA 555 were in a large conference room with members of two other ODAs, talking about the events of the previous day in as much detail as possible. Point and counterpoint arguments that typically arise on any subject were even more in play, with the significant events of the terrorist attacks on New York.

As of that moment, none of the men in the room had been told why they were there. They had just been told to be in the conference room at 0900, and that they would be given further instructions from there. These men were masters of the art of speculation, and the ideas floating around in that room would have made for some very exciting ABC Weekend Specials. Each man was putting in his own two-cents about why they had been chosen to be in that room together at that particular moment. No one knew the real reason yet, but everyone was acting as though they did; no one wanted to let on that he was not "in the know."

The only thing they knew for sure was that all three active combat dive teams of the group were in the room together. For this fact alone, there was always the possibility that this was nothing more than an ass-chewing from the brass for something they had done that was not necessarily legal or politically prudent. These men prided themselves on doing everything better than everybody else, including screwing up.

Every time a new man entered the room, he would look around and say aloud, "Uh-oh, what did we do now?" to the crowd of jesters, who responded with roaring laughter. These men would find any way to make something a joke or belittle a peer. There was nothing more satisfying than entertainment at the expense of a loved one. They started throwing past horror stories around the room, blaming each other for the last time they were all chewed out together as a group.

"Whose house did you piss on this time, Alan?" said Mike Hemmy, the senior medic from ODA 525.

After some laughter from the crowd, a soldier commented, "Oh, I've got to hear this one."

"A few years back, after the bombings in Riyadh," Mike began, "we were partying at the Marine bar on top of the American embassy in Saudi, and Scotty here got stupid drunk." He pointed in Alan's direction.

"The Marines not-so politely, asked him to leave. But he had to piss, so he tried walking back to the bathroom. They just wanted him out, so they started pushing him out the door forcefully. Not wanting to cause any trouble, he stopped resisting and turned to walk out the door." Mike paused and looked at Alan, who now had a growing smile on his face.

"Once they let him go," Mike continued, "he hopped up on the pool table, dropped his pants, and started pissing in the corner pocket."

The other men in the room began laughing uncontrollably and patting Alan on the back.

"He got about three seconds into it before he was tackled to the ground. These Marines start kicking the hell out of him, which of course pissed us off and ended up turning it into the biggest bar fight I've ever seen outside of a movie."

The laughter continued to get louder as the story grew.

"This, of course, was directly above the ambassador's office," Mike went on, "which I guess knocked all the pictures off his wall and made him a tad angry. We knew Alan was an idiot, but we couldn't let some frickin' jarheads kick the crap out of him."

"Yeah, that's our job," Steve chimed in, to even more laughter.

"Needless to say," Mike continued, "it created quite a shit-storm back home and was quickly and quietly dealt with by the command before it escalated into something out of control. They banned us from the Marine bar for the duration of the trip—that was it."

"That was it?!" another soldier asked angrily.

"Hey, man, if they had just let me use the head first, none of that would have happened," Alan came back strongly.

"Just be glad he didn't have to take a shit!" Steve yelled out from the back, creating a hellacious eruption of laughter from the group. This was not the first time this story had been told, or the comment about Alan having to defecate. But every time it was brought up, there was always someone new who had not heard the story yet, and it would be told in painstaking detail all over again.

The story also brought with it a sort of proud feeling from the men of the Triple Nickel for having endured something the others hadn't: a semi-serious incident with serious implications and consequences, one that was kept quiet and brushed under the table because they were the only in-country SF team at the time. And because it was right after the terrorist bombings in Riyadh, it was imperative to keep the men "on station" for security reasons. Their only punishment was being banned from the embassy for the rest of the trip, and a pretty good ass-chewing from the brass upon their return to the States.

Now that it was years later, most of the brass had moved on in their careers, but the men of the Triple Nickel were still here, and the story had become legendary. It was a classic SF deployment story, one to be proud of if involved in, and envious of if not.

"On your feet," barked Captain Luke Walen, the commander of the Triple Nickel. All men snapped to their feet in the rigorous position of attention, with their eyes focused alertly at the door. All signs of joking, fun, and happiness were wiped from their faces with those three little words.

Luke was a smaller man, measuring just five-feet six and weighing around 165 pounds. He was the son of a prominent Iowa lawyer and had plans to return to school to finish his law degree after a few more years in the Army. Everyone liked Luke, not just because he was incredibly intelligent, very physically fit, and operationally sound, but also because he was just a cool guy. A graduate of the historic Virginia Military Institute, Luke was very sociable and always had a smile on his face. He was always fun at team gatherings and social functions, and he could throw back beer with the best of them, only to run like a deer the next morning. He also knew exactly when to be "one of the guys" and when to be a leader.

"Take your seats, men," echoed the command from Colonel John C. Mooreland, the 5th Group commander, who was about two steps behind Luke entering the room. "I heard a lot of laughing on my way down the hall. Still telling that Marine bar fight story, Sergeant Scott?" he said as he approached the podium in the front of the briefing room while pulling papers out of the left cargo pocket of his BDUs.

As laughter once again erupted and fingers were pointed in his direction, Alan stood up sharply in the position of attention and responded, "They just won't let it go, sir."

"Well, it's a funny story. I laughed when I first heard it," replied the colonel.

John C. Mooreland was a monster of a man, standing six-feet four and coming in at well over two hundred pounds. He was known for his straightforward, common-sense approach to leadership. He was direct and to the point when he spoke, and he was well respected throughout the group.

"I'm sure you all are wondering why I called you here today," Colonel Mooreland continued. "By now you all have surely had your fill of television coverage of the events this past Tuesday, and I hope you are all as sickened as I am.

"Terrorism is not new to this world. It is not new to this country and certainly not new to this very unit. We have been there hundreds of times around the world when terrorists have used these types of attacks on our allies, or those with no affiliation to us whatsoever. But this time it's different." He paused as he looked around the room at the young faces staring back at him. None of the men had moved at all since he began speaking.

"This time, they've brought their style of fear and intimidation to our people—our friends, our family, and in our backyard!" He slammed his fist down on the podium. "After my initial reaction of surprise, I was angry. I continued to get angrier, minute by minute, hour by hour, as I am sure you have.

"I have been in my office for the last thirty-six hours, on the phone with everyone you can think of, begging for a hand in this fight. We know the who, we know the why, but we still must follow orders. Trust me when I say this, men—the president is pissed. The whole country is pissed. They want someone's ass, and they want it yesterday.

"A lot of people will be envious of the men in this room right now." He pointed his finger around the room. "This is your call to duty. You have all been chosen to spearhead what will be the greatest mission Special Forces has ever been asked to do. This is what we pay you for. This is for real.

"From this moment forward, you are not to discuss anything you say, hear, or do unless told otherwise. You will be separated, isolated, and briefed. I will issue individual missions for each ODA in its isolation room. You will conduct yourselves as the quiet professionals you are known to be and prove to this nation why we exist."

He paused and looked slowly around the room, "The eyes of the world will be on you, and I know you will not let us down. Good luck, men. And God bless the USA."

As Colonel Mooreland stepped away from the podium, all the men in the room rose up and snapped to a vigorous position of attention. No one would say a word or look anywhere but straight ahead in a dead gaze, trying to take in the few words that had just been spoken to them.

After what seemed like an eternity but was only several seconds, a voice rang out. "ODA 525, go with Captain Miller to ISOFAC Room 13," Sergeant Major Nichols, the group sergeant major, commanded sternly.

"ODA 595, go with Captain Johnson, Room 11," he continued without hesitation or expression.

"Triple Nickel, Captain Walen, Room 15. Don't leave anything in this room and leave it as you found it."

Once the first team was identified, the men stood up and gathered their belongings, pushing their chairs in, and so forth, as if no one was paying attention to anything else that was being said. No one was saying a word.

The Triple Nickel was led down a small corridor to ISOFAC Room 15. Once inside, Frank wasted no time bellowing commands to the rest of the team. "All right, let's get these tables and chairs set up. Alan, I want some lists generated on that wall—at least five, of things

we're going to need right away to begin planning. Maps, intel, supplies, weapons, optics, food, and so on. Blaine, get your stuff upstairs, and start me a list of requirements for the things we want for this mission. It's September now, but I see it getting cold there in the next few months. Let your mind wander, like we have no budget, I'm guessing if Mooreland talked with the president, 'Money is no object' was said at least a half-dozen times."

"Whoa, there, big fella," came the halting words of Captain Walen. "I could have sworn I was the team leader. May I lead for a second, please?"

Steve leaned over and said to Alan, "Yeah, lighten up, Francis."

"Stripes, Sergeant Hulka. Come on, man. That was easy," Alan whispered back.

"Yeah, it's an oldie but goodie," Steve commented.

"Hey, sir, I'm just trying to get a head start on things. I know how this guy works," Frank replied, referring to Colonel Mooreland.

"We may not be going anywhere, and I, for one, would like to. So, you go get set up, and I'll take care of keeping these knuckleheads occupied. The two of us will sit down and talk over some things in private when you are ready, okay?"

"What do you mean, we may not be going anywhere?" Luke asked. "And what did you mean, it will be cold there in a couple months? We don't even know what we're doing yet."

"Come on, man, it's been all over the news!" Frank bellowed. "The secretary of defense has been all over TV saying these are unconventional attacks and this is going to be an unconventional war.

Who do you think he was talking about? The Discovery Channel has had like fifty shows on Afghanistan the last forty-eight hours. What have you been watching, the Cartoon Network?

"And you know as well as I do that there is a chance that all three teams in that room are getting the same mission." He pointed back down the hallway. "And whoever has the best plan of action is going to get it. Well, I don't know about you, or any of you dickheads," he said, pointing to the rest of the detachment, "but I want this fucking mission. And if you don't, then get the fuck out now. Right now! Anyone?"

Frank paused and looked around the room, making eye contact with each team member. "This is no bullshit, and if anyone here lies back or fucks off and screws this up, it will be the last job you have on an A-team in this or any other group—I'll make sure of that."

The men in the room just stood there, watching Frank and Luke stare at each other. It was obvious to everyone that Frank was not kidding around. To him, this was personal. He wanted them to fully understand the implications of what they were about to do. This was no training op. This was no ordinary combat op, either. This was the mission of a lifetime, and he knew it.

Luke cracked a small smile, knowing that he had just the man he needed by his side, to get things done right. The two shook hands and smiled, maintaining the stare they had started a few seconds before.

"Now would have been a better time for that 'Lighten up, Francis' line," Alan whispered to Steve when no one else was within earshot.

"I know. Timing is everything. Damn it."

They both started to chuckle as everyone went back to what they were doing before the verbal outburst had stopped them.

They were interrupted by a knock on the door. Sergeant First Class Tony DeNero, the AST assigned to Triple Nickel, came into the isolation bay.

"Hey, guys, whatcha doing?" Tony said with a huge grin, as if he had no idea what was going on.

"Hey, Tony!" Alan replied and walked over to his old friend to shake his hand. "What are you doing here?"

"I'm your AST, bitch!" Tony said jokingly to the rest of the team.

"If you're our AST, then you're the bitch!" was Steve's immediate reply, conjuring up a bunch of snickers from the rest of the team.

SFC DeNero was a charismatic man who, much like the men of the Triple Nickel, enjoyed a good laugh. He was tall, standing six-feet three, with salt-and-pepper hair. He was known for his love for both the Oakland Raiders and Jack Daniels. He came with the classic Italian mobster vernacular that always brought a smile to those around him and kept the crowds laughing at social functions. He and Alan were close friends and spent many a night throwing back Jack and Cokes while smoking cigars on Tony's back deck, contemplating life.

"Hey, I'm here for you guys," Tony said. "Anything you need, let me know. Here are your first intelligence reports from the Vault." (The "Vault" was the Group Intelligence Office.) "Take it for what it's worth. Some of the information is old, and we are trying to get updates as we speak. Get me a list of gear you might want, and we'll get everything we can for you before you go. The rumor is unlimited budget, so don't worry about what you ask for, as long as it's operational. No mini-bars, Steve."

"Why does he always say that shit to me?" Steve said to Alan with a look of complete surprise.

"You are being released for personal equipment," Tony continued. "Go home, get your gear, and come right back. Kiss the wife and kiddies good-bye, but no stories. Your cover is you are going to a forward operation base to provide assistance for Americans getting out of Afghanistan. Remember, no stories—this is real shit. Those staff weenies over there haven't slept in thirty-six hours and are all on edge. Don't give them any reason to think we aren't ready to do this."

He looked at Frank. "Frank, when you kick these guys out, I have some stuff to go over with you and the captain." Tony turned back to the rest of the team. "Remember—straight home, straight back. There will be no stopping at the Dancing Kitty, Mr. Scott."

"I have too much respect for women to go into those places, thank you very much," Alan replied.

"Oh, come on!" Blaine yelled from the back. "That place gets more of your paycheck than you do."

"Okay, so I have a weakness for a pretty smile," Alan said.

"I thought it was big tits," Steve replied.

"Whatever," Alan retorted.

"All right, you heard him," Frank interrupted angrily. "You have two hours to have all operational and personal gear from your house and team room back here. Better get moving."

"Two hours? Wow, that's generous," JT said very sarcastically.

"Like I said, get moving," Frank replied.

The men scrambled to get their car keys and bolted furiously for the door, pushing each other out of the way to make it out first. Even this small task turned into a competition.

# CHAPTER 5

*Nowhere can man find a quieter or more untroubled retreat than in his own soul.*
-Marcus Aurelius

Alan pulled into his gravel driveway and skidded to a halt, causinga cloud of dust to encompass his old, black pickup truck. It looked like it had never seen a car wash in its life. Hurriedly he exited his vehicle and moved to the gate of the four-foot chain-link fence that protected the backyard of his small home. He had a very simple home: about a thousand square feet with three bedrooms and a single-car garage that was too small for his truck. The home was just enough for him to eat and sleep in, for he spent very little time in it.

Disregarding the gate, Alan grabbed the top rail of the fence and hopped over it. He moved to a large metal shed at the rear of his property and fished for a key hidden in the tall, un-mowed grass at its base. The building looked like something out of a construction-gone wrong TV show. Alan and some friends had thrown it together one weekend, over many beers. Once he found the key, it took some manhandling, but he finally got the large reinforced door to slide open, exposing a well-organized interior with meticulously placed tools and equipment in boxes, on shelves, and against the walls.

Alan maneuvered to the rear of the shed, where several large black plastic truck boxes were stacked floor to ceiling along the back wall. Each box was labeled with a white paint marker, letting Alan know exactly which box to grab and open first. He reached for a set of keys stashed in the corner of the shed along the hangover of the roof, fiddled with them for a second, and removed the Series 2000 padlocks from the plastic storage boxes. He opened several boxes and began gathering his standard green Army-issue gear, along with some personal "cool-guy" gear he had acquired over the last ten years on the team.

He spent the next hour going through the operational gear he had pulled from the boxes. He checked a Surefire flashlight for serviceability. He opened a desert-camouflaged CamelBak water bladder to pour out some water that had been there for several months. He tried on a pair of black Nomex flight gloves, only to notice that half of his fingers protruded. He picked up his rucksack and put it on the bench cluttered with odd bits and pieces. He had sewn some pockets on top of other pockets to add even more carrying capacity. Alan started going through some of the pockets, surprised by what he found in some, disgusted by the contents of others.

In these pockets were half-eaten energy bars, bungee cords that snapped in half with the slightest tension applied, a signal mirror shattered into fragments like a spider web, a headlamp with dead batteries, and small zip-lock baggies filled with different medications with no labels on them. There were two large Benchmade switchblade knives, which he opened to check for functionality. With a flick of his wrist, he extended a collapsible police baton and then pushed it back into its handle by pounding the end on the top of the workbench. From a small side pocket, he pulled a pair of elbow and kneepads with the excess straps held down with green 100-mph tape. A Stillwater personal water filtration system with a Platypus bladder had its own pocket, and he checked the filter date. Still another pocket had nothing but batteries; he removed the obviously eroded ones and discarded them in a large trashcan in the corner.

Other items he removed from the pack in the next hour included a Randall knife with sheath and sharpening stone; an infrared distress strobe that he turned on to check for the telltale sound that strobes make as they build up power; and a small lighter that he pulled out and checked for serviceability, which put a smile on his face because he had used the same lighter for many years and on many deployments, and it still made a flame. There was a half-eaten bag of sunflower seeds that Alan brought up to his nose for a smell, only to wince in disgust at the pungent odor as he threw them in the trash can as well. Several very old ChapStick tubes had melted within a pocket, causing an obvious white area that had bled through the pocket itself. He pulled several very old chemical lights from a side pocket; he cracked one of them and gave it a shake to see if it worked, giving a slight chuckle when nothing came of his labor and throwing it in the trash, which was now starting to overflow. He opened two OD green lensatic compasses and checked them for accuracy. He turned on a Garmin E-trex personal GPS, only to notice that the welcome screen read LOW BATTERY. He opened several camouflage paint sticks to see that there were way too many green ones and not enough tan, again bringing a slight giggle. And, of course, he found a bag of peppermint candies to suck on during the long transatlantic flight, where smoking was extremely forbidden.

He looked up at the wall of the shed and grabbed a black pistol belt off a hook. He wrapped it around his waist and buckled it closed to check the fit. Across the front of the belt were a couple of small pouches to hold small items like latex exam gloves for treating patients, two tourniquets, and a Benchmade rescue hook for cutting off clothes. A large survival knife hung on the belt at his right hip; Alan pulled it from the sheath and felt the blade by running his thumb across it. He smiled as a small drop of blood oozed from his thumb due to the razor-like edge of the knife.

Most of these items had been left in the pack since his last deployment, and it was obvious to him now that he had to replace most of the things he had neglected. It was much easier to come home, throw everything into the shed, and worry about it later. Later had arrived, and rather unexpectedly. As he went through his gear, he made entries in a small notebook on the workbench to fix or replace each item he came across.

Alan tossed items haphazardly into the main compartment and side pockets of his pack, knowing that they would soon be dumped out in the ISOFAC and sorted through. Once all the items had been replaced in the pack, he cinched up all its straps and threw it over his shoulder. He glanced around the shed to make sure that everything was back in its rightful place, reached down to grab a green aviator's kit bag with some more gear in it, and headed out of the shed. He pulled the doors shut and replaced the massive lock, looked around to see if anyone was in the immediate area, and tossed the key into its hiding spot. Alan made his way back to the truck and tossed both packs into the bed. He took a walk around the outside of his home to check all the doors and window for security and turn off the main water supply and fuse box to the house. Once satisfied, he jumped back in his truck and sped out of his driveway with the same intensity as he'd pulled in, again kicking up a cloud of dust.

He reached down and gave his radio volume a boost, lit a cigarette, and glanced into his rearview mirror. He managed a small smile, wondering how long the grass would be when he returned home next time.

# CHAPTER 6

*In time of test, family is best.*
-Burmese Proverb

Steve Greenwell walked silently into the nursery of his home. The room was quiet, with the only sound that of a child's mobile hanging over a crib. He hovered over his newborn daughter, holding a small stuffed bear in his hand, giving it a squeeze to hear the squeak it produced. He delicately placed the bear at his child's feet to provide some sort of comfort, which he hoped might fill his upcoming absence. His little girl was his first child, and whenever he looked at her, he was amazed that anything could be that beautiful. He rubbed his left hand gently across her forehead, feeling her softness and warmth, which brought a slight smile to his face.

"Daddy has to go to work, sweetie," Steve whispered with a hint of sadness. "Take care of your mother for me."

He kissed his left hand and gently placed it on her temple. Taking a step back from her crib, his eyes never left her. He glanced around the room to embed the picture deep in his memory, for he knew he would be returning to the scene in his mind many times in the days to come. As he turned to walk out of the room, he glanced at the wall next to the door to see the picture hanging there. It was a snapshot of the day they had brought her home, with him holding his daughter awkwardly, so new to parenthood. In the photo, Steve looked enamored and a little disbelieving, with an incredible grin on his face that only a new father could make. It was his favorite picture; he looked at it nearly every time he left this room. He reached up and gave the picture a slight correction, even though it was unnecessary; it let him feel an ounce of power in an environment in which he knew he was completely powerless.

When he reached the front door, his wife handed him a black backpack and his truck keys. This was a scene they had played out many times, and she was carefully businesslike in her demeanor.

"Kit and keys," she said as she helped him sling the pack over a shoulder and placed the car keys in his hand. "I put some snacks in the bag in case they forget to feed you on the plane."

This came from the experience of previous deployments when he couldn't tell her where he was or what he was doing, but he could definitely complain about the lack of Oreo cookies, Snickers bars, and juice boxes. It was her way of feeling an ounce of power in an environment in which she knew she was completely powerless.

"You're the best," Steve said, and he leaned forward to kiss her on the lips. "You know this one is different," he said, with an almost questioning tone.

"Just make sure your ass is home for her first birthday," she replied with mock sternness. "And tell Alan if he lets anything happen to you, I'll kill him myself."

"I don't need a babysitter," Steve barked scornfully as he made his way out to the driveway.

"Both of you do!" she said. "How they let you two juvenile delinquents go gallivanting across the globe without supervision is beyond me."

Steve tossed the pack into the bed of his truck and opened the driver's door, with his wife in close pursuit.

"We got this one, baby," he murmured as he turned to give her the bittersweet embrace of goodbye that they had shared much too often.

Before Steve got in the truck, she squeezed tighter for one last feeling of warmth before she released him. He noticed a single tear falling down her check before she turned to walk back to the house without even a parting glance. She was a strong, powerful woman who refused to show any weakness; she always wanted to give Steve the confidence that she had the house in order while he was gone.

"Stubborn," Steve muttered under his breath, shaking his head. He started the truck and pulled out of their circular drive, glancing up to his rearview mirror to see her peering through the drapes of the front bay window. A small smile began to form on his face: his thoughts about her vulnerability had just been validated. But he also knew he had a strong wife who would be able to handle even the worst situation.

It was slightly comforting to him knowing that they had discussed what to do if something terrible happened on one of his deployments. Being a good operator, Steve had planned out every intricate detail of his demise: what to do with his remains, whom to contact in the family, what music he wanted played, the name and address of his hometown newspaper to contact for the obituary, who were to be his pallbearers, and what was to be placed in his casket with him for all of eternity. It wasn't morbid or excessive; it was just another aspect of his life that he had under total control.

As Steve prepared to enter the main traffic control point to Fort Campbell, he reached down to grab his wallet from the cup holder of the truck so he could pass his government identification to the gate guard, allowing him access to the base. Opening his wallet, he noticed that his wife had hidden a wallet-size copy of the picture hanging on the wall in his daughter's room. A smile began to fill his face as he went through the gate and toward the isolation facility in the group area. He held the picture with his right hand and steered the truck with his left, only glancing up occasionally to watch the road. Normally he would have no problem dealing with the good-byes, but he knew that this was no ordinary good-bye and could very well be his last.

# CHAPTER 7

*I will prepare and someday my chance will come.*
-Abraham Lincoln

The men of Triple Nickel began the rigorous tasks of mission planning. Each man was busy and completely focused on the task at hand. Very little conversation was going on, as each member of the detachment had his own job to do during this phase of the operation. Frank and Luke were sitting at a long desk with "ruggedized" laptop computers that were hooked up to the secure servers from Group Headquarters. They were typing furiously and looking at aerial photographs of Afghanistan. At this point, they still had not received a definitive mission statement from higher up. Alan and Steve were hanging a large topographical map of Afghanistan on the far wall, so large it took two men and handfuls of thumbtacks.

Normally the task would be simple, but these two adjusted the map and pins repeatedly to have it perfectly level. Alan had a small spiral notebook in which he jotted down notes as Steve pointed out different areas on the map and disease processes endemic to them. Things like malaria, cholera, dengue fever, and leishmaniasis were all found in Afghanistan, and they needed to plan for them and order the proper medications necessary for their treatment.

Across the room, Sergeant Speakman was spray-painting an SR- 25 Stoner sniper rifle desert tan. At first glance, it might have seemed that there was no order to what he was doing; he appeared to be covering the entire weapon in paint with long, flowing passes of the spray can. He paused, put the can down on the table, looked at the weapon carefully, and began slowly removing the tape that he had placed on the weapon before painting it, revealing a meticulous desert camouflage pattern of several different colors. Shane took one step back and bent his knees slightly to put him at eye level with the weapon, giving it a visual once-over from butt to barrel. He cracked a little smile and whispered, "Perfect," to himself. He moved it to the floor, where there were several M-4 carbines, already painted with similar camouflage patterns, drying.

Blaine was in the corner of the bay, conducting an inventory of several large Pelican cases that contained a myriad of electronic and optical devices. As the engineer on the team, he kept track of all the supply issues and was accountable for all equipment. He always knew what every piece of equipment was and where it was located.

He was going through his demolition kit, piece by piece: demolitions bag, M-34 blasting machine, the plastic box containing blasting caps, an M2 crimper, a pocket knife, a hundred-foot measuring tape, and a blasting cap test set.

He would spend the next several hours going through all of his Pelican cases and counting every piece of equipment the team had in its inventory. Some boxes were put along the wall to be palletized and taken with them, and others were stacked against the back double doors to their isolation room, to be returned to their storage container, as not everything would be needed for this trip.

Optics such as ACOG optical scopes, carbine visible lasers, M-68 reflex sights, AN/PEQ-2 Target Pointer Illuminating/Aiming Light (TPIAL), and night optical devices (NODs) such as their PVS-6, 7B, 10, 14, and 17A were all inspected and checked for batteries and functionality. He put these items into an empty Pelican case, along with an inventory sheet of what he was placing in each box. The fact that his team sergeant, Frank, had been an engineer prior to being promoted made Blaine step up his game a little, because he always felt like Frank was watching his every move. On more than one occasion, Blaine had looked up to the sky with arms outstretched and asked, "Why couldn't he have been a medic?"

Upstairs in the sleeping area, JT was busy going through cardboard boxes of brand new IMBTR radios that had just been dropped off at their bay. Normally the heaviest boxes on the team were always the communications gear. The invention of wheeled boxes was probably the biggest advance in Special Forces in the last twenty-five years. Each man was only allowed so much space on one pallet to deploy with, so they would all figure out what gear was mission essential and pack it in large boxes.

There was an unwritten assumption in Special Forces that the medics were the smartest men on a team because their education was twice as long as all of the other career fields. Although it was very demanding being an SF medic, being the communications sergeant was akin to learning a new job every year. By the time one got comfortable with the radio he had, a new model would be put into play that needed to be integrated into use. This not only involved being competent on the radio; it also required the communications sergeant to teach the new device to the other members of the team.

These tasks kept the team busy well into the night, and one by one, without direction, they would venture upstairs to the sleeping area to get some needed rest. They had been going non-stop for many hours since the brief by Colonel Mooreland, and they knew what pace they had to maintain throughout isolation. There was much more to be done before they received a direct mission statement from higher up, because once that happened, it would consume all their thoughts, and some of the basics might go undone. Pilots called this instrumentation fixation; a pilot would get so fixated on one instrument that he neglected everything else around him that might lead to a crash.

With so many moving parts, it was the job of the team leader and team sergeant to have everything planned out so that after the receipt of the mission, all that needed to be done was to fill in some blanks with critical information to focus on. Luke and Frank worked well into the morning at their computers, silently typing away. Every once in a great while, a new cup of coffee would be fetched and shared, questions were posed to each other, or one of them would stand up and stretch his legs for a few seconds. They would set a cut-off time to keep themselves from working through the night. No matter where they were in the plan, when that time came, they would just stop and retire. Although each had his idea of what time it should be, they settled on 3:00 AM and concluded the first day of isolation without any serious problems.

They briefed each other quickly on their progress so far, decided what should be accomplished in the next twenty-four hours, and headed off to bed. It had been an incredibly hectic day, but both knew it would get worse before it got easier. At the stairs, Frank held out his left hand as in an "after you" gesture to Luke, who walked up the stairs first, only to be tripped by Frank grabbing his ankle, sending Luke falling into the stairwell. Laughing loudly, Frank leapfrogged the downed captain and ran up the stairs, holding his arms high in the air as if he had just won a gold medal in the Olympics.

"You better hope you don't fall asleep first," was Luke's only response as he picked himself up and walked up the remaining stairs. This would be his first real-world combat operation, and although he was experienced on the team and had done several training ops with them, his only thoughts now were of the literally hundreds of ways this could play out.

With sounds of snoring coming from all directions, Luke lay in bed and stared at the streetlight out the window, his mind racing so fast that there was no way he would fall asleep. As he stared at the light, his thoughts switched to the planes crashing into the twin towers in New York. How could that have happened? What exactly happened on those planes that would allow someone to take over flying them? Why didn't anyone stop them?

Slowly he drifted off to sleep, playing through the scenario of his detachment being on a civilian flight, returning home from a long training mission, and two men with box cutters trying to take over the plane. The scenario would obviously have a different outcome, with the men of the team pushing each other out of the way to be the first to subdue the hijackers. The thought of that particular scenario brought a smile to his face. He knew that he had been assigned to a great team, and he wanted to show them all that he was up to the challenge. This was the crux of the men in Special Forces: they were all great at what they did, and even better when together, but no man wanted to be the one who failed his peers. Mistakes were rare in this community, but when they happened, they usually yielded catastrophic results. The fear of letting your teammates down exceeded the fear of combat, and this was what drove these men. For some, this would be the only family they would ever know.

They still had no idea what awaited them, but each knew that whatever it was, it was something none of them had done before. The anger over the preceding events had fed their determination up to this point, but they would need more than determination to accomplish

what might be considered the greatest mission these men had ever heard of. The events of history were happening to them in real time, and they were at the epicenter of it all. They were about to learn what the phrase "tip of the spear" really meant.

# CHAPTER 8

*We are what we repeatedly do. Excellence therefore, is not an act, but a habit.*
-Aristotle

The next morning, the team wasted no time jumping right into the fire. There had been a dramatic increase of maps on the wall, boxes stacked up, computers on the planning table, and lists on the wall with checkmarks next to lines on them signifying their completion. There was also noticeable facial hair growth on the men. Part of their mission was to go in under cover of humanitarian assistance as American civilians, so not looking like an army unit was imperative.

Since the image of the military man was that of a clean-shaven young man with a short haircut, in uniform, the way to avoid seeming military was to not wear a uniform, have longer hair, and grow a beard. In Islamic culture, the beard was a sign of manhood and wisdom, so facial hair was necessary for them to be able to gain rapport with whomever they were to meet.

SFC DeNero made several trips into the room, delivering different boxes of supplies, maps, stacks of intelligence reports, and grocery bags full of snacks and sodas. With each successive trip into the planning bay, the walls became thicker with reports, maps, and lists. The trash can was full and had several full trash bags next to it for removal. Because of the sensitive nature of this operation, all trash leaving the room had to be burned under supervision, for security.

Steve and Alan had several medical trauma bags open on their work area and were going through their equipment meticulously, checking the functionality.

Down the hall from the rest of the team, Blaine, JT, and Rusty were in the ISOFAC weight room, exercising. They were performing a circuit routine consisting of dead lifts, bench press, pull-ups, and squats, moving from one exercise to the next with no rest in between. While one person performed the entire set, the other two monitored their watches to keep track of the time it took. Each time they finished, the time was announced verbally and became the new time to beat when the next person began his set.

Even though there were only three men in the gym, the loud rock music, grunting and groaning, and cheering on of each other could be heard throughout the ISOFAC. As each man moved from exercise to exercise, the weights being dropped to the ground with force were both heard and felt throughout the entire building. In planning cells on the other end of the building, coffee cups and water coolers could be seen shaking with each repetition.

Back in the team's bay, Tony opened the back double-doors to the room, exposing a large gray van he had backed up to them. He and Shane began loading the team's weapons into the van, along with many crates of ammunition. The ammo was separated by caliber— 5.56, 7.62, and 9mm ball along with a couple boxes of 40mm—and checked off on the hand receipt signed by Shane.

The team was gathered and put into the van as Tony took his position behind the wheel. With Luke in the passenger seat looking over the scheduled shooting range logistics, Frank was putting out the information of how the range would be broken down to maximize their training time. There would be multiple things going on at the same range, and with so many moving parts, safety was always discussed.

The van pulled into a secluded range complex at the rear of the post, down a long gravel trail off the main road. Once they arrived, each man went right to his assigned tasks to prepare the range for operation. JT immediately opened his pack, pulled out his IMBTR radio, and contacted range control to let them know the range was occupied and what weapon systems would be emplaced. Shane and Rusty delivered the ammo boxes to different parts of the range so each member would have the right ammo for the particular stage of fire he would be conducting. They also put up a large, plain, red triangular flag on the flagpole at the entrance of the range, signifying its occupancy and "hot" status. Alan and Steve went in opposite directions with their trauma bags and placed them at opposite ends of the range to prepare for any mishaps and returned to the van to secure their gear.

Frank gathered the men in a semicircle around him and started dictating which member would go to which part of the range and what would be done there. Once the information was put out, Tony reached in and gave the van radio a boost of volume while the rest of the team grabbed their individual bags and headed to their respective parts of the range.

On the far west end of the range, Shane, Steve, and JT were shooting their M-4 carbines with attached M203, 40mm, on the underside. They were standing abreast, separated by several feet, and repeatedly bringing their rifles from the high ready position to the firing position and engaging paper FBI silhouettes at distances of roughly twenty-five meters. In each man's target, there was a distinct area missing in its center mass, or kill zone, that had been removed by the steady double-tap or "controlled pairs" put into it by the shooter. As their magazines ran dry, they finished off the round with a 40mm to the abandoned vehicle that was roughly two hundred meters downrange.

There were several of these vehicles scattered throughout the range to shoot at, into, and around. They were all bullet-ridden and missing glass and had tall grass growing up around the sides, covering the undercarriage.

Alan, Blaine, and Rusty were at the next section of the range, doing transition drills against each other. While one man stood in the ready position, facing his set of three targets fifteen meters in front of him, another held a shot-timer to his ear, which would signal the beginning of the drill. A shot-timer used sonic waves, or the concussion of each round fired, to give the elapsed time down to the hundredth of a second, along with the time between rounds, which could be annotated after each round of the drill.

Upon hearing the start tone of the timer, Alan brought his rifle to the firing position and engaged three silhouettes from left to right with two shots each. After he put two shots in the third target, he rapidly changed magazines in his rifle and reversed his direction, putting two more shots into each target from right to left. After firing the last shot with the rifle, he lowered it while simultaneously drawing his 9mm Beretta from his thigh holster. He then reengaged each target with the pistol, for a total of twelve shots with each weapon and two magazine changes.

Once he completed the round, he cleared his weapons, and Rusty showed him his elapsed time on the shot timer. With a smug smile for his rapid execution of the drill, he grabbed the timer from Rusty, and the two switched places so Rusty could perform the same drill while Blaine loaded his magazines and waited for his turn. This continued for some time, with each successive round getting faster until all that was heard from their area of the range was a rapid barrage of controlled pairs, with very short pauses during the magazine changes.

Luke and Frank were standing some distance behind them, so they had a good view of both groups of men on the range. They discussed the different attributes of each detachment member with weapons, pointing out Shane's ability with the M203, Alan's pistol skills, and JT's prowess with both. It was their responsibility to make sure they played to the strength of each man's ability with different weapons, so they could best employ them in a combat environment.

Shane, Rusty, and Steve moved down to the known distance range to set up the M24 and SR-25 Stoner sniper rifles. Shane and Rusty got down into prone firing positions, while Steve sat in a lawn chair with a twenty-power spotting scope on a tri-pod to read the trace and spot the targets.

Reading the trace of a round was not easy and being a spotter could be as difficult as making the sniper's actual shot. It involved seeing, through the spotting scope, the shock wave of the round as it traveled from the rifle to its target, and this could easily be missed if you didn't know what you were looking for. Frank had been an instructor for the Special Operations Target Interdiction Course (SOTIC), better known as "sniper school," and had brought the long-range shooting skills of the entire detachment to a better than average level of competency.

Both weapons sergeants on the team were proficient with both sniper systems, and since it hadn't yet been decided which rifle would accompany them on this mission, they alternated between the two. As always, this turned into a small competition, with Steve calling out the proximity to the center of the target at each distance. After each round of shots between Shane and Rusty at different distances, the results were tabulated, and the victor received a handful of cash from the loser. With the quality of marksmanship of these two snipers, the same cash was passed back and forth several times between them until it settled in the hands of the original owner, with no actual winner of the contest.

After lunch, the men move to the van area and started donning their protective gear. With Velcro straps, they secured body armor to their torsos that had the ability to stop up to a 7.62-caliber round. These vests had pouches sewn to them to hold multiple rifle and pistol magazines, flash-bang grenades, and radios for internal communications.

The radios were handed out by JT and hooked up to throat secured microphones that picked up vibrations from the vocal cords through the neck, and earpieces that secured over the ear and went into the ear canals. The men donned their eye protection and baseball caps with the familiar scuba logo embroidered on the front, with TRIPLE NICKEL and their initials on the back strap.

The men moved to the familiar "tire house," which was a small building with several rooms and hallways that were movable and could be configured in a myriad of ways to give them multiple scenarios of room clearing and close quarters battle (CQB) drills. Luke and Frank set up the targets in each room, so the team would be unaware of what awaited them as they entered the rooms.

The targets were responsive steel targets that were shaped like large bowling pins spray-painted white. The targets were attached to a vertical rail system that allowed the target, once shot, to slide down the rail, signifying that the target has been put down. The men could also see where the bullets struck because of the marks they left on the white paint.

After setting the first round of targets, the two leaders made their way up the stairs to the catwalk overlooking the rooms. From this vantage point, they could assess the speed, surprise, and violence of action necessary for good CQB. The rest of the ODA were stacked outside the first room along the exterior wall, with Alan in the first position, holding his weapon on the door, and the rest of the men in line behind him with their weapons at the high ready position, ready to enter the room. Blaine was crouched near Alan's feet, setting a breaching charge on the door and fixing the detonation cord running from the charge to an M60 firing device.

Blaine made eye contact with Alan, gave him a slight nod, ducked his head, and pulled the firing device. The blast obliterated the locking mechanism of the door, allowing it to be opened with a slight kick. Alan entered the doorway and continued to his point of domination along the side wall, firing two shots to the target in his sector of fire.

He was immediately followed by JT, who entered the door and went the opposite direction in the room, clearing his corner target with two shots and assuming his point of domination opposite Alan. Shane entered and followed the path made by Alan but stopped short of the corner and engaged the target in the center of the room. Steve was the last into the room and followed JT's path, again stopping short of the corner and engaging the same target as Shane in the center of the room almost simultaneously.

After the last target fell down its rail, signifying that all targets in the room had been neutralized, a short pause was followed by JT calling out, "Doorway front!" Unlike the movies where everyone yells "clear" in each room they enter, real CQB need to have violence of action and speed. Yelling "clear" from every room not only would alert everyone in the rest of the house of what was coming; it also would slow down the flow. The men in the room are professionals and know that when the firing stops, the room is clear, and they move on.

JT's command was followed immediately by Alan removing a flash-bang grenade from his vest, pulling the pin, and throwing it into the newly discovered room. Once the grenade detonated with a thunderous explosion, Rusty and Blaine flowed between the men and into the second room in the same fashion, engaging more targets. This bounding, flow-through action was repeated throughout the structure until all rooms had been cleared of their targets.

Once this was completed, the team moved outside of the structure and refilled their vests with ammo, breaching charges, and flash-bangs while Luke and Frank reset the rooms and moved targets around. This continued for several hours, with multiple room configurations and a rotation of the team so that each member got to perform in each position in his stack. Every so often, they would break to discuss different scenarios and positioning that would optimize the

violence of action and speed. Rooms were made larger and smaller, with different props placed strategically in each room to add confusion and provide obstacles for the men moving throughout them.

It is said that in every art, there are many techniques but very few fundamentals. Because of their experience, they had grown accustomed to sticking with the fundamentals of combat and mastering them. If they started incorporating techniques into their training, the

first time the situation didn't allow that technique to be used, it would cause a chain of events that could be detrimental to the mission. By sticking to and mastering the fundamentals, they would be able to adapt to whatever situation arose, with very little change from what they trained on.

This mentality of adaptation allowed them to be employed in many different environments and situations, giving their command a greater use of combat power. Some military commanders tended to overanalyze and make intricate plans for operations that looked great on a slide presentation, but that if not stuck to in every detail would cause a failure in every phase of the operation after the initial mishap. For this reason, planning at the team level stayed very basic and covered all contingencies. These men planned on things going wrong from the beginning and dealt with problems as they arose. This was in stark contrast to planning the "perfect" mission, which is doomed from the start.

After Luke was satisfied with the training value of the shoot house, he gathered all the members of his team for the final training event of the day: the beer shoot. They gathered back by the van and laid all their kit in piles around it. Each man now only wore a concealed-carry holster on his hip with a M-9 Beretta 9mm pistol. Shane and Rusty set up the range for the beer shoot: two identical target setups, side by side. Each consisted of five bowling pins on a small rack, three feet off the ground, and two three-foot steel silhouettes stood in between them. Each steel target was set up so that one round contacting it in the center would cause it to fall to the ground. The targets were set up close enough and in such a manner that two shooters could stand several feet from one another and begin shooting at the bowling pins from outside to inside, finishing with the steel silhouettes side by side in the center. The shooter could not engage the steel target until all the bowling pins were shot down; the winner was the one who made the first steel fall.

It is very difficult to simulate the stresses of combat in training situations. It's almost impossible to initiate a sympathetic nervous system response to stress in training that mirrors what is felt when real enemy are confronted. Dry mouth, sweating hands, jerky hand movements, and the inability to focus are just a few distractions that may keep a well-trained operator from accurately engaging targets in a real-world scenario. Because these men had been in many stressful situations in their careers, it was even more difficult to stress them in training by using the usual Army tactics of yelling or throwing small firecracker-type devices or smoke grenades. The best way to cause them stress was competition. The desire to beat one of their peers at a skill they all shared would cause them to push themselves faster and amplify any little mistake. It was a fun way to end any day of training, but it also gave the leaders a realistic look at how these men handled stress and shot under pressure.

Two at a time, the men approached the starting boxes and placed their hands in the high ready position: arms in the air, with fingers resting on the hearing protection each man wore. Rusty stood behind the men with a whistle, and on his signal, the men reached down and drew their pistols and engaged the bowling pins, from outside to inside, finishing off with the steel target in the center. With each successive round, the men locked, cleared, and holstered their pistols before moving downrange to reset the bowling pins and steel silhouette.

The big lesson in this exercise was not the speed of engaging targets or who was the best shooter of the day; it was training in the ability to deal with difficulties such as weapons jams and magazine malfunctions. The weapons these men used were far from brand new, and faulty magazines and ammunition were just occupational hazards endemic to the profession. But if a man had a weapons malfunction in the middle of a stress-shoot, he needed to fight through it, correct the malfunction as quickly and smoothly as he could, and get back in the fight.

One might think that just the slightest pause in shooting would doom a shooter to an immediate loss in the competition, but that is not always the case. The competitor may also suffer a malfunction, miss targets, or realize his opponent has suffered a misfortune and slow down because he feels a win is imminent. Many a winner who at first encountered a misfortune has persevered to overcome his opponent. In combat, the enemy does not care how old your weapons are, how dirty the magazines have gotten, or how nervous the shooter is; the fight continues. The only thing that contributes to success in these situations is the mentality to stay in the fight.

The men watching in the back wagered on the projected winners and then exchanged handfuls of cash after each round. After several iterations in the double elimination tournament, the last two shooters were Steve and Alan. Everyone knew Alan had the greater advantage, because he was known for his pistol skills and spent much of his personal time at the range with one of his many personal pistols. As the two stood next to each other and prepared for the final round, they gave one another a scornful look.

Rusty initiated the competition with a blow of his whistle, and the men began shooting their targets. One by one, the bowling pins fell, and as expected, Alan reached his steel target first. But due to the off-center impact of his round, the steel did not fall. Realizing his target was still standing, he reengaged it with several more rounds in rapid succession. This slight hesitation was all that was needed to allow Steve to reach his steel target, and the two silhouettes fell simultaneously.

Steve immediately holstered his weapon and raised his hands in victorious celebration. Behind them the bettors argued about which steel target had fallen first, and after a few seconds of watching, Luke declared Steve the winner, because it had taken Alan so many rounds to put down the steel. Hearing the final decision, Steve walked to each man and triumphantly pulled the handfuls of cash from their hands, one by one.

At the end of the training, the men began their respective tasks of shutting down the range. JT contacted range control to close the range; Shane pulled the range flag from its pole; Blaine, Rusty, and Alan helped Tony pick up some empty brass shell casings on the range, while Steve loaded equipment back into the van. Frank and Luke continue discussing the training as they joined the other men in the van. They stopped at the entrance of the range and picked up Shane with the flag.

Tony sped the van down the trail, kicking up a cloud of dust from the gravel road, which obscured the range in his rear-view mirror. The dust settled to the earth along with the sun, bringing the second day of isolation to an end. They still had not received any type of mission statement, and they were beginning to throw around speculations about what might happen.

Normal isolation prior to combat operations was seventy-two hours, and they were more than halfway there. Frank assured everyone that they would find out soon enough and told them to remain focused on their individual responsibilities. He knew that it was a distraction to spend what little time they had speculating on things they had no control over. This, of course, was completely ignored by the rest of the team as more and more elaborate missions were discussed, until it became another competition, to see who could come up with the most interesting one. Even with the stressful events of the previous few days, a few hours on the range were all these men needed to settle them down and get them relaxed for what was ahead.

As they returned to the ISOFAC, Luke stared intently out the window, knowing that once a mission statement was given to the team, things would get considerably more difficult. Although he was starting to feel some stress, it was quickly averted when Tony informed him that there was chow waiting for them back in the ISO bay.

Little did he know that chow was not the only thing waiting for them upon their return.

# CHAPTER 9

*To live effectively is to live with adequate information.*
-Norbert Wiener

The men of Triple Nickel were busy at the tables in their planning bay, eating pizza and cleaning weapons. There was a vast array of weapons parts in front of them, laid out meticulously on towels in order of their removal from the weapon. Each piece was cleaned individually with brushes, cotton-tipped applicators, lubricating oil, and white cotton towels until it was as clean as the day it was first put into operation. Rifle barrels were held up to the light to peer through them, noting any irregularities or carbon remains from the day at the range. M92 pistols had their triggers squeezed several times to check the ease of pull after being properly lubricated.

Shane tightened the screws on the ACOG atop his M-4 and held it up in a firing position toward the empty wall to check its sight picture. Alan was adjusting his PEQ-2 with a laser bore sight, a device that was inserted into the barrel of the weapon, projecting a laser onto a target taped to the wall twenty-five meters in front of him. He adjusted the PEQ-2 laser to cover the bore sight laser, giving him accurate target acquisition.

The door to the planning bay opened, and Captain Walen announced, "Group, attention." Immediately the men sprung to their feet and assumed the position of attention. Through the door walked Lieutenant General Jeffrey Lombard, commander of the United States Special Forces Command (USASFC), followed by the group commander, Colonel Mooreland, and another gentleman who was in civilian clothes and unknown to the men.

"Please relax, guys," General Lombard said, and the men relaxed slightly but remained standing. "If I could get you to gather around the table for a few minutes, I'd like to talk to you about a few things." He assumed his seat at the head of the long table. Colonel Mooreland remained standing at the rear of the room with the unknown civilian. The men put down their weapons and cleaning kits and joined the general, with Luke and Frank sitting closest to the general and the rest of the men filling in the other seats.

"First off, I'd like to thank you men for your patience thus far with this situation," the general began. "I understand that although you have been alerted and isolated, you have yet to be given a mission statement or any other details of what lies ahead of you. From what I hear, you have handled everything with the attention to detail and sense of urgency that this particular group is known for. Colonel Mooreland has a lot of faith and respect for this detachment, and I can see why. It looks like you men are already set to go, regardless of the mission."

"We are, sir," replied Luke.

"Well, that's all about to change. I am sure you men understand the importance of the events of this last week and the role that we will play in the immediate response to this attack on our country. We have the intelligence that al Qaeda is responsible for the attacks, and we are going to do everything we can to bring these men to justice and prevent this sort of thing from ever happening again.

"I am tasking you men to infiltrate Afghanistan, link up with friendly host-nation forces known as the Northern Alliance, and occupy and secure land for conventional forces to be brought in.

"We have connections through another governmental organization that have established rapport with a small group of Northern Alliance that is willing to meet with you and begin operations. You will be going into the area known as the Panjshir Valley, just north of the capital city of Kabul." The general used a red laser pointer to highlight an area on the large map hanging on the wall.

"The city is under the control of Taliban forces, a fundamentalist Islamic organization that rules most of Afghanistan. These Taliban are severely anti-American and view us as a threat to their way of life. They are a very strict and controlling force for the local populace." General Lombard continued, "Along with the attacks on New York City and the Pentagon last week, the Taliban assassinated the leader of the Northern Alliance, General Ahmad Shah Massoud. He had a growing force of more than fifteen hundred troops located in the Panjshir Valley, hiding in the mountainous hills and valley there.

"If you know anything about the Russian invasion of Afghanistan in the 1980s, the Panjshir Valley is where the Afghans were able to hold off the advancing Russian tank units from their positions in these hills. It is extremely rough terrain, and it's easy for the Northern Alliance to conceal their position and defend against Taliban forces.

"There has been a hiatus of action in this area, as the Taliban do not want to venture into the mountainous region, and the Northern Alliance does not have the manpower to move south and attack the Taliban in direct combat. As I said, the Northern Alliance in the area number roughly fifteen hundred men, with experienced military men in command. These are not militia—these are men who have been fighting for many years. The Taliban, however, have about fifteen thousand troops in Kabul and the area north of the city, all ready to fight to the death for their beliefs.

"A small airstrip in the town of Bagram will be the focal point of your mission." Again, the general highlighted the map with his laser pointer. "This airstrip is the key to our ability to bring in follow-on forces and supplies to assist the Northern Alliance in the retaking of the capital city. The goal of this operation is to rid Afghanistan of the Islamic fundamentalist Taliban and restore freedom and democracy to the region. What I need from you men is that airfield," the general said, pointing to it on the map.

As the men stared stoically, he continued, "Now, I would love to tell you that you will be given the best available support, with all the resources we have at our disposal, to assist you with this mission. But due to the urgency of the situation, the president wants boots on the ground and real-time ground truth as of now. For this reason, you men will be going in alone, with no backup, no support, and no means of exfiltration aside from the boots on your feet. There is no Big Army to call if things go bad—you're on your own. Make no mistake about this, men—this is a die-in-place scenario." He paused to let that statement sink in.

"The odds are considerably in the favor of your enemy, and the Northern Alliance is undermanned, under-resourced, and overwhelmingly outgunned. When the president issued the order, he was informed of the potential unfavorable outcome that this might produce. He is confident that our men are the best the world has ever seen, and we as a nation have made a habit of overcoming tremendous odds in the fight for freedom. This is a risk he is willing to accept for the greater cause. What we are doing right now and in the coming months will be incredibly historic. Its significance will not be fully comprehended for decades."

He looked around at each man individually and said, "I need to know right now if there is any reason any of you do not think you can do this. And I mean any reason—you're sick, tired, broken, have family issues that are unresolved, or are just plain scared of dying." He paused to allow the men to respond. There was nothing but silence in the room for what seemed like minutes but was actually a few seconds. "I take it that means you are all on board, then?"

"Yes, sir," was the reply from the team, but not in the typical simultaneous and boisterous military fashion. The responses were more individual and at different tones, so you could almost make out each man's answer.

"Okay, then. I have given Colonel Mooreland the entire operational plan, and he will have it in your hands before the night is over, so you can adjust what you already have going here," he said, waving his arm to indicate the room.

"At this point, I'd like to introduce you men to Mr. Charlie Jacobs." He gestured for the civilian standing in the rear of the room to come forward. "Mr. Jacobs works for our government and is in direct contact with your Northern Alliance counterparts. He is here to answer any questions you might have and give you a better idea of what to expect once you hit the ground. If there are no questions of me, I will leave you men to discuss what you will with Mr. Jacobs."

As General Lombard rose from his chair, the entire detachment popped to its feet and into the position of attention, giving the general the utmost respect as he made his way toward the door along with Colonel Mooreland. Along the way, he shook each man's hand and wished each of them good luck.

When he reached the door, he paused for a moment and looked around the room as if he was searching for something in particular.

"Captain Walen?" the general said.

"Yes, sir?" Luke replied.

"Remember, I have been doing this a long time," the general stated matter-of-factly. "Where's the beer fridge?"

"Sir, with the sense of urgency we were under when we moved in here, it was left behind," Luke answered with a slight smile on his face.

"Well, that's no good. Hard to plan the mission of a lifetime without good beer, don't you think?" the general said, looking around at the members of Triple Nickel.

"It would definitely help, sir," was the immediate response of Master

Sergeant Galliano, answering for the rest of the team before they had a chance to embarrass him.

Looking at Colonel Mooreland, the general asked, "Can we do something about that, John?"

"Consider it done, sir," Mooreland replied with a slight grin, and the two exited the room, pulling the door closed behind them. On hearing the reply, Alan looked at Blaine, smiled, and reached out his fist for a fist bump from his teammate, who mouthed the word "boom" as if they had scored a small victory.

"Mr. Jacobs, sir, please have a seat," Luke said, pointing at the seat that General Lombard had occupied.

"Call me Charlie, guys," Jacob responded and took the vacant seat. He put a large briefcase on the table and opened it. He started removing stacks of papers and slid them between Luke and Frank. He pulled out a handful of computer-generated maps and scattered them on the table in front of the men, who immediately reached for them and started the process of digesting the hefty amount of information.

"This is exactly what we are dealing with here," he said, handing a stack of papers stapled together to Luke. "You will load a C-17 tomorrow and leave for Uzbekistan. They have allowed us to use a small airstrip along their southern border with Afghanistan to stage from. From there you will be flown into the Panjshir Valley on two MH-47 Chinook helicopters by the 160th Special Operations Aviation Regiment. The trip is long, and fuel will be a premium, so to add another kink in your plan, you will be limited to the amount of gear you can bring in with you, to free up weight for more fuel. I think they will have just enough fuel to make it there and back with nothing but fumes left.

"One of my guys will be on the ground to receive you along with your NA counterparts. You will have to do what you do and establish rapport with these guys and earn their trust. They have been promised a lot by our country, and what you guys bring to the table will go a long way in what we see in the future for this country. Take your time and do this well. We only have one shot at this.

"We will be bringing in arms, supplies, and money to help finance your efforts to equip and train them. Like the general said, the initial objective is to secure the airfield at Bagram. Once we have control of that, we will be able to grow our efforts exponentially in the area and build up a force large enough to move on Kabul—the capital city and Taliban stronghold."

"If it's the airfield you want so bad, why not just jump in a Ranger battalion? Isn't that what they do?" Luke asked with a stern look on his face.

"We thought about that," replied Charlie, "but right now there are friendly and enemy on opposite sides of the Bagram Airfield. They literally look across the tarmac from each other every day. If we were to land three hundred Rangers on that airfield, they would destroy everything within miles of that place, and we need the Northern Alliance to remain on our side for the next phase of taking Kabul. But good question, Captain."

"Wait," Frank chimed in. "Did you say they look across the airfield from each other?"

"Yes, there has been a hiatus for a long time in the area. They just go about their daily business with the unspoken rule of 'you don't mess with us, we won't mess with you.' The Taliban run things a little different that we do here. They bring their wives and families with them as they move around the country, so while the men are busy, the women establish their homes. And take care of the kids.

"You see this area just south of the airfield?" Charlie slid a satellite photo of Bagram Airfield to Frank. "There is a large wadi running southwest along the airstrip that gathers water and is used for irrigation, drinking, and bathing. When the Northern Alliance held them off at the base of the mountains to the north, the Taliban retreated to the nearest water source and set up camp. Over time, this camp became a military compound with housing and families accompanying them. There is a lot of corruption on both sides, as the Northern Alliance get their food and fuel from the city of Kabul, roughly fifty miles to the south along Highway 1 here," Charlie said, pointing to another photo and map of the area. "They bring it right through the Taliban lines and either pay them or trade things with them."

"Trade what?" Alan inquired.

"Water, for one thing," Charlie responded, looking up at Alan.

"The Panjshir River comes directly out of the mountains, and its water is actually bottled and sent to Europe. Opium is another. We all know it is the number-one agricultural commodity that Afghanistan produces, and it runs everything. We all know that when drugs and money are involved, the only side people are loyal to is the side with the cash. We plan on using that loyalty when you guys arrive.

"This is another reason not to use the Ranger battalions. You men will create a smaller signature and will have no United States military affiliation other than some weapons and gear. Right now, the Air Force is starting a bombing campaign in the area south of Bagram. From the initial reports of my guy on the ground and his NA assets, about 95 percent of those bombs being dropped are hitting just dirt. With your laser targeting devices, we can change that number considerably. There are elevated areas here, here, and here," he said, pointing to different areas on a smaller map with his green laser pointer. "From these positions, you can assess the area and call in bombers to hit your targets. Once you have the area around the airfield secure enough, we can bring in more ODAs and supplies to help you guys in the taking of Kabul."

"How long do you think all of this will take?" Luke asked.

"We are planning on about a year before conditions are right to move on the city," Charlie answered flatly.

"A fucking year?" Alan blurted out.

"Dude!" Frank looked at Alan sternly, like a parent visually scolding a child that has made a gaffe.

"It's okay, Frank," Charlie laughed and held his hand up in a calming manner. "Yes, Sergeant Scott, a fucking year. I don't think you realize how difficult this is going to be for you men. Like General Lombard said, there are roughly fifteen thousand Taliban and al Qaeda forces in and around Kabul, and you will be dealing with about fifteen hundred Northern Alliance rebels.

"Organizing, equipping, and training these rebels is going to take time and a lot of patience. These are not the Mujahideen fighters of the 1980s. These are their sons, and most of them are young and have not seen the combat their fathers have. They are going to tell you they are hardened combat soldiers, but walking to a secure front, firing off one magazine at nothing, and returning home hardly makes them what we would consider hardened combat veterans. It is going take your A-game to make this work."

Alan looked at Steve and whispered, "How did he know my name?"

Steve smiled and gave Alan a shrug.

"Everything you guys need to know is in these reports. Now, if there aren't any pressing questions, I have two more ODAs to brief tonight," Charlie said as he stood up and closed his briefcase.

"I have just one thing," Frank said loudly. "Keep those other idiots out of our AO. We tend not to play well with others." By "those other idiots," he meant the other ODAs, and by "AO" he meant their area of operations.

"Don't worry, buddy," Charlie replied. "You are going to be the only team in your area for a long time. Those other guys are not even going to be close to you. You just be smart and take care of these guys," he said, pointing to the other members of the team.

Charlie rose from his seat at the head of the table and shook the hand of each man as he passed, wishing each of them good luck, as General Lombard had done earlier. He went to the door, opened it, and paused just before he exited. He looked around at each of the men in the room, making eye contact with each, as if he were taking a mental Polaroid.

"So this is what crazy people look like?" He cracked a large smile, shook his head in bewilderment, and closed the door behind him as he left.

"Crazy people?" Shane said with a look of amazement.

"I knew I should have become a dentist like my mother wanted," Steve said to himself as he started going through some of the documents Charlie had left on the table.

Within a matter of minutes, Steve had the papers stacked into different piles according to the information contained in them, and he handed each to the right individual, so he could start incorporating the intelligence into their planning.

Charlie had covered most of the essentials of the mission, and all the rest of the details would be in the operations order that would be delivered to them before the night was over. Once again, each man returned to his station in the planning bay, and they began going through their intelligence reports to update what they had already begun.

"All right, men," Luke began, "Charlie says we're moving out in the morning. I want your portions of the briefback done by the end of the day. We have a lot to do, so let's get to work." Without hesitating, the team split up to their respective areas and began the task of putting together the briefback.

As each member began to write his part of the briefback, Tony entered the room with another soldier; they carried a large white cooler and set it down on the floor by the back double-doors. From the sound the cooler made when it hit the floor, and from the look of strain on Tony's face as he carried his end, it was obvious that whatever was in the cooler was extremely heavy.

"Compliments of the general, boys." Tony reached down and opened the lid of the cooler, exposing several cases of beer covered in ice. He started grabbing cans and tossing them to the others in the room like a Las Vegas blackjack dealer.

Upon catching his can, Blaine cracked it open right away, covering the area immediately surrounding him in foam from the shaken alcohol. Unaffected by the shower of foam, he raised the can to his mouth and drank the entire thing, ending with a crushing squeeze. Once he was finished, he held the empty can upside down, signifying that its contents had been cleared. Blaine then threw the crushed, empty can over his left shoulder without a glance, landing it in the large trash can in the corner of the room. He smiled, closed his eyes, and sighed with delight, and then he went right back to the task he'd been working on before Tony entered the room.

The team worked through most of the night, planning, packing, and completing their sections of the briefback. By the time the sun was peeking over the horizon, most of the room was packed up at the back double-doors. There were new maps and photos on the wall, as well as a product folder on the table.

This folder was a large, white three-ring binder with the combat diver logo on the front and the words MISSION UW 001 printed in a large, bold font on the cover. It contained the entire briefback, the mission particulars, maps and photos of the AO, and communication frequencies that were dedicated to the team for their mission.

As Frank and Luke were at the map on the far wall discussing route planning, the rest of the team was asleep up in the sleeping area aside from Alan and Steve, who were sleeping on the floor next to the cooler of beer. Next to them was a large clear trash bag filled with empty beer cans. A loud, thundering snore startled Luke and Frank, and they both looked back to see Steve rubbing his nose, eyes still closed, and laying his head on the rolled-up jacket he was using as a pillow. The two leaders looked up from Steve to each other and started to laugh.

Although this had been a very long three days, the two of them knew it had only just begun.

# CHAPTER 10

*Don't you lock up something you wanted to see fly.*
-Chris Cornell

The next day, just miles from the Afghanistan border, somewhere above the country of Uzbekistan, three Special Forces A-teams were aboard a C-17 Globemaster III en route to Karshi-Khanabad Air Base. This airfield served as the staging area for the Combined Joint Special Operations Task Force (CJSOTF), and it was from where the first SF soldiers into the new War on Terror would launch. Most of the men were asleep, either in the cargo seats against the hull or sprawled out on top of their pallets of operational equipment.

A C-17 was a large cargo plane that could hold several large pallets, over one hundred troops, or a combination of both cargo and troops. Each ODA had its own pallet of gear, loaded down with tough boxes, rucksacks, duffel bags, and weapons. The only light within the plane came from several dull green lights sporadically placed throughout its hull. There was enough light to see only the area immediately surrounding each bulb itself, but not enough to cast light throughout the entire plane or to be noticeable from the outside. The plane itself had no exterior or safety lights on, creating no signature in the night sky other than the sound from the engines. The pilots had flown straight through, with two crews alternating flying and navigating duties, to allow for sleep. The plane had been refueled in the air by tanker planes, and without even the slightest turbulence to alert their passengers that fueling was taking place.

Their cargo was high priority, and the highest levels in the Air Force had established a sense of urgency to have it arrive quickly and safely.

Sergeant Scott was on top of one of the pallets in the rear of the plane, listening to his portable music player, but he was not asleep. Staring up at the green light located near the rear ramp door, he went over scenarios of what could transpire in the near future. He could not get the vision of the planes flying into the buildings in New York out of his mind. He had witnessed tragedy in his life many times before, but never on such a grand scale. With every thought of those scenes that played like a loop of video footage in his mind, he grew angrier.

There definitely had been a feeling of vengefulness in the air during their isolation, although it was never discussed out loud.

These men were no different from any other soldier when it came to their patriotism, and an attack on their country was the ultimate act of war. A terrorist attack on their home soil had always been feared but never considered. Thousands of civilians had been killed and thousands more wounded. The entire country was angry and wanted justice. The men were starting to feel the weight of the responsibility that had been placed on them. To be the ones called upon in a devastating situation like this, carrying the anger of an entire nation,

was somewhat overwhelming.

Through the music playing in his earphones, Alan made out a voice over the intercom system of the airplane. He removed one of his earbuds to see if he could understand what was being said, but between the roar of the jet engines and his music, all he could make out was a muffled human voice speaking in English. He sat up and looked around the plane and noticed that others had gotten off the pallets in front of him and moved toward the front of the plane, where the rest of the men were sitting in the cargo seats. He decided to follow suit and join the rest of his team.

He grabbed his water bottle and made his way to an empty seat between Blaine and JT. While he was fastening his seatbelt, he tapped JT on his leg to get his attention and then pointed toward the intercom speakers in the plane and gave him a questioning look. JT also was wearing headphones and replied with a hand and arm signal signaling a descent. Alan responded with a nod and reached into his shirt pocket for a piece of gum to help him clear his ears during the change in altitude.

The feeling of weightlessness that accompanies a rapid descent, such as felt when making the first big drop on a roller coaster, can be somewhat disturbing when one is not prepared. When experienced in an airplane, it is usually temporary due to turbulence of some kind. Alan immediately grabbed for the cargo straps holding up the rear of his seat for stability. The feeling of weightlessness was not only continuing; it had increased in intensity.

This was not turbulence; this was total free fall. He looked over at Blaine to his left and was in total disbelief to see him throwing his water bottle up in the air slightly and watching it remain there as if suspended in thin air. They were in complete free fall in an airplane, and this man was playing catch with himself, using a weightless water bottle.

Frantically Alan looked around the rear of the plane to assess the situation. The Air Force loadmaster was wearing an olive-green flight suit and flight gloves and had a communications headset on his head, with large earphones fitted with a boom microphone that bent to touch his lips. He was staring intensely out of the small fishbowl window on the rear port side of the aircraft. His demeanor was not that of a man under the impression that the plane was doing anything abnormal. Still confused, Alan glanced to his right to see JT leaning back with his eyes closed and chewing gum, rocking his head from side to side as if dancing internally to the music he was listening to.

They were experiencing what is called a tactical descent. Normally, one would realize that it takes somewhere around 30 minutes for your plane to drop from 30,000 feet down to the runway below to deliver you safely to your destination. With that descent comes your fair share of ear popping and maybe a little bit of shaking and rattling sometimes if you hit some turbulence. However, most of the time, it's a nice and smooth journey, for the most part, down to the awaiting runway below unless something unforeseen happens to pop up. Now, just imagine taking the time that a descent normally takes of that half hour or so and smashing it into less than one minute. The C-17 also has speed brakes. In speed brake mode the flaps extend to dramatically increase drag, and the spoilers deploy to cancel out the increase in lift caused by the flaps and further increase drag. This makes possible a tactical descent well more than 20,000 ft/min. The idea being to arrive directly over the destination airfield in a combat zone at high altitude and then very rapidly spiral down and land before an enemy outside the airport can drop mortars or other weapons on the runway. It works very well.

Having missed the pilot's intercom message informing the passengers in the cargo hold of the upcoming tactical descent, Alan was completely caught off guard. Once safely on the ground, he was informed of the exact reasons for the rapid descent, and immediately he became the butt of several jokes by the others for not being in the know.

Once the aircraft came to a complete stop, the rear ramp started to lower slowly, and the rays of the rising sun came shooting into the cargo hold, blinding all the men, who had been in darkness for the better part of their flight. On the tarmac outside the aircraft was Command Sergeant Major Keith Grainer, CSM of the 2nd Battalion, 5th Special Forces, along with several other staff officers and non-commissioned officers from 5th Group.

Once all three teams were off the aircraft and had gathered around CSM Grainer, he paused and looked around at each of the thirty or so men in front of him, wearing a stoic, almost angry stare and with arms folded across his chest. He reached out an empty hand to his left, and immediately a young staff officer handed him a stack of papers.

Looking down at the paper and not once breaking his demeanor, he announced loudly, "All right, listen up. ODA 525, go with Captain Reed." He pointed with his right hand to the general area where the captain was standing, but he still did not look up from his paperwork. "595, Captain Farrell." Again, he pointed slightly to his right, without looking, as if he could sense exactly where Captain Farrell was standing. "Triple Nickel," he continued, but Alan's voice interrupted him immediately.

"Yeah, baby!"

This interruption caused CSM Grainer to pause and look up at Alan. There was a hint of an upturn in the corners of his mouth as he continued, "You can follow me." Without a word, he turned and headed directly away from the aircraft at a faster-than-normal walking pace.

Frank threw his desert-tan backpack over his right shoulder and followed CSM Grainer away from the aircraft. As he passed Alan, he reached out with his left hand and punched Alan in the right arm, hard.

"What'd I do?" Alan asked with his arms outstretched and an inquisitive look on his face, knowing exactly what the punch was for. Steve reached down, picked up Alan's backpack, and draped the pack over Alan's outstretched arm. He looked at him, cracked a smile, and shook his head as he turned to follow Frank.

"Austin Powers, bro," Steve said as he walked away from Alan. Alan smiled and pointed at Steve with a nod and a crafty grin for his excellent movie awareness, and he followed the rest of the team down the flight line to a row of large, desert-tan tents.

Each ODA was led into a different tent, each with the capacity to house at least thirty men. They were constructed in typical military fashion: equally spaced from each other and oriented in the same direction. Instead of being set up directly on the ground, wooden pallets were used as flooring, and in the far end of each tent there was a stack of Army cots that still needed to be put together. There was a hand-washing station outside, with a plastic bladder filled with water and liquid soap bottles hanging by parachute cord from the corner of the tent.

The SGM entered one of the tents, followed by the men of Triple Nickel. "This will be your sleeping area, planning area, and briefback area," the SGM began, in a very businesslike manner. "Chow is in one hour. I understand you submitted several orders and requests for equipment in the rear and were told it would be here waiting for you. Not going to happen. We have ammunition and chow. We are doing everything we can to get you guys ready to go, but you see what we are working with here. If I were you, I would plan on going in with what you brought with you, and if anything you asked for shows up between now and then, I will make sure it comes right to you."

He continued without changing his strictly business expression. "Right now, the word is forty-eight hours and you launch. That doesn't give you much time, so I would make every hour count. Focus all your efforts on the first couple months in theater and be as flexible with your plan as you can. The commander will be here tomorrow night and will be expecting the briefbacks soon after he lands. Keep them simple and to the point and be confident. He will not hesitate for a second to drop another team in there if he doesn't think you can handle this. It is too important. Roger that?"

"Roger that, Sergeant Major," Frank replied immediately with a more "command" voice than usual.

"Get settled in. It's going to be a long night," CSM grainer said as he turned to exit the tent. "Sergeant Scott … outside." Alan looked over at Steve, opened his eyes wide, and pointed his index finger at his own chest, as if to confirm that he was the person in question, mouthing the word "me." Steve smiled wide and nodded his head several times as Alan walked past him to follow CSM Grainer out of the tent.

Everyone on Triple Nickel knew that Alan had been the junior medical sergeant for CSM Grainer when he was a team sergeant several years earlier. CSM Grainer and Alan had completely different personalities, but Grainer had been a medic himself and became good friends with Alan soon after starting to work with him. CSM Grainer was aware that Alan was a little abrasive and a tad arrogant, but he considered him an excellent medic and operator. The difference between confident and cocky was the ability to perform, and there were never any questions as to Alan's performance.

Early in Alan's career, then Master Sergeant Grainer sat Alan down for a counseling session and explained to him that his aggressive attitude and explosive personality were going to upset a lot of people he met throughout his career in Special Forces. Alan had been told this many times before and was used to being reprimanded for his attitude and mouth. But to Alan's surprise, MSG Grainer had explained to him how much he wanted Alan to keep these qualities, as he felt that they were what gave him his edge. They not only pushed him to be a better operator and medic, but they also made the other members of the team elevate their performance, so as not to be outdone by such an ass. He liked Alan's aggressiveness and explained to him that he only had one person to worry about, and that was MSG Grainer.

Over the next several years, Alan became even more confident in himself, as his team sergeant had given him the green light to be exactly who he needed to be. MSG Grainer knew exactly what he was doing and watched Sergeant Scott turn into an excellent SF NCO. Although he had to rein Alan in many times and remind him exactly who was in charge of the detachment, their relationship grew. Alan knew that he always had a senior leader that he could go to in tough times, one that would give him a straightforward answer. CSM Grainer was not known for beating around the bush when it came to getting things done. He was a "bottom line" leader, and Alan respected him tremendously.

Once both men were outside the tent, CSM Grainer wasted no time in interrogating Alan. With arms again crossed over his chest, and without breaking his emotionless expression, he asked, "Are you ready for this?"

Alan cracked a slight smile and replied, "Bro, I don't even know what this is." He raised his hands slightly and shrugged his shoulders. "This has all happened so fast, I haven't had a chance to even think about it. So, fuck no, I'm not ready for this! Who the hell is?" He cracked an even bigger smile. "But I'm fucking going. I ain't about to miss this one."

CSM Grainer broke character and started to smile himself. "You're ready," he said, nodding a little. "Do you need anything?"

"Yeah, do me a favor and cut my grass, will ya?" Alan replied as he stepped back a little from CSM Grainer to light a cigarette. "And if something goes wrong," he said with a more serious tone, "call my sister. She deserves to know."

"You got it. Just don't do anything stupid," Grainer said sternly. "There are a lot of eyes on this one. I'm not going to tell you to calm down or throttle back—we both know that won't happen. Just remember what's at stake here. And remember you're it—no support at all. It's going to take months before the regular Army gets their shit together and gets over here."

"Keith," Alan said with a calming tone, "I think you're a little jealous."

"You bet your ass I am. Everyone is," the SGM answered matter of-factly. "Make no mistake about it—you guys are in the Super Bowl here. Every dude in this community would give one of his kidneys to be in your shoes right now. There is history being written with every step you take. And much like a Super Bowl, there are thousands of people in the stands and thousands more watching on TV. Everything you guys do, every step along the way, will be analyzed and second-guessed by people who could never do the things you guys are about to."

"You know I've never really cared about what people thought of me, especially ones who can't do what I can. I am good at this—you know I am. Hell, you helped make me. And I could care less about what a buncha virgins think of the way I fuck! I have a good team in there." Alan pointed into the tent to his left. "If I were to hand-pick guys to go in with, I would pick some of those guys. I think everything I have done so far in my career has prepared me for this fight, right now. You ask me if I'm ready—what you need to do is call ahead to those motherfuckers and let 'em know I'm coming and ask them if they're ready. You call this our Super Bowl? Well, get the chips and salsa, bro, because you're going to see some spectacular shit here. If this is it for me—if this is my fifteen minutes or we don't come home—then I'm going to make it count. Just know I'm ready. You made me ready. So don't worry, I'll be just fine," he finished with a smile.

Grainer cracked a smile himself and shook his head. "Go set up your gear, asshole." He tapped Alan on the shoulder and walked back to the operations center.

Alan returned to the tent, where the rest of the men were busy putting together their cots. They had separated the tent into two sections: one for sleeping and the other half for planning and briefing. Two six-foot tables were already set up, with several folding metal chairs around them. Luke and Frank had gotten out their laptops and were busy typing the finishing touches of the briefback when Alan entered the tent.

As Alan walked past, Frank looked up at him and asked, "Did you get your ass chewed?"

"Nah, he's just worried about me. Kind of cute, hey?" Alan said with a condescending tone.

"Just be lucky he likes you," Frank said. "He doesn't seem like the kind of guy I would want to piss off."

"Don't let him fool you. He's a big softie," Alan replied as he began unfolding his cot.

"Didn't he break your nose once?" Steve yelled from across the tent.

"Yeah, but I kind of deserved it," Alan answered.

"He broke your nose?" Blaine asked laughingly. "This I've got to hear."

"Well, we were at the Air Force pool out at Ali Al Salem Air Base in Kuwait one year," Alan began, "and I tried pulling him into the deep end by his shorts as he was getting out of the pool. I was in the water and had my feet up on the side of the pool, so there was no way he was getting away. His shorts started to come down, and it was either get stripped in front of all the Air Force chicks around the pool or get wet."

He started assembling his cot as he continued the story. "I guess he chose to get wet, and he fell backward toward me, leading with a right hand, right to my face."

"And boom goes the dynamite," Steve interrupted as he made a punching motion with his right hand in the air.

The rest of the team started laughing and either pointing at Alan or holding their noses as if they'd just taken the punch themselves.

"Man, I'd have paid to see that one," Blaine said to Steve.

"You would think, after fifty years," Alan interrupted, "and all the technological advances the Army has made, that they would come out with an easier cot. We put a man on the moon in '69, and these things are from like World War I." He held up one of the end bars from the cot and looked at it as if he had no idea how to attach it to the main piece. "This thing is retarded," he said as he threw the bar on the floor and put down the cot with no end pieces.

"Someone didn't get an erector set for Christmas," JT said jokingly from his side of the tent, eliciting laughter from the others.

"Quit screwing around down there, and start setting up," Frank interrupted. "We have a lot to get done today."

# CHAPTER 11

*In union there is strength.*
-Aesop

Over the next several hours, the team set up their sleeping area, unloaded all of their operational equipment from their pallet, and set up their planning area with operational maps, graphics, and charts brought from their isolation area back at Fort Campbell. All the men were busy working in their respective areas of the tent, and Frank was going around and making sure each man had his piece of the briefback completed.

He paused by JT and watched as he put together different antennas on several different radios. He would install the same antenna on each radio to see which ones he could combine to save space. If they were to go in light, he would have to go with as little commo gear as possible to save space, and that meant making the hard decision of which radios to leave behind. With all the factors he had to consider, this was an extremely difficult thing to do. There were different levels of communications training on the detachment, and some men were just not used to the newer types of radios that he had with him. There were also many players in this mission, which meant he had to have a way to talk to each of them.

Probably the biggest challenge was how he was going to power these devices. There were only so many batteries, and most of them were not interchangeable between radios, which meant that for each different radio, he had to hump in a new supply of batteries. Whereas it might be feasible to purchase food, water, and ammunition locally, finding a BA 3030 or BA 5590 battery was highly unlikely.

As was common among most Special Forces teams, the experience JT brought to the table far surpassed what was taught to him in his communications training. He was a master of making things work in situations where they were just not supposed to. It seemed that no matter what the situation was or what shortcomings were involved, he always seemed to get commo with someone. It was a running joke on Triple Nickel that if you gave JT two shot glasses, some string, and a AA battery, he would be talking to his wife on the other side of the globe by lunchtime.

The communications sergeant, much like the medic, was always considered to have a secondary job in Special Forces, because no one ever saw them do their job until it was absolutely necessary. And no one would care what the circumstances were, or how little equipment they were provided, or who was responsible for not giving them what was necessary; the bottom line was that when commo needed to be made, you'd better make commo. Likewise, with the medic, no one cared that you weren't given the supplies you asked for, but if a man was injured, you'd better save his life, period.

"How are we looking, JT?" Frank asked.

"Well, I read the entire manual of these new IMBTR radios, and I think we lucked out," JT replied while looking around at the mess in front of him. "They can do HF, FM, UHF, and SATCOM. That's really going to cut down on what we need to take in with us. They all have spare batteries, so I can charge one while the other is in use. They're also smaller and lighter than what we're used to, which is a big plus as well. The only problem I see with them is the fact that they haven't given me any crypto for them yet, so I don't even know if we can use them."

"English, JT," Frank said as he crossed his arms at his chest and began to look around JT at the mess he had created in his area. There were batteries, radios, antennas, cables, and wires all over the place, in no order whatsoever.

"It means that right now, they can't talk to each other," JT explained as he held up two IMBTRs. "It's like they are all the same radio but speak different languages. But once they get connected to one another with the same crypto, they can talk. So, I need to find out what language these guys are speaking here, so we can talk to them."

"But," JT paused and held one finger in the air. "And like my wife, it's a very big butt—if their language is different from the Air Force, we could talk to these guys but not the planes above us."

"Well, they are going to want us to be able to direct the close air support as soon as we get there. So what's the fix, then?" Frank asked.

"Common sense would tell me that the easiest fix would be to get the Air Force, JSOTF, and the commo guys from each ODA together and marry up all the crypto. But that's about as likely to happen as Alan growing up," he said, pointing in Alan's direction. Frank looked over at Alan and saw him with his earphones on and a cravat wrapped around his head like a bandanna, standing on his cot shirtless while playing air guitar with a broom like a rock star.

"I get your point," Frank said and began to laugh.

"Well, if 160th is here," JT explained, "then they probably have Air Force Pararescue—PJ—and Combat Controller Teams—CCT— with them. I could get with the CCT guys and see if I can get their fill. We have twelve IMBTRs, so if I can get one filled by them and fill one with what the JSOTF has, we will have both sets of crypto. Some of us will just have to carry two radios. The only problem is that if we do split-team operations, I can only go with one, so the other team will have to be read on."

"All right. Keep me up to speed," Frank said, and he walked back to his seat at the long table and went back to typing.

Tony DeNero entered the tent, carrying a handful of water bottles and placed them on the table near Frank. "Hey, Frank, how are things going?"

"We are coming along pretty good," Frank responded. "What's the word on infil? You hear anything yet?"

"Right now," Tony explained, "they are saying three days of rations, fifteen days of batteries. They are looking at pushing out a resupply bundle to you in seventy-two hours. I have the 5th Group parachute riggers getting their stuff together right now to help you build your bundles. Once again, you are going to be limited to the space, so it has to be just the necessities—chow, batteries, ammo, weapons, and medical supplies."

They both walked over to the maps on the wall and began looking for areas to do the resupply. They needed a big enough area for several bundles to be dropped, and in the mountainous terrain of the Panjshir Valley, this would be extremely difficult because of the lack of flat areas. The only area that provided an area long enough at the same elevation was along the Panjshir River. Because of the time of year they were going in, the water levels were considerably lower, and the river had much larger banks on both sides. This provided an excellent area for landing helicopters or dropping bundles from a C-130 cargo plane.

CSM Grainer entered the tent, followed by an unknown man in civilian clothes carrying a large pack over his shoulder. "Frank," he called and motioned him over.

Frank approached them and held his hand out to shake SGM Grainer's hand. "How are you doing, Sergeant Major?"

"Good," replied Grainer as he shook Frank's hand. "This is Tech Sergeant Calvin Michaels. He is Air Force CCT, and he has some things to go over with your commo guy about the SOFLAM."

"Holy shit, Charlie Mike!" JT yelled from down the tent when he recognized TSSG Michaels, and he got to his feet.

"JT, man, it's been a while," Calvin said as he walked over to JT and shook his hand, bringing JT close for an embrace.

Calvin was a larger man, standing six-foot two and coming in at roughly 225 pounds. His head was shaved bald, although you could see the hair coming in the typical fashion of someone who has been losing his hair to begin with but hasn't shaved it in a few days. He had about a week and a half of facial hair growth as well, showing that he had been given similar orders of relaxed grooming in the same time frame as the men on the Triple Nickel.

"You two know each other?" Frank asked.

"We went to dive school together in Key West," JT explained.

"My dive buddy got hurt about two weeks into it, and I got paired up with CM. We had an absolute blast down there." He looked over at Calvin with a huge smile. "Remember those two stewardesses from Seattle?"

"No, I don't remember anything like that," Calvin replied as he smacked JT in the bicep with the back of his hand. "I was too busy becoming a combat diver and never left the compound." He gave JT a dubious look as if he had told a family secret.

"What are you doing out here, man?" JT inquired.

"Right now, I'm covering down for the sorties they are running in-country. I'm the Combat Search and Rescue Team chief in case one of the pilots goes down," Calvin explained. "I heard you guys were going in soon to help spot targets, and I thought I'd come see if you needed any help with the SOFLAM."

"Dude, that would be awesome," JT responded. "I haven't pulled that thing out of the box, except for inventories, in about three years."

"Go get it," Calvin said, "and I'll run you through it really quick. It's easy." The two walked to JT's area of the tent, unpacked their individual SOFLAMs, and began talking and playing with the knobs, buttons, and features of each one.

The Special Operations Forces Laser Marker (SOFLAM) was a device that looked like a large set of binoculars that emitted a coded laser signal to be pointed, or "painted," at a target. This signal code would then be transmitted to a corresponding munitions drop by Air Force fighter planes or bombers. The fighter or bomber was then "talked in" to his target area by the operator on the ground and given the code of the SOFLAM. The azimuth of the laser to the target was given to the pilot, who flew directly down the azimuth and dropped his bomb, which picked up the signal sent out by the SOFLAM and followed the laser directly into the target. This extremely accurate way of destroying individual targets considerably lowered costs of munitions and increased damage to enemy forces. It was first seen in combat in Desert Storm, when Special Forces operators guided fighter planes onto many targets in the deserts north of Kuwait, leading to the annihilation of the Iraqi tank units in less than twenty-four hours. The SGM looked at Frank and asked, "How's it going? You guys need anything?"

"The only issue we have right now is the commo," Frank replied.

"JT says that the radios we have can either talk to the JSOTF or the Air Force, but not both. But he's got a plan, I guess."

"I'll bring it up at the TOC when I get back," the SGM said. "It shouldn't be that much of an issue. Remember, everyone here is 100 percent employed to facilitate you guys. There is no other priority. You tell us what you need, and twenty people are on it."

"All right, then," Frank replied, "how about some cigars? I know one of those staff weenies has some Cubans."

"I'll see what I can do." The SGM smiled as he turned and walked out of the tent.

"Frank," JT called out.

"Yeah? What's up?" Frank replied as he saw JT coming toward him, with Calvin close behind.

"We just had an awesome idea," JT said, pointing to Calvin and back to himself. "Why don't we take Cal with us?"

"What?" Frank looked at him, confused.

"Dude, he's CCT. He would be like having another commo guy on the team," JT replied. "So if we go split-team, we would have a commo guy with each team. He also has all his own radios and SOFLAM, and we know he will be able to talk to the birds," he said, pointing to Calvin.

"That's going to be a hard sell," Frank retorted, referring to the permission necessary to have an Air Force operator join an Army SF team on a mission.

"Not really, Frank," Alan said as he walked up to the group near the front of the tent. "How ya doing, man? Alan Scott." He reached out to shake Calvin's hand.

"Calvin," he replied and shook Alan's hand in return.

"When we were in Bosnia in '95, we had a CCT guy attached to us." Alan looked back at Frank. "It was a total blessing, too. Trying to get CAS through Army channels isn't very, um … efficient. If you know what I mean." Alan looked at JT and rolled his eyes. "Having CCT with us was awesome because they just called up their guys directly, bypassing the whole system, and we would have birds on target, lickety-split, like."

"No doubt," Calvin joined in. He looked from Alan to Frank. "You guys would have to call your people, send the request over to those guys," he said, pointing in the direction of the Air Force area of the compound, "and they would have to approve it and send it back the same way to you. I could get the Airborne Command and Control Center on the horn directly and get the closest thing to us on target ASAP."

"It makes more sense, Frank," JT said. "We could really use the help on this one."

"It would be Colonel Mooreland's call," Frank explained. "He won't even be here until tomorrow, but maybe we can get word to him. It would be nice to not have to find out two hours before we leave that we have an extra body. I'll go talk to Grainer about it. Sergeant Michaels," Frank said, looking at Calvin, "you might want to go tell your people, so we don't blindside them with this. If you were my guy, I am sure I would have a problem losing you for a year."

"No problem," Calvin said and looked at JT with a little grin. He walked out of the tent to go seek permission to accompany the Nickel into theater. He was smiling from ear to ear like a child seeking permission to go to Disneyland with the neighbor. With all the emphasis on this mission, being the only Air Force guy involved would be epic.

"While we are at it," Alan said, looking at Frank, "I saw this hot blonde over by the chow tent. She would be a real asset on this trip too."

Frank just gave Alan a little stare and walked out of the tent, obviously not amused by his request.

Alan looked at JT and pointed his finger at him. "Why do you get to bring a friend?" JT gave Alan the same look that Frank just had and walked back to his area to finish packing his radios. Alan chuckled to himself and went out of the tent to grab a smoke. He looked over at the tarmac and noticed another C-17 landing. They had been coming in non-stop since the team had arrived, bringing in more equipment, tents, and personnel.

Over the next twenty-four hours, the area that began with only a handful of tents grew tenfold. Every few hours, a different person would come into the Triple Nickel tent and drop off another box of supplies, ammunition, or gear for the men. Some of the things had been requested by the team during isolation, and other things were just given to them. Boxes started piling up in the corners of their tent, leaving little room for anything else.

The entire detachment worked through most of the night in preparation for the group commander's appearance the following day. Although each man had done his share of briefbacks, they all knew this one was different, and no man wanted to let the team down by not preparing for every little mishap that could be thrown their way. As the hours passed, each man felt more pressure. The Super Bowl reference the SGM had made seemed more and more accurate as time went by. And kickoff was rapidly approaching.

\* \* \*

"On your feet!" CSM Grainer commanded. From sitting in a row of chairs in front of a large map, the men of Triple Nickel stood erect at the position of attention.

"As you were," said Colonel Mooreland as he entered the tent and assumed his seat at the center of the table, directly across from the men standing at attention. He was followed by several of his senior staff officers.

"Are we ready to begin, Captain?" Colonel Mooreland asked Captain Walen.

"Yes, sir," he replied.

"Well, let's do it. I am sure you men have a lot to get accomplished yet, and I don't want to take too much of your time with this formality. But before you guys start, I want you to know I am not interested in you selling me on this. I don't need long, drawn-out speeches on how awesome you are. Just give me the facts about what your plan is and tell me if you have everything you need to make that happen. You are my guys, period. That should cut your briefback down a tad, so you can get back to your business."

"Roger that, sir," replied Captain Walen as he approached the makeshift podium in front of a large map. Each member of the team in turn described, in a brief but concise manner, his role in the mission and his plan to handle it. Captain Walen talked about the evasion plan for if things should go awry, and he closed the briefing with his conclusion.

Colonel Mooreland looked at TSGT Michaels. "Well, what do you have to say for yourself?"

Calvin got to his feet and looked the colonel directly in the eye with a determined stare. "Sir, I've been doing this a long time. I'm the best at what I do. Everything in my career up to this point has prepared me for this mission. This is what I am meant to do."

"He sounds pretty confident," Colonel Mooreland said to his SGM. "What do you think, Keith?"

"He'd definitely give us a better edge, sir," the SGM replied with a slight grin.

Colonel Mooreland looked around the room at each member of the detachment and then rose from his seat. Each member of the team automatically rose to his feet in the position of attention. "It looks like these guys have their shit together, Keith," he said. "Let's give them some space to finish up. Have they gotten their clothes yet?"

"No, sir. They should be here in a few hours," the SGM said. A large grin began to form on his face.

"Well, I think we should hold off on that little tidbit till they arrive, then."

"Roger that, sir."

"Captain, carry on," Mooreland said, and he grabbed his notebook and pen from the table and headed toward the door of the tent, followed by his staff. He stopped in front of Calvin and extended his hand. "Sergeant Michaels, welcome aboard."

Calvin shook the colonel's hand firmly and said, "Thank you for the opportunity, sir."

"Clothes? What the hell was that about?" Frank asked Tony, who was standing by the door.

"I have no idea, man. Let me go find out." Tony walked out of the tent after the staff to ask what they were planning.

"All right, let's get this place torn down," Frank told the men sternly. "We only have a few hours of daylight left. Pre-combat checks should be done by 1800 hours. I want everything not going packed up and stored in the Conex behind the tent. All personal items with any identification, to include wallets and ID cards, give to Blaine so he can lock them in the safe. I want you to buddy up by job and check each other's gear. I better not see one piece of paper, not one piece of identifying information, and not one picture of a wife in any of our gear. I want nothing associating us with the United States."

"How about other people's wives?" Blaine asked.

"Random naked pictures?" Alan came back.

"Sheep?" Steve inquired.

"How about this?" JT asked, holding up a black leather mask with a zipper across the mouth.

"Oh, for the love of God," Frank said as he left the back of the tent, to the laughter of the rest of the men.

# CHAPTER 12

*Though no one can go back and make a brand-new start,
anyone can start from now and make a brand-new ending.*
-Author unknown

As the sun set against a mountainous backdrop, the team was busy performing last-minute checks of their gear outside their tent: turning on and looking through night vision goggles, checking flashlights, counting magazines, and cinching down straps on their rucksacks. Tony DeNero approached with several other soldiers, all carrying large cardboard boxes, and they put them down in front of the tent. All the men stopped what they were doing and looked over at Tony, who was smiling more than usual as he called Frank over to his location.

"What's up? What's all this?" Frank asked, pointing to the boxes laid out in front of the team.

"Remember the question the colonel asked about the clothes? Well, here you go, boys. Dig in." As Tony finished his sentence, he burst out in laughter.

The men walked over and started going through the boxes on the ground. "The word is," Tony continued, composing himself, "that the Northern Alliance doesn't want you coming in with American military uniforms. So, the supply guys went downtown to get you guys some clothes for your trip. We used your uniform sizes to try to get the right fit. Everyone has a box marked for them."

Each man found the box with his name written on it in black marker, and they began to go through the clothes, piece by piece, with looks of complete amazement at the selection of fashion that was available.

"Oh, hell no," Blaine said as he held up a purple silk dress shirt. "Where the hell are we going, Studio 54?"

Rusty held up a checkered sweater and said, "Oh, this is real tactical. Who am I blending in with wearing this?"

"Dude, check out this hat," Steve said, and he held up a fedora and put it on his head.

"Nice hat, Al Capone," replied Alan.

"Keep laughing, Alan," Tony chuckled. "The word is they had to go to a children's store for you."

"Maybe the little girls' department," Blaine chimed in.

Alan looked in his box, pulled out a pair of blue jeans, and held them up to himself, showing that they were clearly too short. "Aw, come on!" he complained as the rest of the team laughed and pointed at his exposed ankles. "I'm not wearing this crap," Alan said as he threw the jeans back into the box.

"You don't have a choice," Frank scolded. "If this is what they want, then that's what they get. If they want us looking like the French resistance instead of a bunch of American troops, then that's what we do. Unload your deserts, grab a handful of stuff that fits, and repack. Let's go—the clock is ticking. We have our aircrew brief in ninety minutes." Frank donned a wool apple cap, grabbed his box, and went into the tent to change his clothes.

The rest of the men spent the next few minutes making two piles each, one for items that passed their fashion sense, and another that was simply not going to be packed. Each one grabbed the pile that passed the test and moved into the tent to change his clothes and repack his ruck with the rest.

Several minutes later, the team came out of their tent with all their gear and dressed in their new garb. They were greeted by Colonel Mooreland, Sergeant Major Grainer, Sergeant DeNero, and several other staff members. The audience began clapping and laughing at the appearance of the highly trained Special Forces soldiers dressed as if they were going out for a night on the town.

Several cat whistles were thrown their way as they smiled and embraced the moment by bowing, doing catwalk turns, and posing in front of the crowd. This went on for several minutes until Colonel Mooreland quieted the crowd and walked up to the men with a camera in his hand.

"I have to get a picture of this. No one will ever believe me," he said as he motioned for the men to gather for a photograph. Team infiltration pictures were a standard in Special Forces.

They covered the walls in most team rooms and in the homes of most of its soldiers. A typical picture was one of the team wearing standard combat gear, along with a small label of the place where it was taken, adorned with the month and year. The goal, no different than anything else these men did, was to make the pictures as unique as possible. Steve's scuba graduation picture, for instance, was of a bunch of combat divers on a pirate ship—a real pirate ship. The picture also served a purpose as a remembrance of the men that were there and the last photo of them all together. Not only was this a historic moment but combined with the ridiculous outfits these men were wearing, this would be an infil picture to trump all others. Each man took his place in two lines, the front row taking a knee, and everyone putting on their best facial expression, or cool-guy face.

After the pictures were taken with several cameras, Colonel Mooreland gathered the men around him. "Well, men, this is it." He paused and looked around at each man. "I'm not too big on speeches, but to quote Pericles, 'to the brave, few words are as good as many.'

"Half of me thinks you are the luckiest men in the world for going in tonight, and half of me doesn't want to send you at all, because of what I know of what you're up against. This is not going to be easy. The odds are heavily stacked against you. There will be times you question what it is you are actually doing there and days where things don't go your way. Days when you get attacked, shot at, blown up, and look out to see a superior force on the other side of the battlefield. But when those times come, I want you to remember this. You are a Green Beret," he said, pointing at Steve, "and your country was attacked."

"Thousands of Americans were killed in an act of war, and we sent you," he said, pointing at the men before him, "and you. That is a lot of responsibility, and I don't want you to take it lightly. Do not ever forget what started this fight, and do not forget who you represent. Make no mistake about it—although you may look like George and Yortuk Festrunk, you are the best of what the American military has to offer."

Blaine nudged Alan and whispered, "Who?"

"Saturday Night Live, two wild and crazy guys," Alan replied softly.

"Oh, yeah," Blaine responded.

"Get in there, and let us know what the ground looks like," Mooreland continued, "and set us up for success. Although you are going in alone, we will not be far behind you. We will be working hard back here to get more forces in there to back you up. This operation will require everything you have ever been trained to do … and probably some things you weren't. I am confident you will succeed. Good luck, men. God bless you, and God bless America."

He walked up to Captain Walen and shook his hand firmly. He then walked by each member of the detachment and shook their hands, with the men of his staff close behind, who followed suit. Once all the formalities were concluded, the men donned their packs, grabbed their weapons and extra bags, and walked to the flight line for their aircrew brief.

Alan looked over at Steve and commented, "Did he just say he didn't want to send us in because we were all going to die?"

"Yeah, pretty much," Steve answered with a smile.

"Wow, remind me never to have that guy talk to a youth football team at halftime. That wasn't even remotely motivational." Both men chuckled as they followed the rest of the team to the end of the flight line.

The men split into two separate files and went to their respective aircraft: two MH-47 Chinook helicopters. The team was broken down into split-team configuration for the infiltration. This split the team in half, with each smaller team consisting of equal representation of duty position. Team Alpha consisted of Captain Walen, Steve, Shane, JT, and Blaine; Team Bravo had Frank, Alan, Rusty, and Calvin. The men dropped their gear outside their respective birds and gathered in between them. They directed their attention to a soldier wearing a desert flight suit with a green aircrew survival vest around it and holding a flight helmet under one arm.

"Gentlemen, I am Chief Warrant Officer John Bailey," the man began, "and I will give you your aircrew brief for your infiltration. I don't want to question anyone's intelligence. I know you are all experienced operators, so I will make this quick.

"This is the MH-47 Chinook helicopter," he said, pointing to one of the helicopters. "It has two internal fuel tanks that extend our range to 645 nautical miles, and it can carry fifteen passengers with the internal seats. It is radar-evading and has enhanced night optics, active and electronic countermeasures, and refueling capabilities.

"With the gear you men are carrying and the terrain we will traverse, these helicopters will push the limits of their range. During your infil, we will be flying over several mountain ranges that may exceed fourteen thousand feet, so the crew chief will alert you when oxygen will be needed.

"In the event of a hard landing, with the nose of the aircraft being twelve o'clock, move fifty meters to the twelve o'clock position and get accountability of personnel and equipment. The senior person on the ground will take charge, direct security of the crash site, direct treatment to the wounded, and call for evacuation."

Shane leaned in and asked Steve quietly, "Hard landing?"

"That's the politically correct way of saying 'dropped out of the sky in a fireball of flesh and metal.'"

"Oh, okay," Shane replied as he rolled his eyes skyward.

Chief Bailey continued, "We will give you a standard twenty-, ten-, and one-minute warning for touchdown and should be able to monitor your primary frequency for five to ten minutes after we lift off, in case emergency evacuation is required. Take all direction for loading and unloading of personnel and equipment from the crew chief of your individual aircraft. Are there any questions?"

"Is there a movie?" Steve asked, trying to break the silence.

Alan attempted to outdo his peer. "That thing got a shitter?"

"Other than dumbass questions?" Chief Bailey fired back.

"Ouch, meow!" Steve replied, making a catlike scratching motion with his hand as he bent over to pick up his gear.

Chief Bailey walked to the front of his helicopter and looked over at his counterpart in the helicopter next to him. He put his hand in the air and waved it in a circular motion, mimicking the motion of a rotor, signifying starting of the engine. He climbed into his cockpit and began the sequence of his own engine-starting process.

The men gradually donned their gear and moved to their respective aircraft. Steve reached down, grabbed his weapon, and looked over at Alan. "Hey, man, see you on the other side," he said and put out his fist. Alan returned the fist-bump and looked for a few seconds at Steve, trying to come up with the right thing to say. He shook his head and replied, "I got nothing." The two men began to laugh uncontrollably, and they walked up the ramps of their respective helicopters.

With the high-pitched whine of the engines, it was difficult to hear anything within the helicopter. Frank adjusted his seatbelt and put on a small headset connected to the aircraft's port-side communication box. Rusty reached into a top pocket of his rucksack, pulled out a small MP3 player, and put the earphones in his ears. He had his M-9 pistol on his thigh, his M-4 with M203 in his lap, and his SR25 sniper rifle at his feet.

Calvin belted himself in on the starboard side and, like Frank, donned an extra headset to stay informed of the pilots' and crew chiefs' chatter. Alan positioned himself in the rear of the aircraft, buckled himself in, and peered out the back at the large group of people gathered to see them off.

The rear crew chief walked around the rear of the aircraft and performed his pre-flight checks. He moved to the nose of the helicopter and touched a button on his chest, turning on his microphone to the pilots, and gave them thumbs up that his exterior checks were complete. The pilot looked back at the crew chief and returned the thumbs up. The crew chief walked up the ramp and gave a hand and arm signal to the men inside, signifying that liftoff was commencing.

The whine of the helicopter's engines grew, and the dust around the aircraft began to be pushed away with force. A slight shudder of movement was felt as the aircraft began to hover slightly. With the ramp still down, Alan looked out to see the men gathered on the airfield. One by one, they removed their hats and began to wave to the departing helicopters.

Alan noticed Tony in the crowd, holding up a familiar two-finger peace sign, which he returned with a large smile. The onlookers grew smaller as the helicopters lifted higher and flew away into the night sky. Alan looked out at the horizon to an elevated view of the airfield and the surrounding area below. Soon, all the lights in the distance were gone, and nothing but the ambient light of the stars illuminated the terrain.

He looked around the inside of the helicopter at his teammates, each doing his own thing. He caught Frank's eye and gave him a smile and a nod, which Frank quickly returned. He closed his eyes and let the hum of the engines help him drift off to sleep. He knew this was going to be a long night, and he tried to keep his mind occupied with anything other than what he was about to undertake.

* * *

Tony DeNero stood alone on the flight line and stared up at the disappearing helicopters. The other members of the staff walked back to their tents to begin the planning for the other teams in isolation and their infiltration. He watched the aircraft until they were completely out of his sight, like a parent watching the school bus disappear on the first day of school.

He put a cigarette in his mouth and lit it. "Go get 'em, boys. Gadoosh," he said under his breath with a smile as he turned and walked toward his tent.

He found it difficult to be in a support role on this mission, but his work was far from over.

# PART II

# CHAPTER 13

*Go to the heart of danger, For there you will find safety.*
-Chinese proverb

"Ten minutes!" SSG James Lopata, the crew chief of the MH-47 Chinook helicopter barked out loudly to the men in the aircraft. He faced them standing, looking like a robot because of his large aircrew helmet and goggles, and extended both arms in front of him with his hands and fingers extended, showing ten digits.

Frank acknowledged the crew chief's signal with thumbs up and reached down to unfasten his safety belt. He stood from his seat and looked over at Alan, who had his earphones on and his eyes closed. He gave him a slap to the thigh, awakening him from his slumber. Alan looked up alertly to see Frank giving him the ten-fingers hand and arm signal. He gave Frank a nod, pulled the earphones from his head, and stored them in his shirt pocket. He stood from his seat and stretched calmly.

Each man began preparing for landing with a systematic visual inventory of his gear. They put each piece of equipment they were responsible for on the bench seat in front of them, performing a quick functions check, which included the operation of their night vision goggles, laser sights on weapons, and radios.

Alan put the earpiece of his radio into his right ear and did a quick commo check with Frank, who looked back and gave the combat diver "okay" sign: the normal "okay" hand signal brought from the center of the chest out toward the target and back again. Alan put his pack on the bench and sat on the floor in front of it. He reached back and put his arms through the straps, cinching them down securely with a hard pull. He used the straps on the helicopter to get to his feet, only to stagger slightly, startled by the incredible weight of his pack, and he had to grab hold of the bench in front of him to keep from falling.

He looked up to see Calvin laughing at his difficulty in controlling the heavy pack, and he returned the laugh, as he knew just how funny he must look. He pointed down at the rear handle of a folded-up litter with several aviator kit bags attached to it like a spit holding a pig. Calvin nodded, grabbed the back handle of the pole, and faced the rear of the aircraft. Alan picked up his position at the front handle, also facing out the rear of the open helicopter. He had his weapon slung and held it by the handgrip in his left hand; his night vision goggles were around his neck.

He did not have the smile of the arrogant joker he normally portrayed. His eyes were fixed and cold, his expression stoic. He rocked his head left and right slowly, as if to touch each ear to its corresponding shoulder, cracking his neck on both sides to release the tension as he violently chewed a piece of gum.

Frank stood close to the ramp and looked back at the men in line behind him. He made eye contact with each one and received the standard head nod signifying that they were ready. He held up the thumb and forefinger of his right hand one inch apart, indicating the thirty-second warning. Alan, the first man behind him, echoed the hand signal to the rear and sounded off with, "Thirty seconds!"

The Chinook made a high-pitched whine as the engine throttled up to slow its descent. The ramp was still open, but the men saw nothing but darkness from the rear of the aircraft. The only sign that they were about to land, other than the increase in engine pitch, was the large dust storm to the rear of the helicopter, generated by the massive propellers. Alan reached for a hanging cargo strap to steady himself as the Chinook shook violently, touching down to the earth below.

With a verbal signal of landing from Chief Bailey over the headset, SSG Lopata cracked an infrared chemical light stick and threw it directly to the rear of the aircraft. He signaled that it was time to go by extending his hand toward Frank, fingers extended and joined, and then pointing them outside the aircraft. Frank acknowledged him with a nod and moved down the ramp and out into the dust storm to the rear of the helicopter.

Once he was roughly twenty-five meters behind the aircraft and out of the circumference of the tail propeller, he immediately dropped his ruck and turned back to guide the rest of his men. He saw Alan and Calvin carrying the litter between them, kit bags hanging, and guided them to the nine o'clock position of the Chinook with an outstretched arm pointed in that direction. He then focused his attention on Rusty and pointed to the three o'clock position.

Rusty nodded and immediately moved in that direction with a slight jog. Once he felt he was a comfortable distance away, he dropped his pack and went to a kneeling position with his weapon in one hand and night vision in the other. Methodically he began scanning the area around him for signs of movement.

On the opposite side of the aircraft, Calvin began a similar routine in his direction, while Alan dropped his pack and returned to the aircraft. He went up the ramp and into the cargo area of the MH- 47, scanning the empty aircraft with his Surefire flashlight for anything that might have been left behind or dropped.

Once he was satisfied that the aircraft was empty, he made his way back down the open ramp. As he passed SSG Lopata, he tapped the crew chief on the shoulder, leaned in, and yelled above the noise of the engines, "Take it easy, bro!"

Lopata wrapped his arms around Alan and gave a hefty squeeze with a couple pats on his back. Alan, caught off guard by the gesture, smiled at the crew chief and continued down the ramp and back to his position next to Cal. He mumbled to himself, "A simple handshake would have sufficed," and began to laugh at the absurdity of the incident. He went to one knee and began to scan the area through his night vision alongside Cal.

The whine of the engines increased as the Chinook prepared to take off again, which kicked up a large dust cloud that completely engulfed the four men on the ground. The men remained in the same positions but removed the optics from their faces and scrunched their eyes tight to protect them from the dust thrown up by the departing aircraft. Within several seconds, the sound of the Chinook's engine and the windstorm generated by the propellers began to fade away. Frank opened his eyes and looked around. The only thing he could see was a haze of dust in every direction, and his ears were still ringing from the three-hour helicopter flight. Visibility was less than ten feet, and he could not make out the silhouettes of his men. Softly he tried to elicit a response from each man. "Rusty, you up?"

"Right here, boss. I can't see shit," Rusty replied.

"Alan? Cal?" Frank continued.

"We're good," Alan responded. "Where's the other bird? Weren't they supposed to be right behind us?"

"Yeah, what the hell? Cal, can you ask our bird where they are?" Frank directed as he looked in several directions for the other helicopter.

"I'm on it," Calvin said, "Bearcat one-four, this is Tiger zero-one. Over."

After a few seconds without a response, he sent, "Bearcat one-four, this is Tiger zero-one. Do you copy?"

He reached down, adjusted a setting on his IMBTR, and tried again. "Bearcat one-four, this is Tiger zero-one. Over." After several more seconds passed, he said to Frank, "I'm not getting anything. They might be behind the hills by now and out of range."

"This cannot be good," Alan said softly.

"Frank, I've got movement to our three o'clock," Rusty announced anxiously, without removing his night vision from his face, "at a couple hundred meters. Four victors and about twenty dismounted pax headed this way with lights on."

"That's probably our welcome party," Frank said. "Cal, keep trying our bird, and try to get the other team up. Maybe they landed first and are looking for us."

"What do we do about them?" Alan asked, pointing in the direction of the moving lights in the distance.

"We have to assume those are our guys," Frank replied, gesturing to the incoming personnel. "We will have to do link-up without the others. Until Cal gets confirmation, we assume we are alone here. I'll do the link-up."

Frank began removing gear from his body, except for his radio and weapon. He continued, "Rusty, Alan, I need good cover in case things go south quick. We're doing baseball link-up. Rusty, go left. Alan, to the right." He pointed in each direction. "Switch your radios to team internal frequency. Cal, you keep working the commo with that bird, and try to find the other group." Frank began walking away from the men and gear and glanced down at his weapon. He pulled back the charging handle slightly and checked the chamber for a round.

"What's baseball link-up?" Calvin asked Alan as he adjusted the settings on his radio.

"Frank is going to go forward and do a face-to-face with these guys," Alan explained. "We will cover him from there and there." He pointed at areas on either side of Frank, who was walking toward the lights. "He has his little apple cap on, and if things don't go as planned, he will take off his hat. That is the signal for us to pick up sights on the men closest to him on our respective sides and be ready to rock and roll. If everything goes to hell, he will drop to the ground, and we will start picking them off so he can break contact. It's usually done with a baseball cap and much more security. Pretty simple concept, though."

"Yeah, simple, except for the part where we take on thirty dudes with four guns," Calvin replied. "This is nuts!"

Alan held his night vision up to his face and scanned the area quickly. He let it hang to his chest and secured his weapon with both hands. He looked over at Calvin and remarked calmly, "It's what we do."

He reached into his pack, pulled out a small bandolier with several more M-4 magazines, and slung it over his right shoulder. "Stay with the gear and keep trying that bird. We have to know what happened to those other guys," he told Cal. "And if the shit goes down, try not to shoot me as I run past you." He smiled at Cal and began a slight jog in the direction of Frank's right flank.

Once he was a comfortable distance away from Calvin and the team's gear, Alan took a prone fighting position and removed the bandolier from his chest, laying it at his side. He looked through the PVS-14 night-vision monocular mounted to his M-4 and found Frank walking toward the lights that were coming their way.

"Fox-Golf, Alpha-Scott, in position," Alan announced over the radio.

"Roger. Rusty?" Frank said.

"Lima-Jay, I'm set. Let's do this," Rusty replied calmly from his position, with one eye closed and the other looking through his reticle. He was also prone behind his SR-25 sniper rifle with the bi-pod extended. He had his team hat on backward, gum in his mouth, and his left arm bent so that he was grabbing his right shoulder with it, chin resting on his left bicep. He was looking through his scope at Frank, who was roughly seventy meters from the oncoming forces.

Although they were using their initials in the NATO phonetic alphabet as call signs, each man has adjusted his slightly to be better received and used over the radio. Alan's call sign should have been Alpha-Sierra, but Alpha-Scott came off better over the air. Likewise, Rusty should have been Juliet-Lima, but Lima-Jay just sounded cool. Since it was an internal way of communicating within the team, not only did Frank have no problem with the changes, he encouraged the men to use something they liked.

It also gave the men the idea that they could influence what became the standards for the team. The real reason, which Frank only shared with Luke, was so they wouldn't choose inappropriate call signs. And given the chance, each man would outdo the next in choosing something completely ridiculous and inappropriate. To avert that situation, he had suggested that they alter their initials slightly to sound cool, and the men ate it up.

Frank lowered his weapon to his right side, showing vulnerability, but he still had the ability to present it quickly if needed. No matter how many times this exercise was done for real or in training, it was always thorny. It was never easy to be the man who had the rounds whizzing by his head as he dropped to the ground. Frank's mouth became very dry and he put a piece of gum in to help.

"You got this," he said to himself softly. He took one deep breath and pulled out his flashlight to give the oncoming lights a flash and signal his position.

The dust storm created by the leaving helicopter made the lights in the distance glow surreally. With no moonlight, the dancing lights seemed to be suspended in the dusty air like fireflies. By their size and movement, Frank could make out which were vehicle lights, and which were personnel. Frank saw four vehicles and counted roughly a dozen flashlights. Seeing the number of potential adversaries did not help calm his trepidation.

Upon Frank's signal, the oncoming lights began consolidating and moving directly toward his position.

"Here we go," Frank said over the radio, signaling both Alan and Rusty to look intensely into their respective night sights at the situation beginning to form.

Now only fifty feet in from of him, several figures became apparent to Frank. The vehicles behind them stopped several hundred feet away, with several voices yelling commands in Dari, one of the native languages of Afghanistan. Frank made out about a dozen men in front of him carrying weapons and wearing perahan tunban, the knee-length dress with baggy trousers typical of Afghan men. In the center there was a larger figure, much taller than the rest of the men around him. As he got closer, Frank could make out his clothing: khaki cargo pants, a photographer's vest, and a baseball cap. The man towered over his Afghan counterparts, standing six-foot six. He had a gray beard and long, unkempt hair in a ponytail that was pulled through the back of his cap.

As the man came closer, it was apparent by the look on his face that Frank was exactly where he was supposed to be.

"Hey, man. I'm Jack," said the man with a smile. He walked toward Frank with his right hand outstretched, as if they were meeting at a wedding for the first time.

Slightly taken aback by the deliberate and aggressive introduction, Frank paused slightly and returned the gesture. "Frank."

"Glad you guys made it safe. Where's your gear?" Jack asked. "I'll have the boys load it up and get it back to the house," he said, still holding onto Frank's hand.

Frank pulled his hand away from Jack's grip and pointed into the darkness behind him. "They're back there a-ways. But we're missing a few," he replied, still unsettled because of the size of the man and his overt niceness.

"Yeah, they had to land on the other side of those hills there," Jack said, pointing off to the west. Frank followed his hand, but the lack of illumination made it almost impossible to see any farther than a few meters in front of him. "It seems your bird kicked up such a brown-out that the second one had to pull off and move to the alternate DZ."

"So that's why we couldn't get them on the radio," Frank said as they began walking back to the rest of the team and the gear.

"Oh, yeah, line-of-sight comms have no chance in this AO, brother. You'll get a better idea what it looks like when the sun gets up in a couple hours. This valley is brutal," Jack said as he followed Frank into the darkness.

"This is Fox-Golf. All okay. We're coming to you," Frank put out over his radio.

"Roger, Fox-Golf. Charlie-Mike has the Alpha element on SATCOM. They are at the alternate DZ. All okay," Rusty replied from his position.

As Frank, Jack, and several Afghan men arrived at the patrol base, they saw Calvin sitting on his ruck and looking at a small notebook intensely. There was a small satellite antenna on the ground next to him, pointed into the air and attached by coaxial cable to his IMBTR. He held the hand-mic to his mouth and began talking softly into it.

"Is he talking to Alpha Team?" Frank asked Alan as they approached.

"No, he's letting the task force know that we landed safe and conducted link-up," Alan answered from his position next to Cal. "What's the plan for the other guys?"

"I have another group picking them up," Jack replied. "We will meet them back at the Crow's Nest."

"Crow's Nest?" Alan asked, looking up.

"You'll know why we call it that when we get there," Jack replied. "I'm Jack," he said as he reached out his hand to Alan with a smile.

"Alan Scott," he replied with a smile as he stood up. Noticing how he was still dwarfed by Jack, Alan took a quick step backward. "Fuck me. Look at the size of him! How big are you?" Alan said in a horrible English accent. "Hey. Ma, come look at the size of this fella."

"Big man, that's for sure," Cal replied in an accent similar to Alan's as he stood up. "Cal Michaels," he said, resuming his normal accent. He reached out his hand to Jack.

"And that was Snatch. Came out last year," Cal said, looking at Alan matter-of-factly.

"Ooooh, a new player," Alan said with a smile. "Game on."

"Okay, I'm not really sure what just happened there, but it's nice to meet you," Jack said to Cal with a questioning look. "Let's get that gear on the trucks. We don't want to be around here too long. I'm sure those helicopters will make some curious locals check this area out. I'd like to keep your presence quiet for at least a little while."

"At least a little while?" Rusty asked. He stopped repacking his equipment into his pack and looked up at Frank and Jack.

"If you guys are anything at all like your reputation, they'll know you're here soon enough," Jack replied.

"You hear that, Frank? People know me. I'm famous!" Alan interjected with pride.

"Yeah, Screech famous," Rusty chimed in.

"He does kind of look like Screech," Cal piled on.

Alan stopped putting on his pack and looked up at the desert sky as if he were contemplating a decision. "I'll take Screech famous," he said with a nod and continued his task.

It took the four men less than ninety seconds to load their gear onto two small pickup trucks and prepare to leave the area. Frank joined Jack in the bed of one vehicle, while the other three loaded in the back of another.

Cal pulled out his Garmin Etrex Vista GPS and turned it on to get the exact coordinates of their position as he climbed into the bed of the truck. He plotted the landing zone into the GPS and, out of habit, followed their entire path on the device to maintain his awareness while they drove away.

* * *

In his head, Alan was going over the scene he'd witnessed when they landed. He had counted twenty-four Afghan men with weapons. There were no uniforms or military equipment; each man had just his weapon with a single magazine in it. He saw no optics of any kind on the men he counted. There were three men with radios, which were small handheld walkie-talkies like one would give his kids on a camping trip—definitely not encrypted military grade.

Not one of the men was wearing shoes or boots; each had his own style of shower shoe, sandal, or flip-flop. It was hardly the image of the historic Mujahideen fighter that he had envisioned, as not one of them came in at over one hundred and fifty pounds. What he found interesting was that every man wore a watch, and they were what appeared to be nice ones. As he looked closer, he could tell they were cheap knock-offs, like those found on street carts in big cities or at kiosks in malls, but they were shiny nonetheless.

There was still a blanket of darkness around them, but several small buildings could be made out as the trucks slowed to a halt. They noticed they were within a mud-walled courtyard that contained several one-story mud-brick houses with maybe two or three small rooms inside each one. The pungent aroma of waste filled the air, causing the men to crinkle their noses. Several small chickens ran around the courtyard, launching into the air several feet whenever approached by a human.

Small lights emanated from the far building of the courtyard, and several figures inside could be made out through the window. The men unpacked the trucks and laid their gear on the ground, while Frank went into the far building with Jack. The twenty or so Afghans gathered around the trucks and began chatting and pointing at the three Americans. Several men were barking directions to the others; they were obviously in charge of the group. The orders seemed to fall on deaf ears, as the group just continued to stare and point.

Alan took a seat on his pack and lit up a cigarette. He saw one of the Afghan men eyeing him intensely and held out the open pack, offering the man a cigarette. The Afghan politely took one and put it in his mouth. He pulled his own lighter from his pocket and lit it. He coughed violently, to the laughter of several of his peers. "Yeah, they take some getting used to," Alan said with a smile.

He stood up and offered his hand to the fellow smoker. "Sayeed," Alan said as he shook the man's hand. He followed this by placing his right hand to his chest as a sign of respect.

The man pointed a finger at Alan. "Sayeed?" he asked wonderingly. Alan nodded with a smile and sat back down on his pack to enjoy his smoke. The man walked back to his peers and passed the cigarette to another man, who gave it a try for himself. They began talking in Dari, and they pointed back at Alan several times.

"What did you say to him?" Cal asked.

"I told him my name was Sayeed. And a smoke always breaks the ice with new friends, even these cheap commissary ones," Alan said, holding up his cigarette.

"Your name is Sayeed?" inquired Cal.

"It means happy," Rusty interrupted. "Moharej was already taken."

"Very funny," Alan replied to Rusty. Turning back to Cal, he explained, "We all had to go to language school, and the teachers assigned us Arabic names to use in class. When you spend as much time in the Middle East as we do, it's good to have a name they recognize, and it's better than them butchering yours all the time."

"And what did he call you?" Cal asked, pointing at Rusty.

"Moharej. It means clown. It's one of the six words he remembers from language school," Alan said sarcastically.

Cal turned to Rusty. "And what's your name?"

"Jamil. It means beautiful. And ain't it the truth?" Rusty said with a smile and looked skyward, showing his profile to Calvin. Alan noticed headlights in the distance, heading toward the group in the courtyard. He stood up. "That must be the fellas."

The other two men walked around the truck to get a better view of the approaching vehicles. The trucks were weaving their way in a snakelike pattern well below the elevation of the onlookers.

"Wow, we must really be up here," Rusty remarked on the difference in altitude.

"You really think a place called the Crow's Nest would be down in the valley?" Alan asked him with a condescending look.

Rusty looked at Alan angrily and paused. "I'm going to let that one go."

About half of the Afghan fighters went outside the courtyard to greet the incoming trucks and personnel. There were only four trucks this time, with eighteen men, including the five Americans. There was also one of Jack's peers, who was dressed very similarly in outdoor garb. The man was too clean to have been in the area for very long, and he did not look like he was very comfortable in the environment. He seemed completely the opposite of Jack. He was a shorter, thinner, and less rugged-looking individual. He had very well kept sandy blond hair and wire-rimmed glasses. He wore a tan corduroy blazer with elbow patches sewn into it. He never really closed his mouth fully, even when he wasn't talking, and there was a hint of teeth in every expression he made.

"Hi, guys! Good to see you! Where ya been?" Alan asked cheerfully, with his arms outreached for a large hug.

"Where's Frank?" Luke said without acknowledging Alan's horseplay as he walked right past the outstretched arms.

"He's in there, boss." Rusty pointed to the small room in the distance. "With Jack."

"C'mon, Luke, I'll take you inside," the other American said and began walking toward the door of the small mud building.

The men greeted each other with a round of handshakes and discussions of the flight and the mix-up at the landing zone. Once Luke was a comfortable distance away, Rusty announced, "Okay, I gotta ask … what's with Poindexter? Our guy was a beast."

"I don't know where they found that guy, or who he pissed off to be the one who had to come out here, but he's not what I would have expected," came Steve's reply as he began unloading his gear from the back of the truck.

"Dude, our guy is like a wrestler from TV," Cal explained.

"No kidding. The man is huge," Alan said. "Your guy is a little girly-man. I hope he at least cooks well, or you guys are screwed." Even the possession of these advisers becomes a point of competition among these men.

"You have no idea, dude," Blaine came right back. "His name is Cliff, and he's a CIA legend. He's one of those secret-squirrel mass murderer types. He looks all geeky but is in reality a ruthless, vicious killer who disembowels his victims while they remain conscious and watch. He's a real sick fella, that one."

Shane jumped right in. "Yeah, whatever. Why do we get the dork?" His remark caused a wave of laughter to ripple through the rest of the men.

"He looks like a Cliff," Alan remarked.

"He looks like a putz," Rusty said. The group again laughed as they helped each other with their bags and kit.

After a few cigarettes and some chatting in broken Dari with the Afghan men gathered around the trucks, Frank, Luke, and the two American greeters emerged from their small area and came over to where the men are gathered.

"All right, guys, grab your stuff!" Frank bellowed. "There are two rooms back in there." He pointed to the very end building on the opposite side from the room they had just exited. "That's where we will sleep tonight. Don't get too comfortable—it's temporary. We are moving out in the morning to another house closer to where the fight is."

"This is a house?" Steve asked, pointing at the mud building.

"Yeah, I guess so," Frank said. "We will get started first thing in the morning. Alpha Team, you will come with me and do a recon of the target area. From what I saw on the map, it should be a pretty routine recon, and it shouldn't take but a few hours. When we return, we'll start setting up a command area to work out of. I want it up and running by the end of the day, and we can improve on it from there. Let's just get it functional first.

"Bravo Team, you'll go with Captain Walen and link up with the local general in charge of the area. You're scheduled to meet him at 9:00 AM at the airfield, so I need you ready out here by six."

"Whoa, six?" Alan protested. "It's four-thirty now."

"We get Jack!" Rusty yelled from the back of the group.

"Yes, Rusty, Jack is going with you guys. Cliff will be coming with me. He knows the area better and already has it marked on his GPS, so it'll save us some time. Now the bad news. I need someone to stay awake tonight and keep an eye on this stuff, so it doesn't, um, disappear." He pointed to the litter with the aviator bags attached, and to several tough black plastic boxes that had been carried on the second aircraft.

"I'll do it, Frank," Alan volunteered.

"I'll keep him company," Rusty offered, holding his fist out to Alan for a pound.

"All right, just keep an eye on the stuff, and do a little walk around the area for nosy-bodies," Frank directed. "Make sure we are all up and ready by six. I don't know if you noticed, but they don't drive too fast around here, and for good reason, so we need the extra time. Now get some rest, if you can."

With that, the men picked up their packs and headed into the far building, carrying flashlights and bottles of water. The drivers of the trucks got into their vehicles and drove them out of the courtyard and down the road, about two hundred meters below, to another small compound where the Afghan soldiers were gathered.

Alan carried his pack over to the wall by the entrance to the courtyard. He dropped it next to the wall and untied some of the straps holding the top flap secure. He reached in one of the pockets, grabbed an energy bar, and began to eat.

"You got another one of those?" Rusty asked.

"Sure, bro. Got plenty," Alan answered. He reached for another bar and tossed it to Rusty.

"You all right, man?" Rusty asked Alan. "You don't usually volunteer for guard duty."

"Yeah, I'm fine. I took a dex on the bird, (referring to dextro-amphetamine, a stimulant) thinking that we would be going all night anyway, so I'm up for the duration," Alan replied.

"Oh, that's why I don't take that shit anymore," Rusty explained.

"Remember coming home from Bosnia, when we had a layover in Italy and I took that sleeping pill before we took off?"

"Yeah, that was classic," Alan laughed. "Five minutes into the flight, they had to turn back and land. You were out cold, and it took three guys to carry your fat ass off the plane."

"Don't act like you did me any favors," Rusty came back. "I woke up on the tarmac with no clue as to where I was. Everyone else had gone off drinking, so I ended up wandering the streets alone at one in the morning, looking for them."

"Well, in my defense, I'm the one that put the blanket on you," Alan confessed.

"That was a nice touch," Rusty fired back with a smile.

The two walked around the perimeter of the courtyard. The sun was starting to emit a small glow on the horizon, and they could make out some of the area that they had been in the night before. They were obviously several hundred feet above where the helicopters had dropped them off.

They decided to go higher on the hill for a better view of the area. The terrain was drab brown and void of any actual color from vegetation or fauna. There was a small stream to their west that followed the contours of the hills in the area. It was easy to see why their housing area was referred to as the Crow's Nest; it was one small group of buildings high on a hillside, with only one road leading to it. It would be very difficult to actually walk up the hill, which was full of rocks and loose stone and almost impossible with the gear the men had carried with them.

They could see the area below where the Afghan men were sprawled out on the ground around their trucks, sleeping on what looked like rolled-up straw mats and light blankets. Alan counted fifty-three men all together. These would be some of the men they would be working closely with for the next year to take into combat against the Taliban. They had a tough road ahead, almost as hard as the trail leading to their perch high on the hillside.

Alan took a seat on the rocky hillside, about one hundred meters above the Crow's Nest, and lit a cigarette. He stared off into the horizon and watched the sun rise above the mountains of the Hindu Kush. The two men sat quietly and enjoyed the peaceful beauty of the picturesque scene. The entire landscape was a dull brown, with sporadic green foliage surrounding the dark blue of the river below. The rapid flow of the river created a low, calming rumble that filled the air. The two men just stared at the rising sun, each deep within his thoughts of what might lay ahead. The day was already long, and it hadn't even begun yet.

# CHAPTER 14

*Talking just to talk ...*
-Noodles

The fall day was cool and brisk as the sun rose above the hills of the Panjshir Valley. Wearing fleece caps, Calvin and JT were sitting on the dirt floor of their room with several radios spread out around them, hooking up different antennas and hand-mics to each one. They

were deep in conversation about the intricacies of the IMBTR radios. Outside, Frank and Alan had a map on the hood of a vehicle and were going over the terrain and discussing routes and vantage points throughout the AO. Every so often, they would look up at the surrounding area to compare how accurately it matched the aged Russian maps they were using. They were surprised that the maps were extremely accurate when it came to roads, trails, buildings, and rivers and they commented several times on how their own military maps could use some Russian help. Frank had come to the realization that maps would always be more accurate when the landscape remained unchanged for thirty years; America just hadn't had this luxury.

Luke stuck his head out of the building housing the Agency personnel and announced, "Let's get everyone in here real quick, Frank."

"Roger that, sir," Frank replied. "Hey, go grab the guys and meet us in there," he told Alan.

Within several minutes, the entire team was gathered around a large table in a very small room. Jack, Cliff, and another man were standing at the head of the table with Luke. They were holding silver camping mugs with aromatic steam coming from them that was definitely not typical chow-hall coffee.

"Something smells good," JT announced, breaking the ice.

"Italian roast," was the reply from the unknown Agency man. "Want some?"

"Don't mind if I do," JT replied, pushing his way violently past the rest of the men to where the coffee was brewing in the rear of the room on a small camping heater.

As JT helped himself to a cup of java, Luke addressed the rest of the team. "All right, guys, listen up. Good job last night on the infil and link-up. I know there was a little confusion with the birds being split up, but you stepped up and dealt with it smoothly. I am sure there will be many more times for improvisation in the coming months. Let's just hope we deal with them all as smoothly as last night." With an open hand, he indicated the stranger standing to his right. "This is Jerry."

Jerry was an older guy, perhaps sixty. He was roughly five-foot ten, he weighed around two hundred pounds, and he had short gray hair with a well-kept gray beard. He sported clothing similar to his counterparts': khaki cargo pants, baseball cap, photographer's vest, and hiking boots. He carried himself with confidence and was obviously the one in charge of the three men.

"Jerry is the leader of the Northern Alliance Support Team. He will be the one coordinating our efforts with both the Northern Alliance and the intelligence community. We still fall under the umbrella of the Special Operations Command and still must answer to our people, but this is their show, and we are here to facilitate them and the Northern Alliance in any way we can. So please give Jerry your attention, and let's get a one-over-the-world of our AO so everyone is on the same sheet of music. Jerry."

Jerry moved to the head of the table, which was covered by a large map of their target area. There were also several small green army men and Matchbox toy cars spread out on the map as props.

"Thanks, Luke," Jerry began. "Let me be the first to formally welcome you men to Afghanistan. I cannot thank you men enough for coming and for your quick response to the horrific events that took place in New York and Washington DC. I will not go into a long, drawn-out speech on the significance of that event or your presence here now, as I am sure you have heard many prior to your arrival.

"I am sure there is a reason you all have been chosen to be here, and I look forward to watching you men in action in the coming weeks and months.

We each will bring something special to this fight—and a fight it will be, men. I can tell you from experience, as I have seen this country ravaged by war for over twenty-five years. I first came to this country in 1978, and I've been in and out many times since. I'm not bragging if I claim to be the most knowledgeable person they could find to assist you men in accomplishing your mission in the coming months.

"Our job here, as you already know, is to oust the Taliban from its oppressive rule of the citizens of Afghanistan and help the beleaguered Afghan people establish an interim government. It might sound easy enough, but I can assure you men, it will be everything but.

Does anyone here know anything about the history of this area, or Afghanistan in general?"

Frank looked over at Alan. "Sergeant Scott, you want to take this one?"

"Sure, I'll give it a shot. Do you mind?" Alan looked to Jerry for approval with a smug grin as he maneuvered himself between Steve and Rusty at the far end of the conference table, opposite that of Jerry.

"By all means. I'd like to get a feel for what you guys know," Jerry replied as he held out an open hand to Alan.

"The political situation in Afghanistan is a very complex historical soup," Alan began, "largely left over from the ousting of the British Empire in the early 1900s and the unfortunate establishment of the Durand Line, which has had the ultimate effect of making the border between Pakistan and Afghanistan a point of contention to this day. The line effectively isolates large populations of Pashtuns in two countries and divides up other, rival tribal lands in historically untenable ways.

"In the early seventies, the Afghan prime minister, Daoud, took the throne of power from his cousin and was the first president of Afghanistan, establishing its first republic. Much like most barren wastelands, no one in the population knew about it—or really even cared, for that matter.

"Daoud specifically tried to solve the Pashtun problem—that is, Afghani people disadvantaged by the historical effects of the Durand Line—and the Muslim leaders at the time thought it a good change from the previous regime, so they didn't put up any resistance. Until, as fate would show us, about a year later, when Daoud and his commie buddies started cracking down on the Islamic leadership and arresting them.

"This didn't go over well with the Muslim leaders or their followers in the populated areas like Kabul and Kandahar. They tried a coup in '75 but failed miserably, and it only made the regime that much stronger. But like all people in power, greed took over. Daoud started working the Pakistanis and Americans for his own benefit. He began distancing himself somewhat from the Soviets, reaching out toward other surrounding countries and Egypt to attempt to deal with the continuing problem of tribal demographics—Pashtun, Tajik, and others. In 1977, his diplomatic relations with Mother Russia ceased entirely."

Alan talked as he stared at the map on the table in front of him. He wasn't looking at anything on the map in particular; it was almost as if he were reading something on the table.

"Then, in '78, I think, the People's Democratic Party of Afghanistan got a tad upset with the way they were being played and then blamed the Daoud regime for the assassination of one of their members. They staged their own coup, ousting Daoud. The only problem was they had no real replacement for the guy, and of course a bunch of different gangs all stepped up to take control of the country. There were a couple of years in there where these gangs kind of went at each other with no real leader stepping up for control. Just a lot of declining support and increasing hostility pending the Soviet invasion.

"I don't want to go into the why, but we all know that for the last century, the Soviets have been slowly putting their grubby little paws into various strategic countries throughout the globe, and this area was no exception. So with the country in chaos, we all know that on Christmas Eve in 1979, the Russians saw their opportunity and invaded Afghanistan. They took the city of Kabul in like a day, against very little resistance. But you have to admit—when nomadic farmers saw a tank for the first time, they probably thought aliens had invaded. Most of whatever leadership was in the city was either killed or fled to Pakistan, including a young engineering student at the university named Ahmad Shah Masood. More on him later.

"How am I doing so far?" Alan looked at Jerry with a sly grin.

"Who the hell is this guy?" Jerry asked Luke, pointing in Alan's direction.

"My boy's wicked smart," Rusty whispered to Cal with a northeastern accent and pointed at Alan.

"Good Will Hunting?" Cal asked quietly.

Rusty responded with a head nod and a slight smile. "Ooh, Alan said you were a player," Rusty whispered back with a grin, again acknowledging Calvin's expertise on movie quotations.

"Some of you might not know this, but like a month before the Russian invasion of Afghanistan, the U.S. embassy in Pakistan was stormed and burned in a riot."

"I knew that. November twenty-first," Shane chimed in.

"That's Voltaire's birthday," Steve announced.

"Troy Aikman's, too," Blaine submitted.

"And Goldie Hawn," Calvin added.

"Knock it off!" Frank scolded, with angry eyes around the room. "Keep going, Alan."

"Anyway, I am sure the Russians saw that as a great opportunity to move into the area. This might lead one to believe that their ultimate goal might not have been only Afghanistan but maybe all the way to the Arabian Sea. But I digress." Alan paused with one finger in the air, to alert everyone in the room that he had just thrown out another random piece of knowledge that few would have caught without him pointing it out.

"Our boys at Central Intelligence ... well, being intelligent, saw this was not a good thing and started increasing the cash, guns, and supplies to our Mujahideen brethren to help fight the Russians.

"This went on for ... what, ten years, Jerry?" Uncharacteristically Alan looked up at Jerry for a response, although everyone around the table knew he was fully aware of the exact dates.

Jerry nodded and stared. He looked over at Luke, who had his arms folded across his chest and had a large grin on his face. He gave Jerry a small shrug, as if the information Alan was reciting was common knowledge on the team.

Alan continued, "So in '88, defeated, the Russians pulled out of Afghanistan. And needless to say, the place was left in shambles. The Pakistanis saw this as a way to gain influence in the area and did everything they could to get their Pashtun tribal leaders into power in the major populated areas, keeping our Tajik friends here as an unrepresented minority.

"Seeing Pakistani Islamic radical leadership as bad"—Alan lifted both hands and held up two bent fingers in the classic quotation-marks sign—"the CIA maintained its relationship with some minority leaders, including our guy Masood here in the Panjshir Valley," Alan pointed at a picture of Masood that was hanging on the wall inside the room.

"He was a natural leader and an excellent military strategist. His Tajik fighters of the Shura Nazar, or Northern Alliance, made pretty easy work of the Islamic commies in Kabul, and Masood took the city in '92. Bada-bing, bada-boom, new government in place, and Masood is made the minister of defense. Life is good, right?"

"Wrong?" Shane leaned in and asked.

"No, right," Alan replied, pointing in Shane's direction, correcting him. "There was in fact a new era of peace in Afghanistan, which had not been seen in more than a decade. Life was good, and this new era of peace lasted, oh, about six months." Alan looked back at Shane with a smile.

"Now there was peace and the right people in charge. We got what we wanted, so the CIA turned off the faucet of support. The only problem was, the Pashtuns were still being backed by the Pakistanis, and with no support, Masood and his boys didn't really stand a chance. Needless to say, this didn't help their views on the USA. We help them beat the Russians and then walk away without helping them against the Pakistani-backed fundamentalists. My bad," Alan threw in sarcastically.

"Remember, Pakistan is a U.S. ally," Jack interjected. "Part of the problem for the USA in Afghanistan is trying to get what it wants and not alienating Pakistan, which has nuclear weapons and the seventh largest standing army in the world."

"Exactly," Alan said. "Meanwhile, schools of religious fundamentalists were increasingly popping up all over Pakistan, providing food, shelter, and religious teaching to young men, both Pakistani and Afghan. They taught their own twisted version of the Koran, and all the kids drank the Kool-Aid, much like those Christian cult nut jobs in the States. Bad news was, that these nut jobs and their fundamentalist religious teachings slowly started gaining momentum throughout southern Afghanistan.

"Soon a former Mujahideen veteran named Mullah Omar started organizing these crackheads who called themselves Talibs, or defenders." Again, Alan used the quotation-marks hand signal. "It wasn't long before the Taliban took a majority of the country, which was well received, because these were Afghan men, and the population was just plain tired of war. The party would be short-lived, as the rest of the population soon found out that the Kool-Aid didn't taste so good.

"With the Taliban gaining control of the country, a little cash and support got all the freedom that was needed to use the unpopulated areas for whatever crackpot wannabe terrorist organizations that were becoming popular. This included a certain Saudi douchebag who was operating in the Sudan at the time. Osama bin Laden, who we all know helped fight against the Russians, went back to Saudi Arabia but was exiled. Bin Laden was a cash cow to Mullah Omar, who welcomed him with open arms.

"With the influx of Arab terrorists and now bin Laden to Afghanistan, the USA again started gaining interest in the country. They had to find someone they could count on for help—enter our guy Masood, the Lion of the Panjshir. But after just a few years of fighting, he was slowly losing the battle logistically against the Taliban.

"The Taliban took Kabul in '96, I think it was, and Masood fled north. He put up a pretty good fight in the Shomali Plains, there." Alan pointed to a group of green army men gathered in a flat area to the north of Kabul on the map. "This area was easy to defend, with the Panjshir Mountains for elevation and fields of fire and a good source of water here in the valley. Plus, there was the Bagram Airfield, an old Russian airstrip about fifty kilometers north of the city." Alan pointed once more at the map. This time, Jerry leaned forward and placed a green army man directly on the airfield, assisting Alan's class.

"After the loss of Kabul, and even after being ditched by the Agency in '92, it was easy for the CIA to dangle the carrot of cash, guns, and support in front of Masood and get him in their pocket again. With the you-are-the-enemy-of-my-enemy speech, and with Masood's popularity, it was easy for him to gain support in the area. In fact, the rumor was that even some of the men fighting against him turned sides so they could say they fought with the great Masood.

"So, check it out." Alan cracked a little smile and leaned over the map on the table. "We got the Taliban on one side, backed by Pakistan, Osama bin Laden and al Qaeda"—Alan pointed to the southern side of the map with his left hand—"and in this corner," he said, pointing to the northern side with his right hand, "we have the Shura Nazar, or Northern Alliance, backed by the good 'ol CIA. Let's get it on!" Alan said loudly, slapping both hands together.

"The Taliban were cool with having the city of Kabul. That is the capital, you know." Alan looked over at Rusty questioningly.

"Duh," Rusty replied sarcastically. He looked at JT, shook his head, and shrugged, which instigated laughter from several of the men standing around the table.

"Yeah, I thought so," Alan laughed. "Anyway, Masood and his boys were considered an inconvenience at best, but the Taliban wouldn't chase him into the mountains. This allowed Masood to grow his forces and gain more support in the Panjshir over the next several years."

"So where is this guy Masood now? Are we going to meet him?" Calvin asked.

"He's dead," Jerry interrupted abruptly, causing most of the heads around the table to turn his way.

"If I can continue," Alan said sarcastically to Calvin, with a slight head tilt. "Whether the Taliban knew about the U.S. backing of Masood or not doesn't really matter, but the fact was, he was gaining a lot of popularity and amassing quite an elaborate network here north of the city and just couldn't be ignored any longer. So they got a couple knuckleheads to pose as reporters and set up an interview with Masood. They loaded the camera up with some C-4, and bada-bing, bada-boom, kablooey." Alan made a small explosion noise and signaled with his hands by bringing them together and then separating them quickly, up and away from each other. "I guess they figured if you cut the head off the snake—"

Jack leaned in and interrupted. "Okay, I gotta ask. Where the hell did you get all that?"

"Discovery Channel," Alan replied nonchalantly, with a slight shrug of his shoulders.

"Dude, you need a girlfriend," Rusty chimed in, shaking his head back and forth.

"No," Alan replied, with a finger in the air, "I need batteries for my remote. It's been on that channel for two weeks." Alan's self-deprecating humor brought laughter from the men around the table.

Calvin looked at Jerry and asked, "When did this happen?"

"September ninth."

Cal's eyebrows grew wide. "Two days before the attacks? Don't you think that is a little coincidental?"

"Extremely," Jerry replied. "Could it be retaliation for the backing of Masood? Perhaps. You shouldn't have to ask if the three of us believe in conspiracy theories, but this one is an easy sale to me. Bottom line, his guys are chomping at the bit to retaliate. Only problem is, they would get slaughtered if they just took off on Kabul tomorrow. That's where you boys come in." Jerry looked around the room.

"We need your help getting them to the city. The local commanders and I are pretty confident that once they get to Kabul, they should have little problem in taking it, and most of the Taliban will run south."

"What makes you so confident?" Steve asked quickly.

"Well, for starters, the Taliban in the city are true Afghans, whereas the fighters that lay to the north of the city are mostly al Qaeda and Arabs. They are actual fighters who aim their weapons—no pray-and-spray here, boys. They will put up a fight, and a good one. There is also talk of Chechens mixed in there as well. They will definitely be a tough group to bust through."

"Well done, Mr. Scott," Jerry acknowledged. "That was somewhat accurate. I think you might have a skewed opinion of our intelligence community, but I do have a larger respect for cable television now."

Steve leaned in to Alan and whispered, "Somewhat accurate? Dude, you suck," causing them both to chuckle.

"We have already plotted a large amount of targets in our GPS," Jerry continued, "and we will show you some advantageous positions we have scouted for you to direct some CAS from. If there is anything you guys need that you didn't bring with you, or can't get from your people, let us know. We have a pretty good supply of comfort stuff and can get pretty much anything you want. We are here to help you as much as possible."

"I'd dig some of that coffee," JT said under his breath. Jack responded by slowly reaching down, grabbing a bag of coffee, and passing it behind his back to JT, who quickly dumped it into the cargo pocket of his pants with a wink in Jack's direction.

"Thanks, Jerry," Luke said. "We need to get going. Alpha, you're with me. Frank, take Bravo, and check out the positions they have on their GPS. We'll meet back here this afternoon and start getting a plan of action together once we have more of the variables."

"You heard the man." Frank looked at the rest of the team. "Beat it!"

The men began walking out of the small room to prepare for movement. "Get out of my way, nerd," Blaine said and gave Alan a little shove into the frame of the doorway. Alan stopped his violent contact with the door by putting up his hand to absorb the impact.

"You know, it's well known that bullies didn't get enough affection as infants," Alan called as Blaine went through the doorway. "Don't take it out on me because you didn't get enough hugs as a child!"

"Give me a carton of smokes, and I'll protect you," JT said with a smile as he helped Alan to his feet.

"Fuck that. I'll take the beating. You ain't getting my smokes," Alan said with a smile and followed JT out the door.

# CHAPTER 15

*A cat bitten once by a snake dreads even rope.*
-Arab proverb

A convoy of four vehicles maneuvered through the rugged terrain of the Panjshir Valley, led by a Soviet-era jeep, painted olive drab green, that drove off-balance due to the different-sized tires underneath it. It took more than an hour to cover the twenty or so kilometers between their starting point and the tower at Bagram Airfield. After several days of briefings, unpacking, and building changes, the team was anxious to get out to the front lines. Upon their arrival, they were greeted by a dozen-or-so Afghan men dressed in local garb and carrying various weapons.

The airport's tower itself was a long one-story building made of wood and metal, with a two-story control tower like towers at smaller airfields in the USA. This tower, however, showed signs of being part of many years of conflict. There was no glass in any of the windows or the tower itself. Bullet and rocket holes littered the main building's exterior, as well as those of several of the smaller buildings surrounding the parking area. Without windows in the main tower, several men were seen walking around in it.

"These guys need a Home Depot," Calvin announced to no one in particular as he emerged from his jeep.

"I was thinking more of a bulldozer," Rusty responded. Jack and Luke approached several Afghan men at the entrance to the main building and went through some cordial, informal greetings. Several times they made gestures toward the Americans standing by the trucks, which elicited waves from Alan and the others. They began to walk into the building, and Luke waved for the others to follow him. The men grabbed their weapons and slung them over their shoulders. They proceeded to grab large bags from the back of their respective vehicles, and they followed Luke inside the derelict building. They walked through a doorway with no door, into a large room with no windows that had trash everywhere. There were empty water bottles, plastic bags, and empty boxes, along with an incredible foul-smelling stench that would make a coroner retch.

At the far side of the room was a narrow metal staircase that was almost a ladder. It was so steep that it required the use of the handrail to ascend, which was difficult because the handrail itself was missing several attachment points throughout the climb. The men had to readjust their equipment to fit through the narrow opening at the top of the staircase.

Once through the opening, they were in the main control tower with a second-floor view of the surrounding area. The lack of windows in the main room gave it a slight breeze and removed some of the stench from the room below. Several men were sitting at chairs in various positions at a counter below the windows that stretched around the tower. Several old Soviet radios were on the counter in front of the missing tower windows, and every few seconds there would be a squelch through a speaker, followed by an Afghan voice talking loud and fast.

To their south was the airfield itself, with two runways; oriented northwest to southeast. A couple old Soviet MiG-23s, obviously damaged beyond the scope of flight, littered the ground off the airstrip itself. There were several large craters on the actual airstrip from rockets, bombs, or mortar fire, making it difficult for the airfield to be operational.

On the far side of the airstrip, opposite the control tower, were several small buildings with a large number of men wandering about them. They were several hundred meters away, so it was difficult to identify their uniforms and know whether they were friends or foes. In the center of the room, a handful of men sat at a large table, drinking chai, or tea. At the head of the table was a large, overweight Afghan man with a gray beard. He was holding a small commercial walkie-talkie in one hand and a glass of chai in the other. He was obviously the leader within the tower, because everything was brought directly to him: his radio, the chai, and of course, the Americans.

Jack said, "Sir, this is Captain Luke." He gestured in Luke's direction. "He is the leader of the Americans that were brought in last night." A younger soldier standing off to the man's right interpreted what Jack had said to the general. "Luke, this is General Babazheen. He is the commander of the troops in the Bagram area."

Luke reached out his right hand to the general. The large Afghan general paused and looked directly at Luke for several seconds, then moved his gaze to the other Americans standing against the far wall of the tower.

He shook Luke's hand weakly and replied, through his interpreter, "I was told there would be more of you."

"Yes, sir. We have another group out doing a reconnaissance of your front lines. We have a total of nine men with us," Luke replied to the general.

Babazheen continued to stare at Luke as if he were making a complete assessment of the entire American army by what he was seeing in front of him, and it did not look as if he were pleased.

"I am sorry for the loss of lives in your country," the general said to Luke. "This is not an honorable way of war. But I do not think that nine men will help me in my fight against the Taliban. Tell your president we are very grateful for the help. Now, if you will excuse me." The general turned to a soldier standing next to Rusty against the far wall and barked an order at him in Dari, sending him immediately down the narrow staircase as if it were a fireman's pole.

Luke was slightly taken aback by the general's abrupt response to their presence, and he looked at Jack. Jack continued with his introduction as if he were completely ignoring the general's reply to Luke. "Sir, if you don't mind, I'd like to give Captain Luke and his men a tour of your tower and show them the fighting positions we have previously discussed."

The general took a sip of his tea and gave Jack a slight nod; he pointed with his glass to the front of the tower, in the direction of the airstrip. He immediately turned away from Jack and Luke and began talking to one of the other men at the table.

Again, Jack continued his dialogue with Luke, unfazed by the behavior of General Babazheen. "So this is Bagram," Jack said, approaching the south side of the windowless tower, "and that is your enemy." Jack pointed directly across the airstrip to the small buildings opposite the tower where the men had been seen earlier.

"Right there?" Luke asked as he pointed to the same men. "Those men right there are Taliban?"

"Well, it's a mixture of Taliban, al Qaeda, and some others, but yes, right there. Remember, these men are outnumbered almost ten to one. They're in no real rush to go toe-to-toe with those guys."

Jack looked over at the other Americans standing against the far wall. "You guys want to get a look at this?"

Alan and Rusty walked over to where Luke and Jack were standing, to get a look at the enemy area. Calvin bent down, reached into his bag, and pulled out a twenty-power spotting scope. He walked over to the glassless window and began a visual scan of the far end of the airfield.

Without looking down, methodically he began screwing a tripod to the bottom of the spotting scope. He extended the legs of the tripod and set the entire thing on the counter in front of him. Squinting with one eye and closing the other, Calvin started assessing the enemy positions, beginning at the most southern end of the airstrip and working back to the north. He pulled a small notepad from his shirt pocket and began writing. He drew a small rectangle as a reference point for the airstrip and put a small circle on the near side of the rectangle for the tower they were in.

"Doc, can you get a map and compass out for me, please?" Calvin asked, looking up at Alan.

"You got it, bro." Alan grabbed his bags and from one of them pulled a map, a lensatic compass, and a large camouflage case. He opened the case, pulled out a pair of binoculars, and brought them to his eyes to scan the enemy positions.

Calvin had his Etrex GPS on the counter in front of him and was waiting for it to gain full signal to disclose the exact position. Alan reached over and handed Rusty the map and then returned to scanning the far side of the airfield, likewise from south to north. He tapped Calvin, who was now sitting in a chair, still looking through his spotting scope. "Let me know when you get a fix," he said, referring to the GPS position.

"Rusty, write this down," Cal said, looking down at his GPS.

"November-Lima, five-six-three-seven, one-six-five-five."

"Roger, November-Lima, five-six-three-seven, one-six-five-five, aye." Rusty echoed the coordinates back to Cal as he wrote a note in the corner of the map sheet in front of him. When he finished jotting down the number Calvin had given him, Rusty traced the gridlines on the map with his finger to a point in the upper left corner. "Looks pretty accurate on the map. Got us right in the middle of the airstrip, northwest side," Rusty barked out to no one in particular.

Calvin returned to his spotting scope and again peered through it intensely. "Doc, you got that large building that looks like a grain silo or something about two hundred meters off the southwest corner of the airstrip?"

Alan moved the view through his binoculars a little farther to his right and stopped; he saw a two-story cylindrical building made of the same mud and straw most of the other buildings were made of. It had two small windows cut into it at different heights, which might be along a staircase. There were three men and large antennas on the roof, along with a white flag with black writing on it blowing in the wind. "Got it. Ranging."

Keeping his field of view locked on the tower, he reached to the top of the binoculars with his right index finger and pushed a small green button. "Six-three-five," he barked out. "Did you get that, Rusty?"

"Six-three-five, aye," Rusty replied, and he again made a note on his map.

Alan let the optics drop around his neck by the strap and pointed his lensatic compass at the same building. "Two-zero-eight degrees."

"Two-zero-eight, aye," Rusty again echoed.

Calvin paused from his squinting and looked over at Rusty. "Let me know when you plot that."

By this point, several of the Afghan men had gathered around the Americans, curious as to what they were doing. One dressed in brown military pants and a brown shirt with patches sewn on, in no particular pattern, leaned forward and touched the binoculars hanging from Alan's neck. Alan handed them to the man, who immediately held them to his face and began scanning outside the tower at the enemy positions. Alan reached out and took hold of the man's right hand; he slid down to the index finger of the Afghan and placed it on the large button atop the binoculars. The man pushed the button, and a red LED number appeared in the viewfinder.

"It's a range finder," Alan said to the soldier. He then held up both hands, making the quotation sign with them. "Lay-zer!" he said with an accent slightly different from his own.

"Austin Powers, Doc," Calvin announced without looking up from his spotting scope, catching the movie line.

"Bingo," Alan replied while pointing at Calvin.

Alan started scanning around the tower with his eyes. "Where's that dude who speaks English?" He spotted the man looking at the map over Rusty's shoulder, "Hey, bro, can you come here for a sec? What's your name?"

"Akmal," the man replied, grinning slightly.

"So, Akmal, can you translate for this guy here? This is a Viper, a laser range finder. It tells you how far you are from the thing you are looking at in meters. Tell him."

The man translated what Alan had said for the Afghan man looking through it.

"Tell him to push the button on top when he has a target and look at the number."

After hearing the directions, the soldier began scanning back and forth across the airstrip at different buildings. Each time he paused, he pushed the button on the Viper and yelled out the number that came up. After several numbers had been yelled out by the young soldier, an older and obviously higher-ranking man pulled the Viper from the soldier and started scanning the same targets, also pushing the Viper's action button. The small gathering of Afghan men around him began pointing to different targets and telling the man with the Viper to give them the distance to them. Alan couldn't tell exactly what they were saying, but by their body language it seemed as though they had invented some kind of carnival game based on how close they could guess the actual distance to their favorite targets.

Alan saw his opportunity and tapped the man on his shoulder. He pointed at the building he had already ranged and said, "Six thirty-five." Alan tapped the English-speaking man on the shoulder. "Hey, tell him six hundred thirty-five." This instigated several other men to also call out numbers, like a TV game show. The man holding the Viper looked at the silo building and called off a number to the group. There was a large roar of laughter, and some of the men pointed at Alan and patted him on the back several times.

"You are the closest guesser," the interpreter told Alan, smiling. Celebrating his victory, Alan immediately threw both hands in the air and tried eliciting high-fives from his new Afghan friends, only to receive looks of confusion. Alan reached out and grabbed a soldier's wrist with his left hand and then slapped it with his right, teaching him the celebration.

"Cheater," Cal said with a smile as he glanced up at Alan.

"I forgot we even had one of those," Luke told Rusty, as they both looked at the map laid out in front of them on the counter.

"I think Alan keeps it in his golf bag, sir."

A noise in the far corner by the stairs drew the men's attention. They saw a man coming out of the hole in the floor, hoisting a tray of glasses overhead with his right hand like a waiter. He was also carrying two small silver teapots in his left hand.

After he emerged completely through the hole in the floor, he placed the tray on the main table and began filling the glasses with chai. He then delivered a glass to each American, who accepted it graciously.

"You see that guy make it up those stairs with that tray?" Rusty asked no one in particular. "Dude could totally work at the Waffle House."

Luke was again standing near General Babazheen and Jack, trying to instigate more conversation through the interpreter. "General, how many troops do you believe are in that compound on the other side of the field?"

"There are two hundred fifty men," the general replied very matter-of-factly. "Most of them are working intelligence and logistics. There are only fifty combat troops. But they have access to several thousand more throughout the plains between us and Kabul. The commander is General Shir-Wali. He is a very bad man, and he has much combat experience."

"The general seems to have good intelligence on the enemy," Luke observed. "What building do you think he would be in? Sergeant Scott, hand me the Viper, please."

Alan took the Viper from the man still playing with it and delivered it to General Babazheen. He showed the general the large button on the top and simulated pushing it.

The general panned across the opposite side of the airstrip, looking at the buildings, every so often pushing the Viper's action button to give himself a range to his target.

As the general scanned the enemy targets, he called off words in Dari and pointed to various buildings: "Communications. Barracks. Ammunition. Granary. Petrol." Without looking up from the Viper, he paused at the large silo building at the southwest corner of the airfield, the one the men had been eyeing earlier. He lowered the Viper from his eyes and pointed to the building. "This is where Shir-Wali will be."

"I would like the general to please help us by marking those buildings on a map. They will be the first to go." Luke pointed from the buildings outside the window to the makeshift map that Calvin had been drawing.

"What are your intentions?" the general asked Luke.

"We would like to show the general that although we are few in number, we can make a significant impact on his enemy forces and assist his men in the clearing of Taliban from the Bagram area."

Luke turned to his men. "Calvin, I know it's short notice, but do you think you can get us a bird?"

"I can give it a try, sir," Cal replied.

"Set up for that silo. Doc, help him out," Luke directed.

"Roger that, sir," Alan replied and looked at Calvin with a wry smile. Calvin returned the smile and clenched his right fist in anticipation of the coming events.

Calvin reached into his pack and pulled out his IMBTR along with a small satellite antenna and assembled the necessary parts for connection. Likewise, Alan unzipped the SOFLAM and attached the battery pack and tripod to its base. He set the SOFLAM on the counter, facing the southwest, and scanned through its monocle to find the silo building.

Calvin attached a hand-mic to the IMBTR and started looking through a small notebook for frequencies and call signs. Once he found the one he was looking for, he started the process of air requests through his Air Force channels.

"What are these men doing here?" General Babazheen asked.

"They are requesting airplanes to fly here and drop some bombs on those targets." Luke pointed across the airstrip for the general. "If we are lucky, there will be some in our area that can be diverted to us."

"I have seen your air strikes for many days now," the general explained. "They have no accuracy to enemy targets and are ineffective at making any damage. I am not interested in seeing this again."

Calvin interrupted from his seated position at the radio. "I got one, sir. A flight of two F-16s, stacked full. They'll be here in fifteen minutes."

"I'm all set," Alan interjected. "Just need the code from the birds."

"I understand the general is less than impressed with what he has observed up to now," Luke explained. "This is why we are here—to fix this problem. It is very difficult for a moving aircraft at over twenty thousand feet to accurately choose its own targets on the ground. With your help, General, we can accurately talk them in to the correct enemy positions, making them extremely effective."

Luke walked over to the SOFLAM and continued, "My men can point this device at the targets you choose and eliminate them when the airplanes arrive. We have two airplanes on the way here now, and all we need is your approval for a demonstration of our effectiveness." General Babazheen stood stoically with his arms crossed, obviously skeptical of Captain Walen's claims. Jack had warned Luke previously that there had been continuous bombing raids in the

Shomali Plains for several weeks now, which had made little impact on defensive positions of the Taliban. General Babazheen was completely justified in being hesitant to believe the confident claims of Luke.

After several minutes of the general discussing the situation with some of his men around the table, Calvin announced, "Fighters checking in, boss," and he began performing the check-in procedures and CAS brief with the incoming flight.

"It's your call, sir," Luke said to General Babazheen. "This is what we do," he said confidently as he pointed to the equipment laid out on the counter by the tower windows, never taking his gaze from the general.

After several seconds of contemplation, the general raised his glass of chai toward the enemy positions and gave Luke a slight nod, giving the Triple Nickel the green light to begin.

"We're a go." Luke looked over at Calvin, initiating a sequence of events that, although never rehearsed together by this particular crew, seemed to flow as if practiced together for years. Rusty plotted a sequence of grid coordinates from the map in front of him on a sheet of notebook paper, in descending order of importance, and handed them to Calvin.

Alan again checked the positioning of the SOFLAM, peering through its monocular, and made several small adjustments to the tripod to put the reticle directly on the silo building. He grabbed the cord on the side of the SOFLAM and followed it to its end, which contained a red thumb switch, then depressed the button with his thumb for two seconds, producing a clicking sound.

"Laser is functioning," he barked out.

Calvin, finished with his check-in of the aircraft, began his target talk-on calmly. "Wolfpack one-niner, this is Tiger-Zero-One. As you fly north over the city of Kabul, you will see a north-south running road at the city's twelve o'clock position going directly north. Call contact."

"Contact road," replied the voice over the radio.

Calvin continued, "Five-zero nautical miles north on the east side of that road, you will see a small airstrip with two runways, oriented northeast-southwest. Call tally on the airfield. Over." Several seconds passed, and Calvin and Alan looked at each other, awaiting the response. Each cracked a small smile in anticipation of what was about to transpire.

"Tally airfield," replied Wolfpack.

"Roger, Wolfpack. Friendlies are located in the tower of that airfield. I say again, my position is the tower of the airfield."

"Roger, Tiger-Zero-One. Friendlies in tower on northwest side of runway."

"Roger, Wolfpack. Now let's do some damage." Calvin leaned forward and looked out at the landscape in front of him. "There is a row of buildings on the opposite side of the two runways from our position, running parallel to the airstrip, break. The southernmost corner of that row of buildings has what appears to be a tall grain silo, roughly two to three stories. Call tally that silo."

"Contact on the row of buildings, Tiger-Zero-One, but no joy on any grain silo from this altitude. Over."

"Roger, Wolfpack. Are you laser capable? Over," Calvin inquired.

"That's a roger, Tiger-Zero-One. Lead is laser capable. Laser code is one-six-four-niner. Two is on his own."

On hearing this bit of information, Calvin again looked up to Alan and reached out his right hand for a fist bump, signaling that Alan would also play a role in the coming seconds as Alan set the SOFLAM to the correct code. "Roger, Wolfpack, one-six-four-niner. From the southernmost corner of the airstrip, it will be directly south, about one width of the airstrip, so pretty close. Over."

"Roger, Tiger-Zero-One. Tally silo," Wolfpack answered.

"I need you to circle around to the north and fly directly over our position on an azimuth of two-zero-eight, and we will use the laser for that building. Tiger-Zero-One will stand by for laser call and adjust Wolfpack-two off of lead's hit. Tiger-Zero-One has clearance on final. Over."

Calvin looked at Alan. "You ready, bro?"

Again, Alan checked the positioning of the reticle on the silo building. "I'm ready."

"Roger," was the only reply from Wolfpack.

After several minutes of agonizing silence, Wolfpack announced, "Lead is around from the north following two-zero-eight, one minute."

"Roger, one minute," Calvin replied, holding up his index finger to the crowd gathered around him.

"General," Luke said, patting Babazheen on the back to get his attention, "have a look at your Shir-Wali." He pointed in the direction of the silo. Babazheen put the Viper up to his eyes and looked in the same direction.

"Lead is in," said the pilot over the radio.

"Lead is cleared hot," Calvin replied.

"Laser on," Wolfpack announced.

"Laser on!" all three men echoed in unison. Alan depressed the red button, "painting" the target building.

"Bomb's away," Wolfpack stated.

"Bomb's away!" Calvin announced to the tower and stood up.

Simultaneously, each person with any type of optical device held it to his eyes with a fix on the silo. The men were leaning forward, as if getting six inches closer to the intended target would give them a better view. Their hearts began to beat faster with anticipation. For what seemed like an eternity, all that could be heard was the clicking sound from the SOFLAM. One Afghan soldier removed his small binoculars from his face and looked around the target area, wondering if anything had been dropped at all.

The intense sound of the engine of an aircraft passing overhead broke the silence and overpowered the clicking of the SOFLAM. The bomb hit the mud-and-straw silo building in its center, around ten feet off the deck. It exploded in a cloud of dust that extended forward about one hundred meters from the forward throw of the bomb. The sound of a small and distant explosion reached the tower after a delay of several seconds after the impact.

Several men standing around outside of the silo were immediately thrown from the reticle of the spotting scope Calvin was looking through. He looked up from his scope and over at Alan to see if he had witnessed the same scene of carnage. He saw Alan giving him the same wide-eyed expression. No words were spoken, and none were needed between the two, as they immediately returned to their optics.

Calvin put his hand-mic to his mouth and continued his performance. "Shack, shack, shack. Good hit, lead."

"Two is in," Wolfpack replied.

"Roger two," Calvin continued. "From lead's impact, I need you to work your way north along the row of buildings. We have a large gathering of enemy forces escaping in that direction. You are cleared hot to engage troops in the open."

Calvin looked up at the men behind him in the tower and saw a scene completely different from the one they were presented with upon their arrival. Several men were hugging one another and pointing at the destroyed building. General Babazheen was still standing with his arms crossed, facing out the window, but now he had a large grin on his face.

Calvin reached a fist over to Alan and gave him a slightly more violent fist pound. Alan smiled and said, "Say hello to my little—"

Calvin interrupted with a large smile. "Dude, if you say that stupid Scarface line, I'll punch you right in the dick." Rusty, Alan, and Cal laughed out loud at Calvin's quick catch and again held their optics to their faces to watch the second bird's choice of targets.

Seconds later, another small mud building to the left of the silo erupted in another dust storm, to the jubilation of the men in the tower. Alan and Calvin looked up from their optics again and gave each other "the look," as each had been witness to not only the destruction of another Taliban building, but also several soldiers standing in proximity to the building being thrown a considerable distance due to the shock wave of the massive munitions.

"You think they're alive?" Alan asked Cal.

"They may not be dead, but they are not happy," he said and reached his hand overhead for a celebratory high-five.

The man to whom Alan had taught the high-five was now standing by him, holding up his right hand to him. Laughing, Alan returned the gesture appropriately and gave the man a thumbs-up sign for its appropriate use.

Rusty noticed several men standing against the far wall, gathered around a small handheld radio, laughing. He walked over and pointed to the radio, with his eyebrows raised in curiosity. Several men spoke at once in Dari and pointed at the radio themselves. Rusty looked around and found the interpreter. He returned to the men with the radio and asked what they were laughing at.

"There are many dead, and the commander's building was destroyed. He is very angry," the interpreter said.

"Who are they talking to?" Rusty asked.

"They are listening to the Taliban," he replied and pointed in the direction of the newly destroyed buildings.

"You said the commander is angry. He wasn't in the building? Tell them to ask if the commander is okay—and what is his location?" Rusty commanded with a sly grin.

One of the men assumed control of the radio and held up his hand to quiet the men standing around him before speaking into the radio. Seconds later, a voice furiously replied to the inquiry, much to the laughter of the men standing around.

"They say he is afraid and is going to call for reinforcements at the communications building."

"Hey, Captain Walen." Rusty grabbed the interpreter and ran to the other side of the tower, where Luke and Babazheen were. "Excuse me, sir," Rusty said, looking at the general. "The commander was not in the building. He is making his way to the communications building now to call for reinforcements."

"How do you know that?" Luke asked.

"He told us himself." Rusty pointed to the group of men around the radio. "I guess they asked him."

Luke looked at Babazheen. "General, can you tell us which of those buildings is the communications building?"

The general stood behind Luke and held the Viper to Luke's face. He pointed in the direction of the row of buildings and aimed Luke's field of view to a small group of three buildings with many antennas on their roofs.

"Calvin, look about four hundred meters north of the silo, and you will see a group of three buildings with two black vehicles outside and several antennas on the roofs," Luke commanded without dropping the Viper from his eyes.

Calvin lost his smile and immediately went back into work mode. Methodically he panned his spotting scope across the airfield, stopping after several seconds. "I have a group of three buildings with two black SUVs to their north side, several antennas on the center building, and four men dressed in black standing outside between the two trucks. Alan, I need an azimuth."

"That's your next target." Luke looked back to Babazheen and pointed at the building. "Shir-Wali."

"Shir-Wali? Aahh," the general replied with a nod.

"Wolfpack, this is Tiger-Zero-One. We have another target for you. Laser is ready. Over," Calvin barked into his radio.

"Roger, Tiger-Zero-One. Send it," Wolfpack replied.

"I need you to follow almost the same approach. The target is about four hundred meters north of your first, so I need you coming south at ..." He paused and looked over at Alan, who had the number 195 written on his hand in black marker and held it up to Calvin's face. "One-niner-five degrees. How copy, over."

"Roger, one-niner-five approach. Tiger-Zero-One has control on final," Wolfpack responded.

Calvin tapped Alan on the left shoulder and pointed into the sky to the east. Alan looked above the horizon and saw them: two fighters banking hard to the north and coming around for a second run. Alan pointed in their direction, showing that he saw them as well. Seconds later, the jets passed by the tower noisily, causing several men to move to the window and look for the birds.

"Get that thing pointed at the right building, and get ready to rock again," Calvin commanded Alan, who returned to his seat immediately and adjusted the device for another target.

"Can I get some more tea over here, please?" Calvin asked no one in particular. Without warning, echoes of "chai, chai, chai" were sent around the room, and several men fought to be the one who delivered the new, hot glass to Calvin.

Stunned at the hasty delivery, Calvin looked back at Alan. "Oh, now we get good service."

"It looks that way. Ask for a beer, and see what happens," Alan joked.

"Lead is in," came the call over the radio.

"Roger, lead. You are cleared hot," Cal responded.

"Laser on," the pilot called out.

Alan and Cal echoed together, "Laser on!" Alan depressed the thumb switch, which made the familiar clicking sound.

"Bombs away," the radio broadcasted to the room, again followed by the echoes of several men. "Bombs away!"

Each man returned to his optics to watch the next target fall. The anticipation grew as the men in the tower awaited the coming destruction. Moments later, a large dust storm erupted on the opposite side of the runway, followed several seconds later by its sound.

"Shack!" Calvin announced into the radio, letting the pilot know that his bomb had met its target accurately.

"Roger, two is in," the second pilot replied: he was inbound for his bombing run.

"Roger, two. Three-zero meters to the south of lead's hit are several black vehicles attempting to flee the target area. You are cleared hot on those vehicles. Don't let those little bastards get away!" Calvin said with emphasis as he got to his feet.

"Roger that. Wolfpack-Two, bombs away."

Calvin placed the hand-mic on the counter in front of him and peered through his spotting scope. Seconds later, he saw a small black object enter the upper left corner of the scope's reticle, almost as if in slow motion. After a slight pause, the vehicles were thrown in opposite directions from the impact of the bomb. Again, Calvin looked to Alan for "the look," which he received cheerfully. Cal clenched his right hand into a fist and pumped it slightly for a job well done.

"Dude, check this out," Rusty announced as he stood looking at the target area through binoculars. "They look like roaches."

Alan and Cal peered once again through their optics to see dozens of men in black garb running in several directions around the target area. Since the bombs had hit the southernmost building and one more to the north, with a couple more thrown in, the enemy had no real idea where the next bomb would fall. All they knew was that they did not want to be there.

Calvin picked up his hand-mic. "Wolfpack, this is Tiger-Zero- One. What is your weapons status? Over."

"We are Winchester on bombs, but we both have a full load on our Vulcans," explained the pilot, signifying that they were out of precision guided munitions but still had the M61 Vulcan 20mm guns standard on the F16 Falcon.

"Roger, Wolfpack. That last drop sent a few dozen scattering. If you could do us a favor and give 'em one good gun-run to the southwest on your way out, that would be awesome."

"Roger, Tiger-Zero-One. We'd be happy to oblige." Calvin could almost hear the smile on the pilot's face.

"Dude, check this shit out," Cal announced quietly to Rusty and pointed to the airstrip to alert him to the coming excitement. Rusty immediately held his binoculars to his face and looked in the same direction.

Moments later, a line of small explosions erupted along the ground in a southern direction, sending dust into the air to cover the opposite end of the runway like a curtain. This was immediately followed by a deafening sound like a large zipper being pulled closed. A large group of Afghan men rushed to the windows to see what had made the new sound, and they were obviously pleased at what they saw.

Suddenly, the second pilot sent another line of cannon fire exploding across the desert floor, followed closely by the ear-splitting sound of the jets leaving the area. For the first time today, the Afghan men began to cheer. All the Americans in the tower paused and looked at the men, who had gathered together, hugging one another like fans at a sports arena. Then they looked at each other, and with smiles of their own, and gave the slightest of head nods for a job well done.

"Wolfpack this is Tiger-Zero-One. We appreciate the work today. If you're ever in our AO again, give us a call. I'm sure we'll have some work for you. Well done, and have a safe flight home," Cal broadcasted.

"Roger, Tiger-Zero-One. Thank you. I don't know where they find guys like you, but I'm glad you're on our side. Wolfpack is RTB," said the pilot, indicating that they were returning to base.

Proudly Calvin held up the hand-mic so the rest of the crew could hear the pilot's reply. He smiled at Alan and pointed with the hand-mic to the target area, which still had dozens of men running in several directions. "Hey, bro, they may not be dead …"

All three men smiled wide and added loudly, "But they are not happy!"

The Americans laughed and shook hands, celebrating their victorious shellacking of the enemy positions. Although they all knew that this airstrike was only the beginning, bringing a precision attack with substantial results gave them confidence and validation of their mission. Although they enjoyed calling CAS on enemy positions, each one wanted a more personal retribution for this particular enemy. They would not have to wait very long.

\* \* \*

Across the airfield at the northernmost set of buildings, General Shir-Wali peered through a set of binoculars at the windowless control tower. He had a small puncture wound surrounded by dried blood on his left check, from a fragment of one of the American bombs. He stared expressionlessly through his optics at the Americans celebrating in the tower. Although they wanted to keep their presence in theater hidden from the enemy for some time, the precision of the day's attacks had alerted Shir-Wali that something had changed. His suspicions were validated by the identification of the members of the Triple Nickel in the control tower several hundred meters away.

These men posed a serious threat to his forces and would have to be dealt with quickly, as he could not afford many more of these precision bombing strikes. He lowered his binoculars but continued to stare at the tower intently as a slight grin grew on his face. It had been a long time since a worthy adversary had presented itself to a general of his caliber, and he was looking forward to the challenge.

# THE DEGÜELLO

# CHAPTER 16

*In war, numbers alone confer no advantage. Do not advance relying on sheer military power.*
-Sun Tzu

As the sun peeked over the mountains to the east of the Crow's Nest, Steve enjoyed a hot cup of coffee and looked at the scenic landscape below his position. Several days had passed since the bombs were dropped at Bagram, and they had not been able to get dedicated airstrikes diverted to their location since. They had traveled to the front lines daily to assess the area and hopefully hit some targets, but each time they had come up empty on the CAS front.

Steve had spent the entire night listening to the embellished stories of combat and comparisons between directing CAS from distant positions to facing the enemy with small arms on a battlefield or within a city. Although he knew the stories might have been slightly exaggerated, as most good combat stories were, the fact that he was not a part of the first opportunity for contact with the enemy in this fight did not sit well with him. No Special Forces operator came to the unit to watch others perform or listen to others tell stories of combat.

Alan stepped outside the mud-walled compound for a cigarette and saw Steve enjoying the morning view. The decision had been made to continue the split-team concept, with one team conducting operations at all times, leaving the other one to recover from the day before and plan the next day's operations.

"Whatcha doing, bro?" Alan inquired.

"Just enjoying the quiet," Steve replied.

"Everything okay?" Alan asked.

"Yeah, I'm good. Good job the other day, man. Sounds like you guys did some real damage."

"Wow, thanks," Alan replied to Steve's out-of-character accolade. "Any monkey with a radio can sit a thousand meters away and talk a bomb on a target. I might as well have phoned that shit in from Nashville. I was hoping this would be a little more engaging."

"Be careful what you ask for," Steve responded. "I think if we went the next year doing nothing but lasing targets one by one from a mile away and coming home to dinner every night, it would be okay by me."

Steve picked up a few rocks and started throwing them at one of the Russian jeeps in the compound below theirs, roughly fifty meters down the hill. Alan moved closer to the edge of the hill and joined Steve in throwing small rocks like a couple of kids in a schoolyard.

"Where are you guys heading today?" Alan asked.

"We found a couple good elevated positions yesterday," Steve replied. "There's a nice hill in the east with an observation post (OP) that has a good vantage point over a couple pretty heavily populated compounds.

"The area west of Bagram is pretty flat, but there are several small compounds these guys use as OPs that we can use. One of them has little guard towers on the corners, like some sort of medieval castle, and we can get a good view of the forward line of troops from there. I think we're going to the east one today. They really didn't want to make a decision last night, because they don't want these guys knowing where we are going until we leave, for security reasons."

Steve banged a small rock off the hood of one of the jeeps, to the dismay of Alan, who had yet to come close to the vehicle with his throws.

"Security reasons?" Alan said. "You think we have a tattletale among our friends?"

"I don't trust anyone here, bro," Steve replied. "Remember, they told us these guys get their food and fuel from Kabul, a city that happens to be controlled by the Taliban. A little too convenient, if you ask me. I'm pretty sure those guys know that we're here, how many of us there are, and where we are going every day. So, yeah, I agree with not telling them shit until it is absolutely necessary."

"Not going to argue with that," Alan replied. "When are you guys taking off?"

"Should be pretty soon. They were looking for some dude who spoke English that was with you guys at the airfield."

"Akmal. He's a good dude," Alan explained. "He learned English by watching MTV or something. He would be good to have around."

The rock-throwing game suddenly got cut short when one of the rocks Steve threw hit the intended target and skipped off the jeep's hood, right into the windshield. The impact created a large spider-web crack on the passenger side of the vehicle. Steve and Alan looked at each other and reacted like two adolescents who had broken a lamp, and they ran back inside the compound like nothing had happened.

Several men were loading gear into the backs of the vehicles and preparing to depart for the day's mission. Alan saw his English-speaking Afghan friend coming out of the far building.

"Akmal!" he yelled across the vehicle to get the interpreter's attention.

"What is going on, man?" Akmal replied with a smile as he approached Alan and Steve.

"Akmal, this is Steve." Alan pointed at his friend, who reached out his hand to their new Afghan friend.

"How's it going, bro?" Steve asked. "Are you coming out with us today?"

"I go where you go, bro," Akmal responded in heavily accented English to the laughter of the two Americans.

After the convoy brief, Bravo Team—Frank, Shane, Steve, JT, and Blaine along with Cliff and a dozen or so Afghan counterparts— began the long trek to the front lines and the eastern OP. They'd spent the entire previous day driving the AO and doing reconnaissance for good fighting positions, so another hour-long trek to the eastern OP was not what they desired. They had to drive through several smaller built-up areas where the local people were moving about in their daily routines.

They stopped in what appeared to be a shopping district with mud and brick buildings on both sides of the paved road. The area looked like it was straight out of the Old West, but with different characters. It was a one-road town with small mom-and-pop shops on both sides; the only thing missing was a drunken sheriff. There were dozens of buildings that sold a variety of food products and other merchandise. The convoy pulled in front of a food shop, and several of the Afghan soldiers went inside.

"What are we doing here?" Steve asked Akmal.

"They are getting us our lunch for the day," he responded.

Steve began to scan the area from the passenger seat of the jeep Akmal was driving. To his left was a two-story clothing shop with what looked like a living area on the second floor. The shop owners probably lived above their store. He also saw stores for shoes, kitchen supplies, used diesel generators, and a pharmacy. The pharmacy had a familiar sign in the window, and Steve could not resist.

"Akmal, dude, go get us some Coke!" He pointed to the huge Coca-Cola sign in the window, several doors down from where they were parked. Steve handed Akmal a large wad of Afghanis from his pocket.

The exchange rate was briefed at forty-thousand to one, so a couple Cokes had to be a few hundred thousand Afghanis. Akmal jumped from his vehicle and ran into the shop across the street.

"I should have asked him if they had some dip," Blaine said sarcastically. Several minutes later, Akmal returned with two filled plastic bags thin enough to see the familiar red cans inside.

"Yeah, baby!" Steve said with his familiar accent and smile.

"Yeah, baby!" Akmal returned in similar tones but with an Afghan accent. Steve and Blaine began laughing and patted him on the shoulders for a job well done. Akmal handed the bags to Blaine, who filled his pack with the warm cans.

Their counterparts emerged from the store and waved at Akmal to signal that the convoy was moving out. Akmal raised his hand in acknowledgment and followed the vehicle in front of him as it sped away from the shopping area.

\* \* \*

Atop the roof of the two-story clothing store across the street, a large Arab-looking man in black with a full beard walked closer to the edge of the roof, staring at the convoy driving away. He was expressionless and kept his eyes focused on the departing vehicles. He raised a small radio with a large rubber antenna and reported what he had just witnessed. He continued his report as the convoy faded away to the east.

* * *

The eastern OP was atop a large hill, maybe three hundred meters in elevation. The team had to exit their vehicles and hike the long, steep trail that wound up the hill. They also had to carry all their gear, food, and water with them, which would make the trek more difficult. With the extreme slope of the hill, they took several breaks along the route to let Cliff and some of their Afghan counterparts catch up.

"Make sure you guys stay on the path," Cliff said. "Afghanistan is probably the most mined country in the world, and this area is littered in mines left over from the Russians."

The men looked at each other and then at the ground around them, and immediately they filed in behind one another, creating a tighter line on the path.

Once atop the OP, nearly forty-five minutes after beginning their ascent, Frank made a quick visual assessment of the area. Because the hill was used as an early warning OP, there were many fighting positions dug into the side of the hill facing south. These positions were three to four feet deep and had small rock walls surrounding them for protection. Due to the size of the Americans, most of them would be easily seen if they did not squat low inside the dug-out positions.

They could see for miles in every direction, and they had a great viewpoint of their battlefield. They could make out the airfield and tower at Bagram as well as the buildings that were destroyed in the previous attacks. Just south of the row of enemy buildings, they saw a large wadi that had many people and vehicles moving within it. This was significant because the wadi could not be seen by anyone in the tower at Bagram. There were more vehicles and troops in the Bagram area than originally perceived by the team.

To the southeast, the mountains of the Panjshir opened to a large flat area that contained large compounds of mud-walled buildings like the one they were living in. There were various sizes of compounds with walled courtyards oriented like a large checkerboard. There were several small built-up areas that looked like small towns or villages separating the series of residential courtyards between Bagram and the mountains off to the east.

JT set up his radio and assembled a satellite antenna, pointing it to the right azimuth and elevation. Steve pulled out the SOFLAM and hooked it up to the large battery pack and tripod. Blaine and Frank were looking through their spotting scopes at the different mud-walled compounds to the south, while Shane was working with Akmal, assigning positions for the security detachment assigned to them. Cliff was helping some Afghan men set up a small cooking stove and teapot for chai. Several men had been left down the hill with the vehicles, and Shane could see that they were sitting on the ground in a small circle, already drinking tea.

After some time and some discussions with higher command over the radio, JT was having difficulty getting any birds diverted to their AO. It should have been easier after the success of the previous event. One would think that bombers would be lining up to take out real military targets with spotters on the ground, but it was not looking as if they would get any play time today.

Blaine pointed out a large group of military-age men in one of the mud compounds to the south who were amassing near a group of vehicles. Frank trained his spotting scope on the compound and counted roughly sixty men, dressed in black pajamas, gathering with some sense of purpose. Many of the men were carrying rifles on their shoulders, and some were talking into radios. Because the compound was roughly one thousand meters to their south and at ground level, it was difficult to make out anything but vehicles and personnel, even with the precision optics they had at their disposal.

"JT, what's the status on CAS? Can we get some air today, or do I have to go back and get the Air Force guy?" Frank joked.

"Okay, was that really necessary?" JT looked up from his radio at Frank, obviously not amused by his remark. "Give me a break, man. You know how many people are in this chain? Everybody and their brother is getting on, asking what we are going to hit, where we are, where we got the target list from, blah, blah, blah. They want a full nine-line with all the particulars and are saying we have to give twenty-four hours' notice if we want any dedicated air."

"Twenty-four hours? When we were in the desert, we got CAS anytime we wanted it. This is nuts," Shane complained, referring to previous operations.

"Yeah, but those birds were coming off carriers in the Gulf," JT explained,

"That's like a fifteen-minute flight. These guys are coming from the Arabian Sea, which gives them just enough fuel for a trip here and back. And that doesn't give us much play time once they are here—so I suggest we start getting a target list going, so I can talk them right in if they do come."

"Good idea, JT," Frank replied. "Shane and Steve, start scouting some targets, and set up for the first couple runs. That compound there is really jumping," he said pointing to the compound that he and Blaine had been watching. "I don't know what they are getting ready to do, but if we get the chance, I'd like to fuck up their day."

"Akmal," Steve called, "do you know what that compound is down there, with all the people and cars in it?" Akmal came over, and Steve handed him the Viper to look at the compound. "Yes, I think that is a living area. Taliban spend much time there and come out to fight."

"This is some war," Steve said sarcastically. "It's like that cartoon when we were kids, with the dog and wolf clocking in before fighting all day, then clocking out and going home, only to do it all again tomorrow. No wonder this has been going on here for a hundred years."

"In Italy for thirty years under the Borgias, they had warfare, terror, murder, and bloodshed, and they produced Michelangelo, Leonardo da Vinci, and the Renaissance," Frank explained. "In Switzerland they had brotherly love, five hundred years of democracy, and peace, and what did that produce? The cuckoo clock."

"Where the hell did you get that?" Steve looked curiously at Frank.

"The Third Man," Frank answered. "It's an old Orson Wells movie."

"Wow, I bet Alan would have never gotten that one," Steve remarked with a smile.

"I got it from Alan," Frank admitted hesitantly.

Blaine interrupted, saying, "That dude seriously needs a girlfriend. Maybe we should hook him up with a movie critic— probably the only way he'd get a date."

"I don't know, man," Steve came back. "Then he would have to talk intelligently about movies instead of rating them by how many tits he saw in the first five minutes."

"What the hell does that mean?" Frank asked as he continued to look at the map he was holding.

"Well, according to our resident movie guy," Steve continued as he set the SOFLAM on the hill, facing south, "if a movie doesn't have a death, explosion, or boob shot in the first five minutes, Alan gives it thumbs down. And I hate admitting when that guy is right, but it's been pretty accurate."

They all began to laugh at their friend's expense. Shane, looking through the spotting scope to the south, interrupted their laughter. "JT, you think we could get CAS if we were being overrun and breaking contact from the enemy?"

"Probably," JT replied. "E-CAS gets diverted to you from regular flights within a couple hundred miles in any direction. That's a great idea, but I already called it in with a nine-line. Wish I'd thought of that before I made that call."

"Well, you might want to give it a try, just the same. Take a look." Shane dropped the spotting scope from his face and pointed in the direction of the compound they had been eyeing all morning.

All four men came over to where Shane was standing and, using their optics, looked down the hill to the south. A convoy of vehicles was heading north out of the compound, on the only road that led straight to the hill they were on. The lead vehicle kicked up a lot of dust, so it was difficult to make out how many were in the convoy, but Frank noticed that there were only a couple vehicles left in the compound and no personnel. If all sixty men were in that convoy, there had to be at least ten or twelve vehicles. Since the group had about fifteen men, including the five Americans, the odds were not in their favor.

"You think they know we're up here?" Steve asked no one in particular.

"There's no way their intelligence is that good," Cliff responded.

"What do you want to do, Frank?" Shane asked.

"Even if we hauled ass, I don't think we could pack up everything and make it back down the hill before they got here." Frank looked at JT. "Make the call."

JT ran over to his fighting position and began calling for Emergency CAS. Likewise, the other members of the team reacted as if a switch had been turned on: they lost their smiles and immediately gathered their weapons and equipment with a sense of urgency.

"Akmal," Frank said, pointing to the group of Northern Alliance soldiers gathered on the hill drinking chai, "I need you to get those guys over here and have Shane tell you where to put them down on the hill."

He looked over to Shane, "I want them spread out to make it look like we are bigger than fifteen people. Pair them up, and make sure they have enough ammo. What do we have for weapons up here?"

"I have the SR-25," Shane replied cautiously, "Blaine and Steve each have an M203 on their M-4s with about thirty 40mm rounds, a few grenades, and a couple claymores. Not enough for any kind of sustained firefight, boss."

"Well, I say we end it quick, then," Frank responded decisively.

"Put in the Afghans down the hill a little—I want them closer to the road and definitely in front of me in a firefight. You and Blaine set up over there," he said, pointing to a pre-dug fighting position surrounded by stone. "Steve and I will be there," he said, pointing at another one fifty meters or so away from the first. "Split up the 40mm, and let's use as much of it as we can for the effect. From this elevation, we should have easy shots at the first ones who come at us. I need you to have Akmal call down to the trucks and have the drivers move those vehicles two kilometers north, until we call them."

Shane turned and directed Akmal to get the Afghan men emplaced on the hill. Steve separated the 40mm ammo from a long bandolier and gave half to Blaine, who filled every pocket he had with rounds. They moved to their fighting positions on the southwest side of the hill.

Once inside, Blaine laid out the 40mm rounds on the ground in front of him, within easy reach. He opened the long, shotgun-like chamber and loaded a round into his M203. On the right side of the weapon was a flip-out sight, which he engaged, and he picked up an aiming point at the approaching convoy.

Steve ran to the western side of the hill, got into a pre-dug fighting position, and put the half-empty bandolier by his feet. Much like Blaine, he loaded a 40mm round and got a feel for the sight picture to the bottom of the hill. He pulled three M-4 magazines from his pack and put them on the ground in front of him. He then grabbed a metal stake painted alternating white and red and pounded it into the ground in front of him, marking his left limit of firing, to not shoot over Blaine's fighting position.

Shane and Cliff ran to the top of the hill while unfolding a VS-17 panel and staked it to the peak of the hill, in case JT could scramble any CAS. A VS-17 panel was a large, dense, eighteen by-thirty-six-inch fabric signal panel with Day-Glo orange on one side and Day-Glo pink on the other; it was used by American forces to signal their positions to aircraft and could be seen easily from the air. There had been many incidents of friendly fire when working CAS because the ground controllers mistakenly gave their own position to the birds, with tragic results. Calvin was explicit about making sure to describe and mark their position extremely well before allowing any bombs to be released. The short time it took to make sure the airplane knew where friendlies were located was nothing to losing an entire detachment because of miscommunication.

"JT," Frank yelled, "we need those birds!" He looked to the southwest and saw the convoy approaching their position rapidly.

"I'm working on it!" JT yelled back angrily, with the hand-mic still held to his ear.

"What are the chances they drive right past us?" Steve asked Frank.

"We'll know in about thirty seconds," Frank responded.

Without warning, a barrage of gunfire erupted from the fighting positions below them. The Northern Alliance men began emptying their magazines on full automatic fire in the direction of the oncoming convoy. The vehicles were still several hundred meters away and closing fast. The sporadic outgoing gunfire passed quickly among the different fighting positions on the hill and soon was an impressive show of force; it created an enormous stream of bullets in the direction of the enemy.

"Who told those idiots to engage?" Frank said to Steve. He ran over to the fighting position and jumped in. He pulled his weapon to his face to observe the convoy through his ACOG four power scope. It took only seconds for Frank to realize that although the gunfire sounded impressive, it was completely incapable of doing any damage to the convoy itself. Upon further investigation, he noticed his counterparts were not holding their weapons in the manner they were designed to be held. Most of the men were hunkered down in their fighting positions, holding the weapons over their heads, and squeezing the triggers. Although this method kept the shooter safe from return fire, it hardly was a threat to the enemy, as the weapon was not pointed at any individual target.

"They're not even aiming! Oh, this is not good!" Frank exclaimed.

When fired upon, the convoy split into two lines of vehicles. One group headed to the south of the hill while the other continued farther north up the road, to the hill's eastern flank; they intended to come at the Americans from two different directions. Frank used two fingers and whistled loudly to get the attention of Shane, who was in the other fighting position.

Shane heard the familiar whistle and looked over at Frank. He saw him pointing his finger at Shane and then immediately to the vehicles moving off to their south. Shane gave the far signal "okay" sign: fingers of the right hand to the top of the head and elbow out, making a larger O. He extended the bipod of his sniper rifle and brought the butt of the rifle tight to his shoulder. He picked up a good sight picture and began shooting at the lead vehicle methodically, filling the windshield on the driver's side with multiple rounds, causing it to slide to a halt.

Blaine stepped forward, aiming his M203 at the same vehicle and squeezed the trigger, causing a small popping sound, similar to the sound made by opening a can of potato crisps. Seconds later, the lead vehicle burst into a fiery explosion surrounded by a cloud of dust. The trailing vehicles slid to a halt, and the men inside began to exit and scatter, shooting wildly into the hill with the same accuracy as their Northern Alliance adversaries.

"Nice fucking shot!" Shane said to Blaine without looking up from his scope. He followed the explosion with a disciplined and orderly engagement of targets as they emerged from the vehicles toward the base of the hill. Blaine immediately began to shoot targets with his M-4 as they presented themselves down the hill.

On the other side of the hill, Steve picked up a sight picture with his M203 and let a round fly. It impacted just in front of the vehicle leading the second convoy, causing it to veer quickly to its right and come to a halt. Enemy troops exited their vehicles and, in no clear fashion, assaulted the hill from the east. Steve immediately loaded a second 40mm round, held up his weapon in the firing position, and squeezed the trigger. His round impacted the vehicle, causing it to explode, throwing several Taliban troops into the air from the blast.

"Took ya two!" Blaine yelled at Steve with a smile from his fighting position. His reprimand was interrupted abruptly by a short burst of rounds that ricocheted off the rocks in front of him, causing him to duck quickly into the makeshift foxhole.

With the enemy pouring onto their position, and with such a disorganized assault, they were having difficulty choosing an area or direction to concentrate their fire on. Each man would get off several rounds and immediately come under fire from a different direction. What made matters worse was that the initial gunfire from their Northern Alliance counterparts had left many men low on ammunition. Soon after the initial assault on their position, most had completely exhausted their supply. To the surprise of the Americans above them on the hill, many men began to exit their fighting positions and run around the hill to the north side, away from the gunfire.

"What the hell are they doing?" Frank exclaimed as he continued to shoot down the hill. Steve paused his firing and looked down to see his counterparts running away from the barrage of incoming gunfire. Presented with moving targets, the Taliban men shifted their focus and fire to the fleeing Northern Alliance. Seeing his opportunity to strike, Steve loaded another 40mm round and fired it at a group of Taliban that were now making their way up the hill, quickly eliminating several men in one shot.

The sound of a man screaming caught their attention, and they looked down the hill to see a Northern Alliance soldier lying on the ground, holding his right leg, obviously wounded. Another soldier quickly went to his aid and was immediately hit by several rounds to his chest. Frank moved his sight picture to the area where the gunfire targeting the wounded man originated, found his target, and squeezed the trigger, striking the Taliban fighter in the head and causing him to fall backward down the hill several feet.

"There's too many," Blaine barked as he dropped to one knee and reloaded his M-4. "Got any ideas?"

"Give 'em a couple 40mm there." Shane pointed to the far south of the approaching enemy. "And see if it bunches them together." Blaine loaded a 40mm round into his M203 and, without looking through the sights, fired it from the hip in the direction of the enemy's right flank. He immediately opened the chamber of the weapon, expelling the empty shell, and loaded a second round, firing it seconds later in the same direction.

With the impact of two 40mm rounds in one area, the approaching enemy moved to their left, creating a closer group of targets to concentrate on. Shane immediately engaged these gathered troops with the SR-25, sending several falling down the hill in a lifeless tumble.

Suddenly they heard a loud whooshing sound from the peak of the hill, followed several seconds later by what sounded like a handful of firecrackers going off. Steve looked up the hill and saw a white star cluster signal flare burning in the sky like fireworks directly above him. He immediately dropped to a knee and changed his magazine.

"Come on," he said to himself aloud, followed by a deep, calming breath. He returned to a standing position and continued to engage the enemy assaulting the hill; they were now roughly one third of the way up the slope.

Frank squeezed off another round and heard the familiar click of the bolt locking to the rear on his M-4, signifying an empty magazine. "I'm out!" he yelled as he dropped to a knee.

Steve reached down to his feet, grabbed a magazine, and handed it to Frank. "Two more—make 'em count," he replied and continued engaging targets. Frank loaded the magazine into his weapon and slapped the bolt release, sending a round into the chamber. He stood up and began shooting at the men assaulting the hill below.

Suddenly, the ground beneath them shook violently. A large eruption of earth on the hill to the south sent dust and rocks flying off to the west in a massive explosion. Before they even knew what was happening, the Americans instinctively ducked deep into their fighting positions and covered their heads with a free hand.

"Shack!" JT yelled into his radio from his fighting position atop the hill. "Great job! That was right where I wanted it. Two, I need you to follow that strike one hundred meters west at the same elevation on the hill. I stress again, your limit is the hill's midpoint, and I would prefer you to err on the low side."

"WILCO; Vegas One-Four is in from the east," the second pilot replied. ("Wilco" stood for "will comply.")

"You are cleared hot, Vegas," JT calmly answered into his hand-mic. He immediately cupped both hands around his mouth to increase the volume of his voice and screamed down the hill, "Stay down!"

Steve had begun to stand and assess the area below. Hearing JT's direction, Frank reached up and grabbed him by the bottom of his shirt, pulling him back to a squatting position. Seconds later, another large explosion of a five-hundred-pound MK-82 bomb with fuse extender sent a huge cloud of dust and rocks sideways across the hill. The blast vaporized several Taliban, and the overpressure sent ten more troops on the ride of their life.

"Way to go, JT," Frank said aloud.

"Never had a doubt," Steve replied as they watched the remaining Taliban men reverse their assault on the hill and hurriedly move back to their vehicles.

Steve launched out of the fighting position from which he and Frank had been shooting and began a feet-first controlled slide down the hill toward the wounded Northern Alliance soldier, who was still writhing in pain seventy-five meters below him. Once he reached the man, he pulled him back into the nearby fighting position to protect them both from another possible bomb strike. Once inside, Steve pulled out his police model Spyderco knife and cut away the man's pants, exposing the gunshot wound. There was a small entrance wound on the anterior side of his right thigh that went through to the back, creating a large exit wound.

Another Northern Alliance soldier joined Steve in the fighting position and started to talk to the wounded man. Although Steve did not speak Dari very well, he could tell that they were friends and the soldier was concerned for his buddy. Steve grabbed hold of the second man's wrists and maneuvered his hands to the injured man's wounds, one at the entrance and one on the exit wound, having him apply pressure to help stop the bleeding.

"Hold tight," Steve directed and showed the man his own hands squeezed tight for effect. Steve reached into his vest and pulled out two rolled gauze bandages; one at a time, he applied a wad of the gauze under the hand of the man assisting with pressure. He pulled a six-inch elastic bandage from another pocket and wrapped the leg to apply pressure to the wound. He finished the dressing with a circumferential wrap of three-inch white medical tape.

From his shirt pocket, he pulled what looked like a marker and held it against the injured man's opposite thigh, sending an eighteen-gauge needle with pressurized morphine sulfate into the man's leg. After several seconds, he removed the auto-injector from the thigh and showed it to the injured man. "This is for pain."

Steve signaled for his new helper to help the man to his feet and assist him down the hill to their vehicles. Before returning to Frank, he looked up the hill to assess the situation and saw Frank holding up a closed fist in his direction, telling him to halt. Frank then pointed into the air, letting him know that another airstrike was on its way. Steve needed no more direction; he grabbed the two men and pulled them back into the fighting position. He got in himself and hunkered down, covering his head with both hands to demonstrate a futile safe position to his counterparts. Seeing this, the Afghan men looked at each other and immediately followed suit.

Seconds later, the sonic whine of an F-16 Falcon filled the air.

Steve closed his eyes tightly in anticipation of another five-hundred-pounder but was relieved to hear the sounds of the Vulcan cannon instead. He looked up from his position to catch the stream of 20mm rounds cutting through several vehicles in the group to the south. With the vehicles now rendered useless after such an attack, the men running toward them abandoned their first choice, made their way to the last few remaining operational vehicles, and jumped inside.

Several of the men had to stand on the vehicles' running boards and hold onto the roof to catch a ride. Without slowing down for the remainder of the chasing Taliban, the few remaining vehicles sped off to the south in the direction of their compound.

Steve stood and scanned the plains to the south of the hill just attacked; he saw a handful of vehicles speeding away in clouds of dust, both on and off the road, to not be caught in a column by the planes circling above like sharks. The two dozen men fleeing on foot would have put the Kenyan Olympic team to shame. Steve grabbed his M-4 just in front of the ACOG optic and held it above his head, looking back up the hill at the other Americans. He yelled, "Wolverines!"

"What the hell was that?" Shane asked, pointing at Steve.

"Red Dawn," JT answered. "Dude, if you're going to make it on this team, you better learn your movies."

The four Americans gathered at the top of the hill began to laugh at Steve's awesome response to their little battle with the enemy, which helped alleviate the tension they all felt. Blaine walked over to JT and gave him a large bear hug, lifting him off the ground in appreciation for the well-timed air strikes that had turned the tables on the advancing Taliban.

Several minutes later, after everything had calmed down a little, the men began packing up their gear. Frank stood alone, staring at the compound over one thousand meters to his south. The timing of those men leaving that compound minutes after his arrival to the eastern OP could not have been a coincidence. The early initiation of contact by the Northern Alliance was not as disheartening to him as the almost absent marksmanship of the men sent to protect them. Although Jerry had told them that they should concentrate on directing CAS on the enemy because these were "well-trained" veteran soldiers, Frank was not convinced. After the poor display of combat he had just witnessed, training the Northern Alliance had to become a priority. He turned to walk up the hill to where the rest of the boys were and managed a smile as his men greeted him with rounds of high-fives and fist bumps. The celebration would be short-lived, as getting off the hill was now a priority.

* * *

One thousand meters to the south and holding binoculars to his face, Shir-Wali stared intently at the lone American on the hill to his north, who seemed to be staring directly back as if he knew he was being observed. Shir-Wali had a small bandage on his cheek from the wound inflicted in the previous attacks. He scanned the desert floor between himself and the failed attack on the hill and watched what remained of his men flee back to his compound in vehicles and on foot.

He turned from the window and walked to the large table in the center of the room. There was a map of the area on the table, along with several trays of food and tea. In anger, Shir-Wali lashed out with his right hand and swept the area in front of him clear, sending glasses crashing into the far wall.

With the firepower the Americans were bringing to the fight and the support of CAS, a full-frontal assault in open terrain was obviously not the wisest way to eliminate this new adversary. He would have to come up with a more astute way of dealing with this problem, and it would have to be quick, as he was beginning to feel the repercussions of his manpower losses.

Shir-Wali was a veteran of the conflict with the Soviets in the 1980s and had employed many unconventional tactics to help inflict damage to a superior force. Being able to adapt his tactics to the conflict at hand was one of the reasons he had been so victorious. Something different had to be done and done quickly.

# CHAPTER 17

*An ambush, if discovered and promptly surrounded, will repay
the intended mischief with interest.*
### -Publius Flavius Vegetius Renatus

After the attack on the hill the week before, Luke had decided to be more diligent in their security and planning. A concentrated effort to increase the fundamental tactics and training of their counterparts was now as much of a priority as calling CAS on enemy targets. As one team went forward to the forward line of troops (FLOT), the other team trained the remaining forces in an area set up as a makeshift range complex, north of the Crow's Nest.

As the days passed, the training of the Northern Alliance was beginning to show improvements. Small engagements with the Taliban were quickly repelled by the men of the Triple Nickel and their counterparts. With each day's mission, the team would assess the strengths and weaknesses of the Northern Alliance men and adjust their training accordingly.

Several men were preparing to make the trek to the front lines again, and as Steve approached, Alan, Akmal, and Rusty were standing by their jeep, waiting for their departure.

"Alan, can I talk to you for a second?" Steve asked.

"Sure, bro. What's up?" Alan walked away from the jeep with Steve, toward the mud buildings.

"It's Frank—he's not feeling so hot. He's been throwing up and shitting himself for a couple days now," Steve explained, "and he can't seem to kick it."

"Maybe it's fear. Been a while since the old man's been shot at," Alan jested. "You give him anything yet?"

"Standard stuff—Cipro, loperamide, and some Pepto. Nothing is working. He's actually getting worse."

"What do you mean by getting worse?" Alan asked.

"He won't even get out of bed, and now he has a massive headache. I think it's more than just normal gastro," Steve explained, referring to gastroenteritis, a common ailment in austere environments, which presents with diffuse abdominal pain, nausea, vomiting, and diarrhea. "I need a second opinion here."

"All right, let's go check him out," Alan said, and they walked into the back room of the mud building that several of the Americans were using as a sleeping area.

Steve had a litter set up on several boxes, bringing the height to a normal bed level. Frank was lying on the litter with an IV in his right arm and the bag hanging from the ceiling by a piece of parachute cord. The windows were covered with ponchos to limit the light into the room and Alan had to use a flashlight to look around the room.

"Turn that fucking light off!" Frank yelled at Alan.

"Easy, big fella. I'm here to save your life," Alan joked to lighten the mood.

"Great. You got this idiot for a second opinion?" Frank asked Steve. "I'm a dead man."

"I see you've still got your charming personality," Alan said. "That's a good sign. Tell me what's going on."

"It started a few days ago. I threw up a couple hours after we ate lunch, and it's just not getting any better," Frank explained with a low voice, in obvious distress. "I've gotten sick from food before, but never like this. Now I have this fucking headache that won't quit."

Alan went over, put his hands on Frank's abdomen, and began examining the area methodically. "Let me know if any of this hurts," he directed.

After a few seconds of palpation, Alan failed to elicit the response he was looking for in any of the areas of the abdomen that would make him think this was a more serious condition. He put his right hand on Frank's forehead to gauge his temperature. "He's got a little fever going, too."

"I don't think it's his appendix or the gall bladder—the pain is too diffuse," Steve explained. "But with a headache, fever, and photophobia, I don't want whatever he has going septic on me."

"Okay, I don't know what any of that meant," Alan joked, "but I think we should just let it run its course. Let's treat him symptomatically and give it a few more days. You're going to be fine, boss."

Alan reached down and gave Frank a slight touch to his left shoulder, and he and Steve walked back outside.

"We have to tell Luke he'll be out of commission for a while," Alan said. "What are you thinking?"

"Worst case, I'm thinking meningitis. All the signs are there, and he can't move his legs without increasing the pain in his head. And if it's bacterial, he's fucked," Steve answered decisively, referring to the life-threatening infection of the lining of the brain and spinal cord. "If it is, we've got to start the treatment now."

"Well, if it's not and we treat him for it anyway, would that make it worse?" Alan asked.

"Pumping his old ass full of antibiotics isn't going to hurt anything," Steve answered. "And if it's abdominal, it might help kill anything in there as well."

"Half of all belly pain is nonspecific anyway, so maybe a course of drugs will do the trick. I say we hook him up," Alan confirmed.

"Well, the treatment is two weeks. Can we afford to keep him in there that long?" Steve asked.

"It doesn't really look like we have much of a choice. Do we have enough Rocephin to support that?" Alan asked.

Yeah, but it will leave us really low. It would be nice to get some supplies brought in anyway. After the other day, if we take more than a couple casualties, we're screwed," Steve replied.

"I'll see what Luke says. We can't afford to have a man down right now, and it would be nice to have more medical gear out here. I'm on it. You just take care of our boy," Alan said, and he turned to walk back to where the convoy was preparing to depart.

"Have fun storming the castle!" Steve yelled jokingly as he went back inside the building.

Alan briefed Luke on Frank's condition and gave him an update to the status of his dwindling medical supplies. The team was supposed to have a seventy-two-hour resupply dropped to them immediately after their arrival, but it still had not arrived. Now, with combat operations and training in full swing, everyone was feeling the pain when it came to supplies. Jerry helped as much as he could through other avenues, which kept their heads above water, but they were quickly reaching a show-stopping point logistically.

Luke was planning on sending word on their status to the Joint Special Operations Task Force (JSOTF) in Uzbekistan, so that maybe the problem could be resolved quickly.

The plan for the day was to visit the western OP. Due to its larger area, it needed extra attention and troops. There was a larger Northern Alliance presence on their western flank to cover the region. Most of the contact with the enemy from the western OP to this point had been precision-guided munitions with CAS. There had been sporadic gunfire and several incidents with incoming mortar fire, but it was always harassment and never a clear-cut attack.

After a short ride on the familiar bumpy terrain out of the mountains, they hit the paved road that went through the shopping area where they often stopped to get their lunch for the day. Alan was in the passenger seat of Akmal's jeep, with Rusty in the back seat. Akmal had a small CD player between the front seats of his jeep that played music while they drove. Because he only owned one CD, the songs were starting to become familiar to the Americans, who now would tap their legs to the beat of the music in perfect rhythm.

They were discussing Frank's condition when they pulled up to the familiar shop where they purchased their food. Alan looked across the street at the pharmacy, tapped Akmal on his shoulder, and pointed at the Coca-Cola sign in the window. "What are you waiting for? Do your thing, bro."

"I fly, you buy, bro," Akmal responded, holding out his hand.

Laughing hard from the back seat, Rusty patted Akmal on the back several times. "All right, Akmal, pick yourself up something nice for the little lady while you're in there," he said as he handed Akmal a large wad of money wrapped with a rubber band.

Akmal turned and looked at Rusty, confused. "What little girl do you mean?"

Both Americans began to laugh harder, and Alan directed, "Just go get the Cokes."

Akmal grabbed the money and headed across the street to the pharmacy. Alan looked off to his right to make sure the men buying the food had not come out of the store yet, as he had already been spoken to about causing delays in the convoy due to his window shopping. He had noticed that there were less people on the street today and it might go faster inside, which would not give Akmal much time across the street to make his purchase. The food they were served at lunch every day was barely palatable but washing it down with the familiar syrupy nectar made it more digestible.

"What the hell?" Rusty complained as he pointed through the windshield at Akmal, who was returning empty handed.

Akmal got back into the driver's seat of his vehicle and looked at Alan. "They are closed today."

"Why? Yom Kippur was last month," Alan joked.

"Yeah, I bet that one is big here," Rusty laughed. After a slight pause, he said, "Um, Akmal, can I have my money back?"

Akmal looked back at Rusty with a smile. "I want to use it to buy a little girl present."

"It's the little woman," Alan corrected him, "and it means your wife. You got one of those, buddy?"

"No, no, I do not have woman," Akmal responded.

"That's too bad. Maybe when this is all over, we can go out on the town, have a few cocktails, and meet us some ladies. I hear Kabul used to be a pretty good party town," Alan said with a smile as he looked around the area.

Something caught his eye across the street, and he had to lean forward in the jeep to get a better look. There was someone in the window on the second floor of the clothing store, looking at the convoy. When he noticed Alan looking back at him, he closed the shutters of the window completely. At first Alan thought the gesture rude, but then he noticed in his side mirror that people were scurrying off the street behind them into buildings. The smile quickly left his face as he turned around to look at the scene directly.

Noticing the puzzled look on Alan's face, Rusty asked, "What is it?" He too looked back at the scene behind them, and then he scanned the storefronts across the street, which was beginning to empty of any people as well. He saw a figure move across the roof of the clothing store but couldn't get a good look, because of his position in the back seat.

"Rooftop," he said aloud to the other men in the jeep. Alan immediately leaned forward to look across the street at the roof and saw a man pop up over the ledge, holding a familiar but terrifying object.

"RPG!" Alan yelled as he reached out his left arm and grabbed Akmal by the back of the head, pulling it down to his left knee. He covered him up with his right arm and rested his own head on Akmal's back, below windshield level.

In the back seat of the vehicle, Rusty followed suit just as the familiar whooshing sound of a fired RPG quickly drowned out the ambient noise, followed a second later by the explosion of the first vehicle in the convoy. From the overpressure of the blast, their windshield glass shattered, sending glass pieces into the jeep and over the heads of the men who had just ducked for cover.

"Get out, get out!" Rusty yelled, slapping Alan on his left shoulder. Alan immediately swung open his door and exited the vehicle. He stopped suddenly to reach back into the jeep and grab Akmal by his coat, dragging his small frame across the center console and out through the passenger door. He threw Akmal's limp body on the ground behind him, took a half step to his right behind the engine compartment, and brought his weapon up from its slung position around his shoulder. He began to engage the rooftop across the street with well-placed controlled pairs as Rusty climbed out of the back seat.

More figures began to emerge on the rooftop and unloaded a flurry of AK-47 rounds down at the convoy. Rusty quickly joined Alan in returning fire on the ambushers. Rounds were filling the jeep they were using as cover, causing the Americans to duck down behind it. Rusty heard gunfire coming from the rear of the vehicle and quickly turned to face it, bringing his weapon up to engage but then realizing the rounds were coming from Calvin and Luke, who were now out of their vehicle and shooting at the rooftop.

With the new players in the gunfight, the ambushers quickly move their point of aim to the rear of the convoy to engage Calvin's vehicle. Feeling the lull in gunfire on his jeep, Rusty took a crouching step to his left and emerged from the rear of the jeep, again engaging the targets across the street. Alan felt his gun go dry and dropped down behind the engine to perform a quick reload.

"I count at least five, all on the roof!" he yelled to Rusty, and he continued to engage targets as they presented themselves.

Rusty dropped behind the rear wheel of the jeep to perform his own magazine change and confirmed Alan's count. "Five, aye. Are we going?" Rusty paused and looked in Alan's direction.

Alan paused his firing and dropped behind the engine, looking back at Rusty. A slight smile formed on his face, and he turned his gaze to where Akmal was lying on the ground, covering his head with both hands.

"Akmal, get in there," he said, pointing to the doorway of the food shop. Alan took a half step back from the jeep and yelled down to the rear of the convoy, "We're going!"

Calvin, hearing Alan's voice, looked in his direction and made eye contact with him.

"What did he say?" Luke asked.

"No idea," Calvin replied and continued firing at the rooftop.

"Are you ready?" Alan asked Rusty while still crouched behind the engine of the jeep.

Rusty paused his shooting and, without looking over, replied, "Ready!" Rusty again began firing in the direction of the far rooftop, now joined by Alan, who popped up and fired a series of three controlled pairs at the enemy.

"Go!"

Both men simultaneously stood erect, fired two shots at the rooftop across the street, and quickly moved around the jeep they were using as cover. With rounds impacting the dirt at their feet as they ran, both men reached the far side of the street and immediately brought their weapons up to their faces, pointing them at the doorway of the clothing shop while covering the last twenty feet of their trek. They moved to opposite sides of the doorway, now facing each other, weapons at the high ready.

"What the fuck are they doing?" Luke yelled to Calvin as he watched the two men make their way across the street. Seeing the same scene, Calvin ran up the street to Rusty and Alan's original position, to spread out the support fire. Rounds ricocheted off several jeeps as he made his way to the front of the convoy. Once there, he quickly changed his magazine and returned to his active engagement of the ambush.

With a quick head nod as the initiator, Rusty threw his shoulder into the weak door, swinging it open, and quickly moved inside, followed closely by Alan. Once through the door, Rusty moved immediately to the right, clearing his corner, and swept his point of aim back to the left as he moved deep along the right-hand wall. Alan likewise flowed into the room to the left, cleared his corner, and swept his point of aim to the right, stopping just short of Rusty's position, so as not to point his weapon at his fellow assaulter.

"Stairway," Alan alerted Rusty with a loud but calm voice, pointing his right hand at the rear of the room. Without a reply, Rusty moved quickly to the base of the stairway and illuminated it with the bright light attached to the rail system of his M-4, never lowering the weapon from his face. Alan swiftly moved into position on Rusty's heels, and they began to ascend the staircase.

As they reached the top of the stairs and the room of the second floor became visible, Rusty scanned to the left of his position, his weapon following his vision around the room. Alan brought his weapon to his face, and starting from the position Rusty was in, scanned the remainder of the room to the right.

There were no people in the small living area, so Rusty moved to the second staircase that lead to the rooftop, which was immediately in front of him. He was walking Groucho, named after the movie star who had a similar gait, in a slight crouch and exaggerating the contact of his feet with the floor from heel to toe, so as not to cause his weapon to bounce excessively. Rusty ascended the second staircase rapidly, knowing exactly what to expect when he emerged at the top. With the stairs coming right out of the floor of the roof, there would be no cover, and he would be vulnerable to anyone covering the stairs from the roof. Having observed only a handful of ambushers did not mean they were limited to that number. The only way to combat that vulnerability was with speed and accuracy of his shooting.

Rusty increased the speed of his ascent by covering the last few steps two at a time, and he came out onto the roof in a flash. The hole in the floor of the roof was in the far back left corner of the rooftop. Rusty emerged and quickly scanned the small space to his left for any enemy before moving his sights back to the right and the enemy along the front wall. Seeing the row of ambushers with their backs to him, he squeezed off two shots while simultaneously continuing his movement along the back wall, away from the stairs, allowing ample room for Alan to emerge. Close behind, Alan came onto the roof and took two large steps to his right, away from the fatal funnel of the staircase. Alan began engaging the targets against the front wall; the ambushers were now aware of their presence and were swinging their weapons around to fire at the Americans. Before they could bring their weapons up to a good firing position, the Taliban ambushers began to fall to the ground from the quick and accurate fire of the Americans.

Seeing the two Americans and knowing he was outmatched, a Taliban man at the far corner of the roof immediately jumped over the wall to his right, onto the roof of the adjoining one-story building. Rusty saw the man escaping and fired two shots, which hit the ledge of the roof as the man disappeared over the side.

Due to the severe drop in elevation, the man crashed right through the mud-and-straw roof into the pharmacy below. Rusty immediately ran across the roof after the fleeing ambusher.

With his weapon ready, Alan moved cautiously toward the downed men on the roof and began kicking the weapons away from the hands of the lifeless bodies. Suddenly, a barrage of gunfire impacted across the dirt roof ledge in front of him, forcing him to hit the deck.

Across the street, seeing his friend drop quickly to the ground, Calvin looked to his rear to see several Northern Alliance soldiers unloading their weapons into the far rooftop, obviously unaware that Rusty and Alan had begun their assault.

He stood quickly and grabbed the barrel of one shooter with a gloved hand, easily pulling it away from the weaker Afghan man. He looked back to the rooftop to see if Alan was okay, only to catch a glance of Rusty running at full speed across the roof in pursuit of the fleeing ambusher.

Rusty leaped over the ledge and dropped into the hole that the fleeing man had made in the roof. Breaking more of the straw due to his larger frame was to his benefit, as it slowed his descent enough to prevent broken ankles upon his impact with the rigid dirt floor. He immediately popped to his feet, bringing his weapon to the ready to scan the pharmacy for the ambusher.

Realizing he was not injured from the gunfire that had sent him to the ground, Alan got to his feet and ran over to the ledge his friend had just jumped over. He looked over the ledge, down to the hole in the roof made by the two men. "Fuck that," he said aloud, not wanting to make the leap himself.

He slung his weapon behind him and hugged the ledge of the rooftop. He threw one leg at a time over and dropped, feet first, down to the first rooftop below him. He then performed the same action into the large hole in the floor made by Rusty seconds before, turning the trip into two smaller descents.

He made a quick scan of the pharmacy with his weapon and, seeing it empty, moved to the rear of the building. He noticed light coming from an open door in the back of the room and cautiously looked outside in both directions. To his right, he saw Rusty running at full speed down the dirt road behind the row of buildings they had just emerged from. He joined the pursuit; he was not letting his teammate run off by himself.

About fifty meters in front of them, a man dressed all in black with bare feet was running quickly on the dirt road. Alan adjusted his direction slightly to his left, away from the buildings and out from directly behind Rusty, and slid to a halt. He went to a kneeling position and brought his weapon up to sight on the running enemy. Due to his rapid breathing and pulse rate, it took a few seconds to get the correct sight picture. Once he picked up his intended target, he was immediately distracted by an approaching motorcycle. He looked up, only to see the fleeing man jump on the back of the motorcycle, which never slowed down.

Rusty stopped running and brought his weapon up to get a good sight picture. He squeezed the trigger and got off one round before his bolt locked to the rear, indicating an empty magazine.

"Fuck!" Rusty yelled after glancing at his weapon to see the empty chamber.

He looked up to see the two men speed off in the distance on the motorcycle. He reached down and changed the empty magazine in his weapon calmly as he turned and walked back in the direction he had just come from. Seeing Alan, he complained, "Where the fuck were you?"

Alan looked back at him, puzzled, with his arms open. "Dude, that was like a fifteen-foot drop." He pointed back toward the pharmacy. "And I had no idea your fat ass would be outrun by a barefoot twelve-year-old."

A smile began to show on Rusty's face. "Yeah, that fall probably would have snapped those old-ass chicken legs of yours anyway," he said, putting one arm around Alan. The two men walked confidently to an alleyway between the buildings, in the direction of the convoy.

Rusty announced into his radio, "Coming across the street from the south."

"You're good. Come ahead," replied Calvin.

Luke, Calvin, and Akmal were standing by the jeeps with several Afghan soldiers when Alan and Rusty approached. "How about a heads-up before you go running into a hornets' nest next time?" Luke angrily scolded the two men.

"Yes, Daddy. Is that why you guys shot at me?" Alan responded patronizingly.

Calvin silently put both hands up in front of him and shook his head no, and then he pointed slightly toward several Northern Alliance soldiers gathered by another vehicle.

"Let's get back to the Nest," Luke said. "I'm starting not to like this Shir-Wali character."

As Luke and Calvin made their way back to the rear of the convoy, Alan opened his door and moved the seat forward so Rusty could climb into the rear. He looked over the top of the jeep at Akmal entering the driver's side and noticed he had blood running down the side of his face that had already clotted. "You okay, little buddy?"

"You hurt my face when you throw me down," Akmal replied in broken English as he swept away some of the broken glass and got into the driver's seat.

Alan got into the passenger seat and closed his door. He swept some of the broken glass off the CD player and pushed the play button, starting the now-familiar music. He looked up at Akmal with a smile. "A simple thank-you would suffice."

The convoy began moving away from their position, sans the destroyed lead vehicle. As the music coming from Akmal's jeep filled the air, the convoy made a U-turn and headed back in the direction of the Crow's Nest. With no windshield in their vehicle, dust from the vehicles ahead filled Akmal's jeep. Alan turned to the rear, shielding his face from the dust and wind to light a cigarette, and saw Rusty staring back at him with a large smile on his face. He reached up with a fist for a ceremonial pound and returned to a face-forward position. Alan reached down and gave the volume of the radio a slight boost. Both men looked out at the desert and simultaneously began tapping their feet and bobbing their heads to the music as the convoy headed north.

Although the ambush had failed to kill a single man, it destroyed a vehicle and let the team know that they would not have the freedom of movement they originally thought they had. It would also affect the numbers of men going out each day, for had this been a significant force; the ambush might have had serious consequences.

Luckily for the men of the Triple Nickel, help was on the way.

# CHAPTER 18

*The antidote for fifty enemies is one friend.*
-Aristotle

Ten thousand feet above the mountains of the Panjshir Valley, an Air Force MC-130P Combat Shadow airplane flew toward its intended target. Flying in the moonless sky with no external lights, it gave no signature to anyone on the ground besides the hum of the turbo-prop engines. Sergeant First Class Anthony DeNero sat on one of the troop seats against the starboard-side wall, wearing an MC-4 Ram Air Free-Fall parachute. His goggles were around his neck, and his helmet was off and placed on the seat next to him. Much like his predecessors, he was wearing an MP3 player while he caught up on some much-needed rest.

Within the cargo area of the aircraft were several Air Force men wearing OD green flight suits with various patches on their chests and shoulders. Centered on rollers at the rear of the aircraft was a large metal pallet covered with pallet straps, with a G-12 cargo parachute attached on top.

One of the Air Force crew chiefs was performing last-minute checks on the cargo when he paused and put his right hand to his earphone, holding it closer to his head for better clarity. He nodded, stood erect, and made his way over several floor rollers to where Tony was asleep in the troop seat.

The crew chief tapped Tony on the leg, rousing him from his slumber. Tony looked up to see the crew chief staring back at him, holding up both hands with fingers extended: the "ten minutes" hand and arm signal. Tony acknowledged him by giving the thumbs-up sign and reached out his arms in a large stretching motion to help him wake up.

He reached down and unfastened his seatbelt, allowing him to get to his feet. The plane began to descend slowly to its drop altitude of just over two thousand feet. Several times during the descent, the pilots had to make some altitude adjustments to avoid the mountains. On more than one occasion as Tony was performing his pre-jump checks, he had to reach out to the cargo straps to keep from falling over during the evasive maneuvers of the flight crew.

The small lights by the rear doors and tail ramp switched from green to red, signifying that they were approaching the drop area. The crew chief by the aft fuselage power junction initiated the lowering of the ramp, exposing the cool night sky over the Panjshir. Tony calmly stood against the rear of the cargo pallet with a second crew chief and tapped his hand on the top of the pallet in time with the music he was listening to. The crew chief to his immediate left touched him on the left forearm, getting his attention. Tony looked over to see him holding his right index finger in the air, signifying that there was one-minute left before his departure.

Again, Tony gave the thumbs-up sign in acknowledgement. He took two large steps away from the cargo pallet and one large step to his right, to an area clear of floor rollers, giving him a straight, unobstructed path out of the rear of the airplane. He reached out his right arm and braced himself.

Tony stared keenly at the red light directly in front of him and watched it switch to green, seemingly in slow motion. He tightened his grip on the safety strap he was using for stabilization and bent his knees for the coming rise in elevation. He felt the plane violently go nose up, putting him in direct view of the ground below. He looked to his left to catch the crew chief viciously pull the seatbelt cutter through the single cargo strap holding the pallet, sending it sliding swiftly out of the plane and into the darkness.

With the release of the pallet, the aircraft again took a horizontal axis, and Tony relaxed his grip on the safety strap. He then stood erect and calmly walked to the edge of the ramp. Using his right hand, he touched his forehead, chest, and each shoulder in the shape of the cross, and stepped off the ramp into the night.

\* \* \*

"Six knots, one-eight-five degrees!" Blaine yelled from his position. He was several meters up the hill from a large group of men gathered in a large open area the team was using as the drop zone. He had a headlamp with a dull red lens on his forehead and was holding a hand-held wind meter to gauge the speed and direction of the night winds.

"Six knots, one-eight-five, aye," Shane responded. He was well away from the hill, in the apparent center of the drop zone. He was positioning several Northern Alliance men seven meters apart in a makeshift arrow facing the direction of the prevailing winds. In his hands were several infrared chemical lights with six inches of parachute cord tied to each one. Once he had his counterparts placed in the correct position, he gave each man a chem-light by the cord. When the aircraft platform was inbound, he would signal the men to swing the lights around above their heads, or "buzz-saw," as the drop zone marker for the aircrew.

"One minute!" Calvin yelled from a vantage point up the hill near Blaine. He was in constant contact with the aircraft, guiding them in to his position.

"All right, if you are not one of my DZ markers, get off the drop zone!" Shane yelled with his hands cupped to his face. As the handful of men gathered on the drop zone began to meander slowly toward the vehicles grouped on the far end of the empty field, they heard Alan echo Shane's direction. "Ya-leh shibob! Ya-leh, ya-leh!"

"What the hell was that?" Steve asked.

"It's Arabic for 'hurry the fuck up,'" Alan replied.

"Here, let's try this," Steve said. He held a large megaphone to his face. "Get off my drop zone! Move, move, move!"

"Oh, yeah, I'm sure they understood that," Alan retorted sarcastically. "Give me that thing," he commanded. He reached out and snatched the megaphone from Steve's hands and handed it to Akmal. "Akmal, tell those idiots to get off the drop zone, or they are going to get hit with two thousand pounds of Steve's nudie magazines. Hold this button down when you talk," he directed, showing Akmal how to use the megaphone.

Akmal held the megaphone to his mouth and depressed the trigger switch. "Bedo! Bedo!"

"Is that Dari for 'hurry the fuck up'?" Steve asked.

"It is 'run'. I have no word for 'fuck'," Akmal responded politely, to the laughter of the two Americans sitting on the tailgate of a small pickup truck.

The familiar engine noise of a turbo-prop airplane alerted them to the incoming flight. "Here it comes," Steve announced. He stood in the bed of the truck and brought his PVS-7 night-vision goggles up to his eyes.

"All right, swing 'em," Shane commanded, and he started to swing his buzz saw above his head. The men he had set up as drop zone markers all began spinning their strings above their heads.

Steve scanned to the north for the aircraft, and after a few seconds, he spotted the bird. "I got it," he announced. Alan raised his own optics in the same direction as Steve and searched for the airplane himself. After several seconds, he too found the incoming aircraft. Both men watched intently as the cargo plane rapidly approached, only two thousand feet above the floor of the valley.

The plane could be seen moving back and forth in the night sky to adjust itself to the drop zone markings. Once the plane was almost directly overhead, it climbed rapidly, and the large pallet decorated with several chemical lights fell from the open ramp. Seconds later it was followed by a smaller figure, also with infrared chemical lights attached.

Before anyone on the ground knew what was happening, Steve dropped his night vision and exclaimed, "Fuck! Where's that megaphone?" He jumped off the back of the truck and snatched the megaphone from Akmal's hands cruelly.

"What the hell, man?" Alan asked.

"It's burning in," he replied in a panic as he held the megaphone to his mouth.

"Burning! It's fucking burning in! Run!" Steve yelled into the megaphone, across the drop zone.

When the parachute of a several-thousand-pound cargo pallet fails to open on a night jump, the anxiety level for everyone involved goes to new heights. The cargo had now become a two-thousand-pound inert bomb traveling toward its intended target at almost one hundred miles an hour.

Hearing those magical words from the megaphone instantly turned the Americans on the drop zone from performing routine professionals' tasks into frenzied children during recess. Blaine and Calvin looked at each other for less than a second and began to run along the hillside to escape the incoming projectile.

Shane ran toward the men he had swinging the buzz-saws above their heads and grabbed the first man as he went by, dragging him.

"Run, run!" he yelled back to the others, echoed by the man he was dragging.

Steve and Alan each grabbed Akmal by an arm and ran away from the vehicle they had been sitting on. "What about Tony?" Alan asked as they ran.

"He's probably a two-hundred-pound Italian lawn dart now, bro," Steve responded jokingly. "I'll help you search for the body at first light."

They found their way to a small depression near a stream running off the Panjshir River and slid down the slope to apparent safety. Steve immediately held his night vision to his face in search of the falling cargo, only to duck behind cover instinctively on seeing the cargo pallet's imminent impact.

The impact was felt immediately by everyone in the surrounding area and caused each man not only to dive to the ground for self-preservation, but also to perform a complete self-assessment of his body parts after the impact.

Peeking their heads over the crest of the depression, Alan and Steve saw the large dust cloud well off to the north. The projected release time of the cargo was done by computer, taking into consideration the aircraft speed, forward throw of the cargo, weight of the cargo, drop rate of the attached parachute, and the prevailing winds. Without an open parachute, all bets were off, and the cargo would obviously fall well short of its intended target.

They stood up and scanned the sky for their incoming friend. Because of the infrared chem-lights attached to him, they found him immediately, floating through the sky on a controlled descent. "There he is," Steve said, pointing to the approaching canopy. Tony was slowly maneuvering back and forth in the night sky, coming closer to the desired impact position.

Most of the people in the drop zone were now running toward the crashed cargo pallet, which was now buried several feet in the desert floor. Alan and Steve, however, jogged to the pre-planned point of impact to meet Tony before he landed. "Here he comes. He better not frappe in with all these people watching." Alan joked.

"He's coming in too fast," Steve commented. "Oh, this one's going to be painful."

Now easily seen without optics and still well north of the intended impact point, Tony reached up to one corner of his parachute and pulled hard. Known as a "hook-turn," this was a way to build up speed at the last few seconds before landing, and when followed by a flare with both toggles, it resulted in a spectacular landing in which the jumper skimmed mere inches above the ground at thirty to forty miles per hour, for up to a hundred yards. The downside to this maneuver was that if the jumper flared too late, it could result in a different spectacular landing in which the jumper hit the ground painfully, leading to medical bills, orthopedic surgery, or death.

Tony pulled it off perfectly, coming to rest within mere feet of Alan and Steve. He took several steps forward after landing and turned around to collect his still-floating parachute. Seconds later, he unfastened his helmet and looked at his two friends with a large smile on his face. "Hi, fellas. We're the flying Elvis's, Utah chapter."

"Honeymoon in Vegas," Alan responded with an equally big smile, shaking his friend's hand. "Well done, my friend."

"Let me see one of you fag combat divers pull that one off," Tony said arrogantly. "You see that cargo chute? Ah, gadoosh!" Tony joked, demonstrating with his right arm something falling and coming to a sudden halt.

"Well, if the Air Force ever runs out of bombs, we can just call in a bunch of resupply south of Bagram," Steve fired back, to the laughter of both men.

"Let's get you out of that kit, turf surfer, and go see how much shit we just lost," Alan said as he helped Tony unbuckle his chute. Moments later, the three men walked north toward the impact area of the cargo pallet. They saw several men with flashlights moving about, and every so often they caught a glimpse of a flashlight illuminating the overturned pallet, which generated a new bout of laughter from the three approaching Americans.

Once they arrived at the chaotic scene, they heard JT and Shane yelling at each other from the other side of the pallet. Glancing around the area with a flashlight, they noticed that the equipment that was supposed to be contained in the pallet was now strewn so far away that it extended well beyond the capabilities of the flashlight. This discovery caused a louder laughter attack from the new arrivals.

"How about you quit fucking around and help us over here?" JT yelled when he heard Alan's familiar loud laugh. Alan walked around to the far side of the pallet, which was now on its side and buried several feet in the ground, with the parachute open and beginning to gather wind. Several Afghan men were trying to flatten the large parachute by pushing down the inflated section from the top.

"No problem," Alan said as he pulled his knife from his jeans pocket and began cutting the parachute's suspension lines.

"What the fuck are you doing? You're destroying the parachute!" JT scolded Alan.

"Dude, it burned in. You want to jump this thing again?"

"Good point. Move," JT told an Afghan soldier standing between him and more suspension lines. He pulled his own, larger knife from the sheath in the small of his back and, grabbing several lines in his left hand, cut right through them.

"Whatcha doin', boys?" Tony asked as he walked up to the two knife-wielding Americans.

"Tony! Good to see you, man," JT fired back and reached out his right hand. "You really know how to make an entrance, brother."

Tony shook JT's hand and again began to laugh uncontrollably at the scene they were all now a part of. He grabbed a handful of suspension lines to join in the cutting.

"We're glad you're here," Shane said as he helped gather more suspension lines.

"Thanks, Shane," Tony replied. "The staff back there is saying     great things about you guys, and I was kind of hoping you'd call me in. There are like twenty other teams sitting up there, just watching what you guys are doing down here. It's crazy."

"You know what's going to be crazy?" Alan interjected. "Watching you go into these mud houses. It's going to look like Gandalf walking into Frodo's house."

"Okay, two things," JT replied. He paused in his work to look up at Alan. "One, that was a Lord of the Rings reference. You're a dork," he said, looking at Alan. "And B," he said, turning his gaze to Tony, "we just needed someone to put the blame on when we screw something up."

"Ah, gadoosh!" Tony exclaimed, making all four men laugh raucously. "You know I brought another mission with me, right?" Tony announced to the group. "And it's right up your alley, Alan."

"What, does someone need some Legos put together?" JT joked.

"Hostage rescue," Tony fired back in a condescending tone.

"Excuse me?" Alan paused cutting and looked over at Tony.

"Well, it seems there are some Christian missionaries locked up in a jail in Kabul," Tony explained. "I think a dozen or so from around the world, but two chicks from the States."

"And they want us to go get them?" Alan asked.

"Sending this idiot after them," JT commented, pointing at Alan, "would be like sending in a cat to rescue a bunch of mice. It would be like sending in Tony to rescue Jack Daniel's. It would be like sending in Steve to rescue a bag of doughnuts. It would be like—"

Alan interrupted. "Okay, I get it."

"Do they want them sent home pregnant?" Steve piled on.

"Why? Are they hot?" Alan looked up at Tony with a serious expression on his face.

"I have no idea, but I brought a target packet with me that has pictures of all of them," Tony explained.

"Yeah? And just where is that target packet, Tony?" JT asked, looking over at Tony with a large grin.

Using his flashlight, Tony looked around their position, pausing periodically. "Um....There's some there ... and some more over there. Oh, and I think that might be some. No, wait—that's an MRE wrapper." He looked back at JT and admitted hesitantly, "Yes, I put it on the pallet," causing all four men to laugh uncontrollably.

Within several minutes, the parachute was gathered up, rolled, and placed off to the side. JT systematically began unwinding the cargo straps holding what was left of their equipment onto the pallet.

Luke and Rusty were off to the north, collecting whatever bags they could find and making piles of like items on the ground. This would continue for several hours until the sun started to emerge, showing the true devastation and the immense area over which their gear was now spread.

Once they had a visual on all their gear, they separated the piles of like items into further piles of functional versus destroyed gear. Considering the rate of descent and the incredible impact of the cargo pallet, they were able to salvage more gear than they had originally anticipated.

They spent the entire day collecting gear, inventorying equipment, and moving it all back to the Crow's Nest. Even though Tony was intricately involved in the team's communications back at the JSOTF and was already familiar with what had transpired up to this point in their operation, he was still subjected to inflated war stories for most of the day. Although he was only several months from retirement and had already been in many combat situations himself, hearing the stories all day made him wish he had been there from the beginning.

# CHAPTER 19

*War is the only proper school of the surgeon.*
-Hippocrates

After several days of going through all the equipment and supplies recovered from the bundle drop, the Triple Nickel was again ready to conduct operations. Most of the durable items that burned in were unsalvageable, including several radios, laptop computers, and optics. Many items, however, managed to survive the crash, including much-needed ammunition, batteries, medical supplies, rations, and more clothes. These items filled their shortages and would be able to keep them operating for several more months. Because the team had operated successfully up to this point with the equipment they had brought with them, losing some of the new equipment did not hamper them too significantly.

Because of the increase in enemy contact in recent weeks, Luke had made the call that the entire team would be involved in all further operations, to maximize their combat power. Frank was gradually recovering from his bout with meningitis and was now driving their CIA counterparts crazy by hanging out in the operations center all day. Everyone was ready for him to rejoin the team in their daily trips to the FLOT, especially Frank.

Unlike the resupply methods of Special Forces, the Agency relied on more traditional methods and finally received the weapons and uniforms for the Northern Alliance by helicopter. They were now ready to conduct some good training with their counterparts and get them ready for full force-on-force maneuvers against the Taliban. With the devastating air strikes and the damage inflicted during previous contact with the Taliban, they were starting to see large gaps in the enemy defenses between Bagram and Kabul.

Although Frank and Luke did not feel that the Northern Alliance was remotely close to being able to move on the capital city, Jerry was more optimistic. They had created a list of high-priority targets and hung it on the wall in the operations center, and when a target was destroyed or neutralized, they crossed it out with a large red marker. When all the targets on this list were taken out, they would have created enough damage that a movement on Kabul would be met with little resistance.

The priority right now, however, was the hostages in Kabul. With his assets, Jerry had arranged a ransom for the twelve hostages, and the drop was supposed to occur on the tarmac of Bagram Airfield. The timeline had not yet been established, but it would have to be soon. Luke was determined to have the team perform the entire operation independently, but his counterparts in the Northern Alliance had other plans. This included General Babazheen, who would not give his permission for the operation to be conducted at his airfield unless the Northern Alliance played a larger role in the exchange.

With such a high priority placed on this operation by the JSOTF, and with all the publicity these hostages were receiving in the news in the United States, Luke could not afford for this to be a half-assed operation. The bigger problem was that Luke did not feel he could trust the Northern Alliance with the security of the ten million dollars they were to exchange for the hostages. He had objections knowing his own team would be that close to so much money, but he definitely thought that kind of temptation put his team at an increased risk for danger from any unsavory characters who might find out about the exchange.

The entire team was now at Bagram Airfield so that Jerry and Luke could convince Babazheen to let them use his airstrip for the exchange. Luke and Jerry were in the tower with Babazheen and some of his men, all gathered around the map table. JT and Calvin were also in the tower, setting up their radios and observing the enemy activity on the far side of the airfield. The mood was light as they discussed the hostage exchange while drinking chai.

The general could not understand why he was not getting any of the ransom money for "improvements" of his tower. And considering that he was "allowing" his men to help with security, he felt they should be compensated appropriately for their efforts that were obviously not related to the combat operations they were supposed to be conducting.

Luke was completely against any Northern Alliance involvement and was extremely upset when Jerry told the general the exact dollar amount that would be exchanged for the hostages. This information would spread through their Afghan counterparts quickly, putting the entire operation at risk. This was Jerry's call, and Luke would have to conform to whatever decision he made. How the operation would be conducted, however, was Luke's call. He was the tactical commander on the ground, and even if he was directed to use the Northern Alliance in the operation, how he employed them was his decision.

Outside the tower, the rest of the team was gathered around the bed of a small pickup truck filled with boxes. A few dozen Afghan men stood in a line leading up to the truck. In the boxes were uniforms for the Northern Alliance, provided by Jerry. The weapons would be issued later, and only after the NA had been trained and qualified on them to the standard of Shane and Rusty, who had already begun training on the new range north of the Crow's Nest.

While Frank and Shane were in the truck handing out uniforms, Blaine was walking down the line with a large black magic marker, writing sizes on the back of each man's right hand. He would stand in front of each man, look him up and down, and estimate his size. Although there were a significant number of "smalls" in the line, most of the men had "medium" written on their hands, to the irritation of Frank in the truck.

"Blaine, come on. Does this guy look like he could fit a medium?" Frank chastised as he pointed at an undersized Afghan with a long beard.

Blaine paused in his writing and leaned back to look at the man standing to the rear of the truck. "He'll grow into it," he replied sarcastically.

"He's like forty. I think he's done growing," Frank responded as he handed the man a uniform.

Across from the men being issued new uniforms, Alan and Tony were handing out new boots to each man. They had several boots on the tailgate of their truck for sizing, and when a soldier approached, they would have him lift one leg and rest it on the tailgate like a ballerina, so they could hold up a boot to estimate the appropriate size.

"I hope you have some bleach to soak my hands in when we're done with this," Tony complained as he held a boot up to a bare foot.

"You know how much fungus I've touched today?"

"Quit complaining," Alan responded. "It's not that bad. But I wouldn't eat with my hands for a few days, if I were you."

Tony held his left hand under Alan's nose to give him a whiff of the horrible scent emanating from it. "Wow, that is rancid," Alan remarked, with an expression mirroring that of a child eating spinach for the first time, causing Tony and the Afghan man to laugh aloud.

"What's up with the hostage thing? Is there any more news?" Alan asked Tony.

"The captain is up there briefing the general on it now," Tony replied. "Shelter Me is a Christian organization that runs humanitarian aid projects in Pakistan and Afghanistan. They've been doing this for over twenty-five years. In early September, twelve members of their organization, including two American females, were found guilty of spreading Christian propaganda and breaking several of the laws imposed by the Taliban. Aside from the many rules broken by having women perform humanitarian assistance, the fact they had passed Christian literature carried with it a sentence of death in Taliban law. We think they are being held in Kabul, in a jail somewhere, but we are waiting on more intel."

Several very distinct popping sounds were heard coming from the southern edge of the airfield, which caused the Americans to stop working on their assigned tasks and look in that direction. Frank looked over at Tony who had lost his normal large grin and was concentrating his gaze on the far side of the airfield. Frank held out his empty hands, palms up, as if to ask, What? Tony returned the gesture with a shrug of his shoulders. After several more seconds with no further sounds, he cautiously returned to his task.

"Get down!" Frank yelled almost simultaneously with a loud whistling sound above their heads. This was followed closely by an ear-piercing wham that sounded like someone hitting a sheet of corrugated steel with a hammer.

Tony dove to the ground close to the vehicle next to him but still felt the overpressure of the mortar round. The impact was immediately followed by a handful of small plinks: the mortar's fragments hitting the truck's metal exterior.

Hearing the impact of the first round, several men in the tower ran to the window to assess the damage. Without warning, a second and third round hit the tower itself and the roof of the adjoining building. The second round went right through the roof, into the room below, and the third ricocheted off the roof into the wall of the tower, shaking it violently and causing a large fireball to climb up the tower's exterior wall. The men at the window dove back into the center of the tower, covering themselves from the heat of the blast.

A frenzied group of Afghan men fought with each other to be the first down the shaky staircase out of the main tower. JT and Calvin, now on the floor but still at their positions near the south window, looked at each other with wide eyes.

"You all right?" Calvin asked.

"Well, that was the prettiest round we've taken so far," JT fired back, eliciting a small smile from Cal. Both men rose up and begin scanning to the south to find the origin of the incoming fire.

With the chaotic and frantic reaction to the incoming mortars by their Northern Alliance counterparts hampering their movement, Frank and Tony made their way to the impact point of the first round to perform a quick crater analysis.

The direction of flight could be determined fairly accurately from the projectile crater. It was possible to obtain the azimuth that would pass through or near the enemy position by accurately locating the crater and determining the direction of flight. Due to the proximity of the origin of the mortar team, the impact crater had been made by a projectile coming in from a very steep angle, but it still showed signs of a cardinal direction.

Akmal emerged from the doorway of the main building, crying,

"Doktoor, doktoor!" Seeing Alan, Akmal ran up to him and grabbed him by the arm. "Men are injured inside," he said, pointing to the building he had just left.

Alan reached into the bed of the nearby truck, grabbed his large aid bag, and followed Akmal into the building.

"You want some help, bro?" Steve asked as Alan walked by his position.

"Check around the building and in the tower. If anyone is hurt, bring them down."

Steve had made his way to the bottom of the tower when he heard another short whistle followed by the impact of another mortar round fifty meters north of where the vehicles were parked. He immediately dropped to the ground for protection. Frank and Shane made their way to a small mud wall and hunkered down on the north side with their truck in front of them, providing protection on that side.

Alan followed Akmal inside the building and saw several men lying against the far wall, with several others gathered closely around them. Alan pushed his way through the gathered men to get to the casualties. A younger man was writhing in pain on the floor, holding his left leg, with blood flowing freely between his fingers.

Alan put his bag on the ground next to the wounded man and unzipped the top pocket, exposing a large array of dressings and supplies. He reached in and donned a pair of latex exam gloves. From a small pocket in his bag, he pulled a large seatbelt cutter and carefully but quickly cut the wounded man's pant leg from his hip to his ankle, exposing his entire leg. Multiple small puncture wounds on the lateral side of the left leg oozed a steady flow of venous blood. Two rather large entrance wounds, one under the man's hand on his thigh and another closer to the ankle, had begun to form a small pool of clotted blood on the floor next to him.

"Akmal, get his shirt off. Let's see if there are any more," Alan commanded his friend. Akmal directed the man to remove his shirt, and several onlookers bent down and assisted him with the task. Alan wrapped the man's leg tightly with gauze followed by an elastic bandage, stretched tight for compression. He placed one dressing on the thigh wound and another covering the entire lower leg from knee to ankle. By this time, the man's shirt had been removed, exposing several small puncture wounds on his left side, from his belt line up to his armpit, along with several others on his left arm. Alan inspected the wounds and found them all superficial, aside from a large laceration just proximal to the elbow that was easily controlled with a small pressure dressing.

They heard another mortar round just outside the south side of the room they were in, and the entire room shook from the overpressure, causing the gathered observers to drop to the floor. Alan looked around the room and saw several tables on the far side.

"Let's get them over to those tables," he told the other men. He mimed picking up the man and pointed to the far tables.

Several men gathered the wounded soldiers and moved them across the room. Alan bent down to zip up his aid bag, and a group of men entered the room, carrying two more wounded soldiers. Alan moved across the room with his bag and pointed at the second table next to the first wounded man. "Put him on that table," he commanded the men who had just entered.

Steve poked his head in the room. "I got these two. I think there are a few more out by the tarmac that should be coming in as well."

Alan, now assessing the man on the second table, acknowledged Steve by holding his right hand in the air for a second and then returned to the casualty.

This man was wounded considerably more than the first one he'd worked on. He had multiple puncture wounds and lacerations to the left side of his face and head, along with damage to his right hand. He had probably been standing close to the impact of one of the mortar rounds and held his right hand up to his face to protect it, causing the damage to his hand and the unprotected portion of his head. Although his face was bleeding profusely, it looked mostly superficial, but Alan could not get the man to open his left eye to inspect it, which caused him some concern. The real trouble was the man's right forearm and hand; there was a large through-and-through wound in his forearm, with exposed bony fragments, and two digits of his right hand were missing. The first and second fingers were missing at the second joint away from the fingernail, and the third digit was partially amputated but still attached by the skin.

The man's hand and forearm had been wrapped tightly by Steve before he'd been brought into the room, and the bleeding was well controlled. Alan grabbed a bottle of water and rinsed off the bloody face of the man on the table to get a better look at where the blood was coming from. Aside from the multiple small, oozing puncture wounds along his cheek, there was one large laceration bleeding profusely right next to his left eye and extending up toward his hairline. Alan quickly loaded a needle driver with suture material and put two very tight tack sutures into the wound, sealing it shut and stopping the bleeding.

He had begun to assess the man's fingers more closely when he heard two more mortar rounds hit outside the room, causing several men to drop to the floor. Alan leaned over his patient to shield him from any falling debris.

The room became more chaotic, with people yelling and running around. Several men came into the room to check on the injured men and help render first aid. Although there was a large language barrier, with the help of Akmal and with Alan's experience in these situations, there was a sense of order in the chaos. Alan directed helpers where to move the injured, where to set up tables and boxes for treatment, and to help wrap dressings and hold pressure when needed.

Outside the tower, Frank and Shane were directing the pandemonium of men running around between mortar rounds. They were placing them into fighting positions in case the mortar attack was followed by an assault and putting them into positions where they would be best protected from the incoming fire. Frank was startled by a familiar loud whistle coming from the main tower. Turning to look in the direction of the whistle, he spotted JT leaning out of one of the empty windows of the tower, trying to get his attention.

Once they made eye contact, JT held up three fingers and pointed toward the south end of the airfield, telling Frank that three mortar teams had been spotted. Frank acknowledged the information with the far "okay" sign: fingers to the head, elbow out. Once acknowledged, JT held up six fingers followed by two closed fists in succession.

"Six hundred meters," Frank muttered to himself and again responded with the far "okay."

The mortar attack had been going on for about two minutes when Frank yelled across the dirt parking area, "Shane!" getting the attention of his senior weapons man. "Get up there and put an end to this shit!" he said, pointing to the top of the tower.

Without hesitation, Shane ran to the rear of the jeep he'd arrived in and threw open the canvas cover, exposing the rear compartment. He reached in and opened a long, hard-plastic weapons case, exposing his SR-25 sniper rifle. He slung the weapon across his back, reached behind the case and grabbed the M49 spotting scope and tripod from a smaller bag, and turned to the tower. Walking quickly and confidently, he screwed the tripod to the base of the scope.

He spotted Rusty and Steve bringing another casualty into the building Alan was in. Steve was carrying the torso, with Rusty supporting the legs in front. He followed them into the room where they laid the man on a table for Alan.

"Rusty, you want to spot for me?" Shane asked, handing him the twenty-power spotting scope.

"Hell yeah, I do!" Rusty exclaimed with a smile and grabbed the scope.

The two men made their way to the far corner of the room and the unstable staircase leading to the interior of the tower. They quickly ascended into the main room of the tower, drawing the attention of the few remaining men. JT and Calvin were on their knees, peering out of the tower to the south, exposing no more of them than was necessary. Shane made his way to the far north side of the tower and climbed a narrow ladder leading to a trapdoor in the roof.

Seeing Rusty waiting his turn, JT started feeding him information. "I've got three teams south at one-five-seven degrees, six hundred meters out, roughly ten meters apart." JT synchronized his words with the hand signs for each number he gave to alleviate any confusion. "Look for two black vehicles.

The tubes are off to the left about a reticle and a half."

Looking up at Shane on the ladder, Rusty released his right hand's grip on the ladder to give the thumbs-up sign to JT. After Shane was through the opening in the roof, Rusty began his ascent. Once through the opening himself, Rusty took a quick look around the corrugated tin roof for a clear path to where Shane was setting up. Several damaged areas in the roof exposed the room below. Stepping onto the wrong piece of tin would quickly send Rusty falling into the main room of the tower.

Rusty slowly walked across the roof, carefully looking down before each step as if he were walking on a thin sheet of ice. He looked up to Shane, who was on his knees, with the butt of his rifle on his left hip, barrel pointed to the sky, extending the bi-pod legs. Shane locked the bolt to rear and loaded a magazine into the weapon. He looked up to Rusty and gave a small giggle at his large friend walking so cautiously.

"Keep it up," Rusty said irritably. "I'll throw your little ass right off this roof."

"Just do me a favor and set up over there," Shane responded with a smile, pointing to his right, several roof tiles away. "I don't want us both falling through."

Rusty reached Shane's position, and they both took prone positions facing south and began scanning in the direction of the enemy mortar tubes. Shane got into a comfortable firing position and popped the front and rear covers off the M3A scope on his rifle. Several feet to his right, with his left eye closed and right eye peering through his spotting scope, Rusty found the black vehicles and panned a little to the left for the mortar tubes.

"I've got two black vehicles with a half-dozen men gathered around them about six hundred meters south-southwest," he said calmly. "Pan left twenty meters. There are three separate mortar tube emplacements, ten meters apart, with one man each. Start on the far left and work back to the right."

Rusty continued, "Let's try six minus one. Winds are quarter value from the east, less than five. Hold left chest."

"Ready," Shane declared.

"On you," Rusty replied.

Shane took a deep breath and held it while slowly squeezing the slack from the trigger, until a round was fired from the SR-25. Across the open field, a Taliban soldier was holding an 82mm mortar round with both hands above its tube and was about to let it go when a bullet struck him in the chest. He fell backward while still clutching the round in both hands.

Shane immediately called his shot. "Chest, ten inches off left."

"That's one minute," Rusty responded.

Shane reached up with his left hand, adjusted his scope for one MOA correction, and again assumed a firing position. "Ready."

"Let it go," Rusty commanded, followed almost instantly by a round at the target from Shane.

"Bingo," Shane called after the shot, telling Rusty he was right on target.

Looking through his spotting scope, Rusty noticed that the other Taliban men were just standing next to their downed compadres as if they were unaware why they had fallen.

"Again," Rusty directed, followed closely by a shot on the next target.

Looking through his scope, Rusty saw the men around all three mortar tubes now lying motionless on the ground. Realizing what was happening, the other men quickly ran to their vehicles to leave the area.

"Throw a couple in the first vic," Rusty told Shane, referring to the vehicle trying to escape the target area.

Shane adjusted his body position slightly to get a good line of sight to the moving vehicles and squeezed the trigger several times, hitting the first vehicle in the windshield on the driver's side. Seconds later, the vehicle slowed to a crawl, with the driver slumped dead over the steering wheel. Several men threw open their doors and escaped the vehicle at a full run.

Rusty looked up from his spotting scope at Shane and praised him for his shooting. "Now, that's the way you—" Suddenly the corrugated tin roof he was lying on began to buckle underneath him, from his movements. Rusty braced himself as the thin roof dropped several inches, making a loud noise and a crease in the tin. He looked up at Shane with panic on his face, to find him laughing uncontrollably at the fate of his friend and teammate.

"Karma is a bitch," Shane said with a large grin as he got to his knees and collapsed the bi-pod of his SR-25. Cautiously moving on his hands and knees, Shane made his way back to the ladder. Rusty used his palms to slide his body back several inches at a time, away from the damaged part of the roof. Once he was on a different tile, he rose to his knees and began crawling to the ladder.

When both men were in the main tower, Luke greeted them at the bottom of the ladder.

"Nice job, you two," he praised them. "I think Steve and Alan need your help downstairs."

Both men made their way to the staircase leading down to the main room below, which was now a small emergency room. "You should have seen the look on your face," Shane said, still laughing hard. "That just made this whole trip worth it."

Both Steve and Alan were working diligently on patients in the room below. They had several trauma tables set up along the north wall and were using Northern Alliance soldiers as helpers on each one. A handful of men were sitting on the floor along the south wall, wearing various bandages and dressings. At least a dozen men had been injured, and the medical supplies were quickly becoming scarce.

Steve had coordinated a good triage system, and he was dealing with the less injured patients, while Alan and Tony attended to a seriously injured man on the far table. Seeing Shane and Rusty come down the stairs, Steve waved them over to brief them on the situation.

"Go out and check with Frank if you're needed out there on security, but tell him I need at least one more body to help in here,"

Steve directed. "We've got about a dozen wounded, mostly pretty minimal, with just some superficial peppering, but at least three serious. I'm trying to knock out all these walking wounded quick, so I can go help Alan with the serious guys."

"I'll stay in here. You go check with Frank," Shane told Rusty as he handed him the SR-25. Rusty grabbed the weapon and headed out to the parking area.

"You remember how to do stitches?" Steve asked Shane.

"You think Frank's going to let me slack on my cross-training?" Shane responded.

"All I need you to do is close the wound and approximate the edges the best you can. I'm not worried about making it pretty—all that does is make a smaller scar. What I need is a few boxes of water, so we can irrigate the shit out of these wounds before we close them up."

"I'm on it," Shane said and disappeared out the door with urgency.

Steve had a door stretched across two stacks of boxes as a table for treatment. Shane returned with two cases of bottled water and set them down under the table for quick access. He assisted a man with a leg wound over to the table and unwrapped the elastic bandage from his lower leg.

"So, what's the plan, Doc?" Shane asked Steve.

Steve had set up a small suture tray on a box next to the table and was filling a large syringe with lidocaine to anesthetize the area prior to closing it with stitches.

"Unwrap the dressing, and let's clean the wound. Stick your knife into the top of the water bottle so we can squeeze a stream into the wound. I'll freeze it, you close it. Savvy?"

"And if it's still bleeding?" Shane inquired.

Steve held up his right hand, showing a needle driver loaded with a large cutting needle with a thick piece of silk suture material attached. "We ligate." He held up his left hand, showing a disposable high-temperature cautery device. "Or we burn it." It looked like a thick magic marker with a filament from a toaster attached to the end that turned bright orange and hot with the push of a button on its side.

"Got it," Shane said, and he inspected the small wounds on the injured leg. There were several small puncture wounds in the calf muscle that were no longer bleeding. He gave the punctured water bottle a small squeeze, rinsing the leg, and wiped it clean with a handful of gauze.

Steve injected several milliliters of lidocaine around the wound and handed Shane the needle driver. Shane positioned himself perpendicular to the wound and began sewing. After each suture, Steve reached in with scissors and cut the attached ends, freeing the remaining suture material for Shane to continue.

"Hey, man," Tony said to Steve as he approached their table, "Alan needs your help over there." He pointed to the far side of the room.

"Okay, take over for me here," Steve replied and handed Tony the scissors and the syringe of lidocaine.

Steve walked over to where Alan was working and removed his exam gloves. He donned a new pair and squeezed between two Afghan men standing around the table.

"What's going on?" he asked Alan.

Alan explained his patient's situation, pointing to each area with a bloody glove as he talked. "I've got a guy hit almost directly by a mortar round. He was unconscious when they brought him in, breathing on his own, with a good radial pulse. He has traumatic amputations of the left leg below the knee and the left arm at the wrist, both controlled with tourniquets. There is peppering to the entire left side, including the thorax, with decreased breath sounds on the left side. I've performed two needle decompressions already with a fourteen-gauge catheter, to buy some time, but he's going to need a chest tube."

Looking up at Steve, Alan continued, "I've got two large-bore IVs going, with two hundred micrograms of fentanyl and fifty milligrams of ketamine on board. I need you to work the amputations while I put the chest tube in before this ketamine wears off."

"How are we doing on supplies?" Steve asked as he looked around the table Alan had set up for the procedure.

"We should have enough, but we are running low on suture material, so be conservative with your sewing."

Steve positioned himself on the patient's left side and began assessing the left arm. There was a tourniquet just distal to the elbow and a traumatic amputation of the left hand, midway through the carpal bones. Steve looked at the table of equipment next to the table to assess the tools he had available.

The difficulty in this procedure lay in the available tools. In a controlled environment with unlimited supplies, completing an amputation was pretty routine. But having to carry the equipment you were going to use required cutting down your supplies to only what was absolutely necessary. Single-use items were replaced with similar items that were multipurpose. Nice-to-have items were omitted to save on space and weight.

Steve grabbed his Metzenbaum tissue scissors and began radically cutting tissue from the man's wrist and hand. He isolated the radial artery and ligated it with a large strand of silk suture material. After removal of the last few remaining carpal bones, he had a good view of the distal end of the radius and ulna. Having left enough viable skin to cover the end of the wrist, he sutured the flap closed, making a good stump with the suture line on the anterior side of the forearm.

Meanwhile, Alan has cleaned and prepped the left chest for a tube thoracostomy. He made a five-centimeter incision along the fifth rib and then grabbed a pair of nine-inch forceps, using them to separate the skin from the chest wall to the next higher rib. "Sorry, guy," Alan mumbled, using heavy pressure to push the forceps into the chest cavity and causing the unconscious man to lurch upward from the pain. Alan stuck a gloved finger into the widened hole, feeling for any adhesions between the lung and chest wall.

He reached for the chest tube and pushed it into the new hole, toward the head. Using his hand to temporarily seal the new hole in the chest, he watched a large amount of blood exit the chest cavity through the tube. He attached a one-way Heimlich valve to the end of the chest tube and then sealed the wound with two layers of petroleum gauze.

He grabbed a preloaded suture and made a purse-string tie through the skin around the tube to seal it tight. He dressed the wound with a handful of four-by-four gauze pads and three-inch tape.

Once this was complete, he reassessed the man's chest by listening to his lungs with a stethoscope, and he began to suction the distal end of the chest tube with a portable suction device to help re-inflate the lung. Once a normal negative pressure was established to the chest wall, Alan conducted a full reassessment of the patient and assisted Steve in completing the amputation of the left leg.

After several hours, all of their patients were completely stabilized and treated. Because of the limited supplies they had available, most of the wounded would have to be evacuated to the compound north of the Crow's Nest, where Alan and Steve could administer nursing care and follow-on antibiotic therapy. With the accuracy of the mortar attack, they were lucky not to have had a single fatality.

Frank had the rest of the men gather all their equipment and prepare to move back to the Crow's Nest, while Steve and Alan cleaned up the area they had used. They emerged from the room with several plastic trash bags full of dirty bandages and clothes, which they threw into a pile of trash to be burned.

Seeing his worn-out teammates approach, Tony reached inside the jeep he was leaning against and tossed each one a warm Coke. Alan caught it and popped open the top. Disregarding the foam billowing from the opening, he tilted back the can and drank half of the liquid.

"You guys all right?" Luke inquired.

"I'm beat," Steve responded, and he let out a large belch from the warm, carbonated thirst quencher. "We can't afford to keep losing handfuls of men out here."

"My feet are killing me!" Alan exclaimed, and he hopped onto the tailgate of a nearby truck and let his feet dangle. He sat back, lit up a long-overdue cigarette, and looked at Frank. "Let me guess. Shir-Wali again."

"We think so, but Blaine's got a fix for it," Frank said with a smile, pointing to Blaine.

"Oh, yeah? What's that?" Alan inquired.

Shane, Rusty, and Blaine all paused what they were doing and looked up at Steve and Alan. Almost in unison, they replied, "Stop sign."

"We're doing a stop sign?" Steve asked with a growing smile, as if he'd just heard he had won something.

"What the hell is a stop sign?" Jerry asked Luke, instigating laughter of the men gathered around the truck.

Luke couldn't help laughing himself. He couldn't have thought of a better fate for his adversary, and he knew exactly what the potential benefits would be from cutting off the head of this snake. Although they had taken more casualties, a definite momentum was building amongst the Northern Alliance. With new uniforms and weapons, they looked like soldiers.

Now it was time to give them the rest of the tools.

# CHAPTER 20

*If the wind will not serve, take to the oars.*
-Roman proverb

With the range complex fully operational north of the Crow's Nest, the Triple Nickel began training their Northern Alliance counterparts intensely. Giving their trainees credit for being combat veterans, they ran an accelerated marksmanship program, with new weapons provided by the CIA. Every morning prior to movement to the FLOT, they logged several hours at the range, giving training in marksmanship, combat reloads, and shooting while on the move, and performing malfunction drills.

Shane and Rusty acted as the experts, with other members of the team assisting. They had already demonstrated the combat effectiveness of well-placed rounds and controlled pairs versus spraying targets on full automatic fire. The Northern Alliance men were good students and progressed quickly, with several standouts who became their star pupils.

They also incorporated movement and patrolling techniques into their training. As they were a smaller force fighting against superior numbers, using movement-to-contact drills allowed them to patrol the FLOT and expose the enemy for precision bombing campaigns and sniper fire. Being familiar with break-contact drills allowed them to come into contact and successfully disengage with minimal casualties or loss of life while inflicting serious damage on the enemy. Setting up and executing ambushes against lines of supply and communication disrupted their enemy and left them vulnerable to further attacks. Combined, these small-unit tactics, along with a concentrated air campaign, not only evened the battlefield, but over time they would also allow them to achieve their goal of taking back the capital city of Kabul.

Shane chose several of his star pupils to train on the new Dragunov SVD Russian sniper rifles supplied by Jerry. He taught his handpicked sniper crew use of the optics, positioning, target acquisition, breathing control, and how to gauge distance and wind speed. Having this capacity greatly increased their support of patrolling units on the FLOT and covering movements.

Luke also began an intensive physical fitness program with his Northern Alliance troops. Alternating long runs up and down the mountainous terrain with days of shorter, faster runs was beginning to show benefits when the units were out on patrol.

Being in a deployed environment and not having access to a gym did not stop the Triple Nickel from maintaining an intense physical training regimen. They were used to making due with less and had improvised ways of staying strong in austere conditions. Hanging a pole between two buildings for pull-ups, using water cans attached to a pole for a barbell, using sandbags as dumbbells, and setting up a makeshift obstacle course were some of the ways they stayed active and kept the Northern Alliance men focused on increasing their fitness levels.

They incorporated fitness into their training on the range as well, by making the trainees do sprints, push-ups, and pull-ups before firing, to gauge their accuracy of fire with an elevated heart rate. This simulated the adrenalin rush of an active engagement, and the more they used it in training, the easier it would be to use it to their advantage in a real firefight.

After several small successful missions, the Northern Alliance men were gaining confidence, which only made them want to learn and do more. Shooting contests, fitness challenges, and hand-to-hand matches were now daily occurrences. Each member of the team would work with a select individual of the Northern Alliance on his fighting skills, and every few days they would have small, controlled matches that drew several hundred onlookers. The Americans would referee the bouts and try to stay clear of the betting.

Destroyed vehicles were brought to the compound for parts, as well as to shoot in and around on the range. Jerry watched intently as Blaine and Alan removed the hood from an incapacitated vehicle and carried it behind their team hooch. This was the second hood he had witnessed them remove and take to their private area behind the far building. They had asked that this area be left alone for the team to be able to have meetings and conduct personal business, and their Northern Alliance and CIA counterparts honored that wish and never went into the area. When asked what the hoods were for, Alan would joke and tell them it was a surprise.

Several days throughout the week, Steve would conduct medical training with the Northern Alliance soldiers to teach them the basics of first aid and how to control bleeding. He chose the several helpers that had shown a propensity to not vomit during previous engagements and conducted live-tissue training using the animals that were to be eaten each night. Using scalpels, knives, axes, and sometimes his pistol to wound the animal, he would show the soldiers how blood clotted, where pressure points were to slow a hemorrhage, and how quickly and effectively a pressure dressing could stop bleeding. They could have a vascular trauma surgeon with them, but if the casualty bled out before being evacuated, there was nothing even the surgeon could do. Stressing the importance of point-of-injury intervention and showing quick techniques would help to maintain the limited number of soldiers they were working with.

Jerry and Luke were working closely with the Northern Alliance leaders, creating battle plans and target packets and deciding how to shape their battle space. Each time a high-priority target or building was destroyed, they would cross it out on their master list and celebrate with a meal together. Having a quantifiable plan with accurate intelligence was building trust between the Americans and their working partners.

Transitioning from active combatants to combat advisers had been the goal from the beginning, and it was getting closer and closer every day. Shane would set up ambushes and stand off several hundred meters to watch his men assault their Taliban enemy with violence and aggression. JT was working his magic with his handful of radio operators, showing them how to use their radios effectively and incorporating them into signal intelligence collection. He would routinely accompany a sniper mission with one of his radiomen just to listen and report what the enemy was discussing in that area. The reports would be sent back through Luke and Jerry, who were training their own mix of intelligence operatives.

Shane and Rusty routinely performed strategic reconnaissance in the target area to gather intelligence and find new targets. They would set up a hide-site by digging into a hidden position during hours of darkness and watch a certain area for twenty-four hours at a time, to report back to the operations center. Several times on these recon missions, they took pictures and gathered intelligence on high-ranking officials, including Shir-Wali himself. They were noticing patterns and habits, which were documented in targeting packets. Assets were routinely met with and paid for information concerning their Taliban counterparts. Human intelligence was the most accurate and available form of intelligence they were using, and although it was not always on target, when matched with signal intelligence and aerial or satellite photography, it gave them everything they needed to be successful in their combat operations.

Calvin went out every day to the FLOT and paired with each member of the Triple Nickel to give them experience with calling in air strikes and the use of the SOFLAM. Talking an airplane traveling at five-hundred miles per hour onto target twenty thousand feet below was no simple task. Getting bombs on target when all the buildings looked the same from that altitude required a skilled operator. With Calvin's experience as both a combat controller and an instructor, he was able to take even the most novice member of the team and bring him to a level where he could operate independently; this increased their combat power dramatically.

After several weeks of calling in air strikes, the pilots were becoming familiar with the target area and could easily find many of the terrain features on the ground to use as reference points. Having this rapport with their air crews greatly reduced target talk-on times and started paying dividends in the number of enemy targets destroyed. If they were working out of the tower at Bagram, the pilots knew exactly where to fly and position themselves for accurate bombing and gun runs. Targets on the team's priority list were rapidly being destroyed and crossed off.

Blaine and Frank began training select individuals on improvised explosive devices. The chemical makeup of explosives, different initiating devices, emplacement techniques, and when to best incorporate them into battle scenarios were now being taught and applied in combat daily. Blaine had his favorite crew on the demolitions range and was demonstrating improvised platter charges by taking a thick piece of steel and building up one side with several blocks of C-4 explosive. Once detonated, the steel would be thrust in the direction away from the charge with severe force as a projectile— in this case, through the door of a vehicle.

Behind the group, Frank and Alan were removing several blocks of the C-4 from the box and putting them into a small bag, which they then took back to the team hooch, out of sight of the rest of the compound.

Having better than average language skills, JT spent much of his time with

Akmal, visiting the local populated areas. There were roughly fifty thousand people living in the Shomali plains north of Kabul, in over a dozen built-up areas controlled by the Northern Alliance. Having an unlimited supply of cash from the CIA, JT and Akmal went shopping several times every week.

JT had a knack for fixing things, and it wasn't long before he had the entire compound lighted with fluorescent lighting hooked up to car batteries. He found an old diesel generator that he paid a ridiculous amount for, but soon he had it up and running the entire camp. Returning from a recent shopping trip, JT removed a large metal pipe and a roll of wire from the back of the truck. The pipe was maybe ten feet long, and he had enough wire to string lights throughout most of the Panjshir Valley. These were also brought behind the team house to be added to the secret that Alan and Frank were working on.

Like a child on Christmas Eve, Jerry meandered to the corner of the building to peek at what was going on in the secluded team area. He caught a glimpse of Alan with safety goggles on and watched him use an electric drill with a grinding bit to work on a large piece of sheet metal. They had cut down the hood he had seen them disappear with earlier in the week; it was now a circle roughly three feet around. Frank leaned on it, holding it steady on a large table, as Alan ground the edges clean, covering him with a shower of sparks.

"Need something?" Tony asked as he and JT pushed past Jerry with a smile, knowing they had caught him spying. Having been caught, Jerry hung his head and went back to the operations center. Tony gave a little giggle and followed JT into the team area to lend his assistance. Tony lifted a blanket, exposing another large piece of steel already cut and ground into a perfect thirty-inch octagon. He picked up the piece of steel and laid it flat on the table next to the one Frank was holding down. He pulled a tape measure from the toolbox on the ground and locked it open to three feet. He laid the tape measure on the table, and JT handed him a three-foot piece of rubber hose. He matched it to the tape measure in front of him and used a black permanent marker to mark the hose at half-inch intervals. Once he had sufficient pieces marked, he pulled a pair of trauma shears from his back pocket and began cutting the hose into pieces, letting them fall onto the metal octagon on the table.

Once all the hose pieces were cut, he put them into a large coffee cup off the table. Using double-sided foam tape, Tony covered one entire side of the steel octagon on the table. Once it was completely covered, he systematically placed pieces of hose at equally spaced intervals onto the tape. After some time, the entire piece of steel was covered with the cut hose pieces; it looked like he had cut down a bunch of birthday candles to the nubs. Smiling, Tony held up his masterpiece for the crowd to admire and received a weak round of applause for his efforts.

On a smaller table to the rear of the area, Blaine was working diligently with the C-4 explosives Frank had confiscated from the demo range. He removed the plastic covering and worked the clay-like material into several loaves. Rusty sat next to him, cutting pieces of detonating cord into two-foot sections and crimping an electric blasting cap onto one end of each piece.

JT put a small bucket down next to Blaine and opened the lid. Blaine looked down into the bucket and grabbed a handful of ball bearings, holding them up to JT with a smile. "Perfect!" He proceeded to layer the ball bearings atop his loaves of C-4, like sprinkles on a cupcake. Blaine took a roll of duct tape, wrapped blocks of C-4 into small loaves, and placed them in a large wooden box with rope handles. Several hours later, the box contained almost a dozen of these loaves.

When Alan was finished grinding the second octagon, he brought the large piece of steel over to Tony. Tony covered one side of the steel with two-sided tape as before and placed it directly atop the first piece. This created something that looked like a sandwich cookie, with the steel on the outside and a layer of tape and the cut hose pieces in between, providing a nonmetallic barrier between the two pieces of steel.

Frank handed Tony two small blocks of wood with slots cut into them. Using a rubber mallet, Tony pounded the blocks of wood onto opposite sides of the "cookie," holding the steel together securely. He then used a drill and bored two holes into one edge of the steel sandwich.

Alan took the finished product and, using a can of red spray paint, covered both sides of the octagonal sandwich with several layers of paint. Once it dried, he used a small brush to finish his masterpiece with white letters across each side. Using rocks and a few handfuls of earth, he pounded and scratched the sign on both sides to give it a weathered appearance. When it was complete, he held up the sign with a smile, to the approval of his teammates.

Tony stripped the ends off a long piece of electrical wire and attached it to the holes he had drilled previously. When both pieces of wire were attached to each piece of steel, the opposite ends of the two wires were run through the long pipe the team had acquired. After the pipe was securely attached to the finished product, Tony grabbed the pole and stood it upright next to him with a large smile.

Sitting around the table, the rest of the team stared at the magnum opus with pride as they discussed its construction.

Luke brought Jerry into the team's area for a view of the finished product. Looking at the large red sign, Jerry was confused about the elation of the men on the team. He said, "It looks like a stop sign."

The men gathered at the table laughed at his observation. "That's exactly what it's supposed be," Luke explained as he walked Jerry over to get a closer look at the sign.

"There are two pieces of steel separated by rubber insulation, less than a half inch apart. Each piece of steel is attached to an electrical wire that goes down through the pole and is attached to a power source—in this case, a small car battery. The wire continues out to det-cord that is attached to these C-4 cakes," Luke explained, pointing at the box of loaves Blaine had constructed.

"We plant the sign at an intersection and bury the explosives in the ground where the vehicle will stop. Once the target vehicle is stopped at our little sign here, all it takes is a shot from Shane several hundred meters away to hit the sign, which touches the two metal pieces of the stop sign together, completing the circuit and—"

"Ah gadoosh!" Tony chimed in, pounding his right fist into the palm of his left hand.

After several minutes of laughing and joking with each other, the Triple Nickel gathered around their finished work of art for a team photo, which Jerry gladly volunteered to take.

Were they to pack up their gear and leave at this point, the mission would still be regarded as a tremendous success and be talked about for many years to come. But for the men of the Triple Nickel, there was still work to be done, and they had no intention of stopping or even slowing down.

# CHAPTER 21

*To eat an egg, you must break the shell.*
-Jamaican proverb

November 1, 2001


As the morning sunbeams came through a far window, General Shir-Wali gathered with several of his senior leaders around a large conference table to eat breakfast and drink chai. Wearing a calm and stoic face that now displayed a scar from the American attacks, he pointed at different locations on the large map in front of them. They discussed plans for an upcoming attack on Northern Alliance fighting positions.

Once the briefing was complete, Shir-Wali stood up at the head of the table, and all his subordinates stood out of respect. Shir-Wali went around shaking their hands and embracing each man before he left the room.

Outside, his driver handed him a stack of papers containing reports from his front-line commanders. He was briefed daily on the status of each subordinate unit under his command. These units had been severely reduced in size due to the devastating air strikes, ambushes, and contacts with the Northern Alliance.

He had a much superior force in the area surrounding Bagram, but they had to cover such a large area that they were spread too thin. This created smaller elements that could not withstand the violence of the Northern Alliance, who had concentrated large assaults against the smaller targets.

With the increase in action the last few weeks, Shir-Wali had decided to consolidate several of his smaller units to defend some of the more strategic locations between Bagram and Kabul. By having a larger force in these areas, he was confident that he could repel any attack from the Northern Alliance and prevent them from gaining any momentum. He was replacing the lost troops with new ones from Kabul, but he was starting to feel the effect of the constant small attacks on his supplies and communications. He had commanded this area for many years, and he was extremely confident that his superior numbers could handle any kind of invasion by the smaller Northern Alliance.

Shir-Wali was angered by the increase in attacks on his position by his adversaries, but he considered the attacks harassment and had no reason to believe he was in any danger of losing his terrain to such a minimal opposition.

A black SUV lead a convoy of four vehicles out of the gated compound south of the Bagram Airfield. Sitting in the back and smoking a cigarette, Shir-Wali continued to read the daily reports from his front-line commanders. He was not pleased as he read report after report of the losses of personnel and equipment he had recently sustained. Replacing the men was easy with the large reserves in Kabul but replacing the vehicles and other equipment would be more difficult, as most of their arsenal was either captured from or left behind by the Russians many years ago.

* * *

"Target on the move," Calvin transmitted into his radio headset from the tower at Bagram. He was watching the convoy pull away from the mud buildings through his M49 spotting scope.

Along the southern edge of the airfield, in a fully camouflaged hide-site in the grasses between the airstrip and the enemy compound, Steve had just enough daylight to poke a pair of M22 binoculars through to make a positive identification of Shir-Wali. "Tango is in the number-one victor," he confirmed over the radio.

After several weeks of intelligence gathering and reconnaissance, they had noticed that every few days, Shir-Wali would visit different command posts in the area east of Bagram. He was constantly on the move, and it was difficult to predict exactly which commander or compound he would visit, because of the way he varied his movements. Even though Shir-Wali was extremely confident in his forces and his ability to command them, he had not made it this far by being predictable.

The convoy made its way down the dirt road leading away from the airfield to the east. They were traveling at a high rate of speed, with a large dust cloud forming behind the lead vehicle, which was followed closely by security forces in the three trailing vehicles. They approached a populated area and maintained their high speed as they passed Afghan locals walking through the streets. People quickly ran out of the road as they recognized the speeding black SUVs, knowing they would not slow down. Shir-Wali's driver paid no attention to the people vacating the streets and he repeatedly blew his horn to signal the pedestrians to vacate the road ahead.

The vehicles passed through the far side of the small village, covering the populace with a cloud of dust as they watched the convoy speed away. JT was inside a small clothing store, watching the convoy pass. He stepped out into the street, wearing a new pakol hat he had just purchased, and eyed the dust cloud as it disappeared down the road to the east. He reached up to his collar, which hid the microphone attached to his earpiece and radio, and calmly announced, "Target is through checkpoint one."

Several miles away on a rocky hilltop, Rusty followed the convoy through his spotting scope as it sped in his direction. He had a rubberized communications earpiece coiled around his right ear and had been monitoring the chatter about the convoy from its origin.

"Couple more minutes, buddy," he said aloud to Shane, who was lying next to him.

Shane pulled his SR-25 tight into his shoulder and peered through the M3A telescope at the populated area nearly eight hundred meters west of his position. He found the main street running directly through the center of the built-up area, oriented east to west, and followed the south side of the street until he identified the stop sign.

He cracked a sly grin as he watched people walk right by the sign without paying any attention to it. He watched as several pedestrians looked up at the sign and then looked both ways in the intersection, as if the newly placed sign would increase vehicle traffic in the street. Tony and Alan had worked through the night, planting the sign and burying the explosive charges while the streets were clear of any people. With no streetlights in the village, it was easy for them to sneak in and spend more than an hour digging without being seen. Tony was positive that it would be noticed at first light, as there were no street signs on any dirt road in the target area, but Alan was more optimistic.

Rusty noticed something on the north side of the intersection and panned right slightly. He saw about forty sheep in a small herd being corralled by a bearded man in a perahan tunban and headdress carrying a large walking stick. The man was toward the front of the herd, and Rusty commented on how the sheep tend to stay bunched together. "Why don't they just run off? I'm pretty sure they know they're about to be someone's lunch."

"It's safer in the herd, especially in the middle, close to the shepherd," Shane answered without moving his reticle from the stop sign. "Normally, a dog will circle the herd and nip at the legs of any sheep that stray from the rest. It doesn't take long for them to realize that the middle, by the shepherd, is the place to be. After a while, they don't even need the dog anymore."

Rusty opened both eyes and looked at Shane. "Have you been going over to Alan's house for Discovery Channel Tuesdays?" Shane began to laugh and looked over at his friend. He shook his head and returned to his rifle scope. "I did go to high school, you know."

"Oh, yeah? And what class were the sheep in, sex education?" Rusty fired back as he too returned to his spotting scope.

"Here we go, boys," Frank said over the radio. He and Blaine were positioned in the small village, near a shop that sold auto parts, which had several broken-down vehicles out front. They had the hood of a small pickup truck open of and were leaning into the engine compartment. With their now-full beards and local garb, they blended well into the surrounding scene.

Shir-Wali's convoy had just passed their position and was heading toward the intersection with the stop sign.

"You know if those idiots didn't connect the right wires, we're screwed," Blaine declared.

"They know what they're doing," Frank responded while still eyeing the last vehicle making its way toward the intersection. As the vehicles approached the charges buried in the earth, the lead vehicle hit its brakes hard, sending a large cloud of dust forward and obscuring the entire intersection.

"What the hell?" Blaine exclaimed. "Tell me those guys stopped because of the sign."

"Nope, look," Frank answered, pointing at the intersection.

The driver was not inclined to stop or even slow down through the intersection, but with almost forty sheep walking in the middle of the road, he was left with no other choice but to slide to a halt.

Agitated, he laid on the horn to get the sheep to move faster, but they were staying to the herd and fighting frantically for position close to the shepherd.

Shir-Wali was thrown forward slightly by the sudden stop, and he looked up to see the sheep crossing in front of his vehicle. He looked around at the shops and pedestrians outside the vehicle for anything suspicious. Satisfied, he looked back at the shepherd, who was now hitting his sheep with his stick to hurry them through the intersection. Shir-Wali waved his hand and commanded, "Run them over."

The driver inched the vehicle forward, bumping several sheep, which reacted by tightening up their herd on the shepherd. Seeing his animals being bumped by the SUV, the shepherd angrily looked through the car's windshield at the occupants. Shir-Wali leaned forward and yelled at the shepherd to get out of the way. He sat back in his seat and again looked around the vehicle.

This time, however, Shir-Wali didn't see any pedestrians on the road next to him. He glanced to his right and noticed the stop sign. His eyebrows furrowed with confusion, as he did not remember there being any street signs this far north of the city. He looked over at the shops next to the intersection and watched the workers hurry inside. Shir-Wali leaned forward to yell at his driver to get moving but paused when he saw the shepherd still staring at him intently. He made eye contact with the bearded man and watched him reach up with his right hand and slowly remove his headdress.

Shir-Wali again looked at the stop sign; as if he had just realized something, he quickly looked back at the shepherd. His eyes grew wide as he saw not an Afghan sheep herder but Luke staring back at him, a large grin forming on his face.

"Go, go, go!" Shir-Wali yelled, slapping his driver on the right arm. Before the driver knew what was happening, he watched Luke dive to the ground behind a dozen sheep.

"Hit it," Rusty announced as both men stared intently through their optics. The 7.62 mm Special Ball bullet left the barrel of the Stoner SR-25 at twenty-five hundred feet per second. It reached the stop sign before Luke made it all the way to the ground. When it hit the stop sign, it collapsed the gap between the two pieces of metal, completing the circuit. A small burst of electricity from the car battery traveled down the wire and into the det-cord, initiating the blasting caps within the loaves of C-4.

Hundreds of 5mm ball bearings shot skyward, ripping through the undercarriage of the vehicle above and cutting the occupants to shreds. The overpressure of the explosion threw the vehicle several feet into the air in a burst of flame.

The sheep in front of the vehicle scattered in every direction, leaving Luke exposed on the street. He rolled furiously away from the explosion and covered his head with his hands before the vehicle returned to the earth.

Seeing the explosion on the street below, Rusty slapped Shane on the back and said, "We're out of here." The two men jumped to their feet and quickly made their way down the far side of the hill from which they had made the shot. Rusty hopped onto a small motorcycle and started the engine. Shane slung his weapon behind his back and jumped on the back of the bike, wrapping his arms around Rusty's waist. Rusty gave the motorbike full throttle, and they sped off to the north.

Luke looked up from his protected posture to see Shir-Wali's vehicle completely ablaze. As he slowly got to his feet, he laughed hard at the fate of his enemy. The laughter would be short-lived, as Luke watched the other vehicles in the convoy begin maneuvering around the burning vehicle.

He jumped to his feet and began running fast through the intersection, away from the convoy. He pushed his way through dozens of onlookers, who were now on the street, watching the burning car. He heard gunfire and immediately changed direction to cut between two buildings. Once he reached the street on the other side, he headed north, still at a full run.

Without looking back, Luke could hear a vehicle coming up hard behind him, and he increased his speed even more.

"Want a ride, boss?" Blaine asked, leaning out of the passenger side of the truck as it pulled even with his running team leader.

As soon as the convoy passed their location, Blaine and Frank had lowered their hood and followed the convoy to the intersection. Had the stop sign not worked, Frank was to pull up next to the driver, so Blaine could shoot him and toss a hand grenade into the vehicle. Shane would cover them from any vehicles that gave chase. Not as flashy as a stop sign IED, but still effective.

Hearing Blaine's voice, Luke looked to his left and, without slowing down, jumped into the bed of the pickup. Frank sped off to the north as a large crowd of civilian onlookers now started to gather behind them, curiously heading to the burning car down the street. Several of the Taliban men from the trailing vehicles were now on the street with weapons, looking into the SUV for Shir-Wali. With the large fire within the vehicle coming out of all its windows, the only thing they saw were two human figures, frozen in the position they were in when the fire started and rapidly losing all recognizable features.

A man dressed all in black and carrying an AK-47 assault rifle was standing on the corner of the intersection, looking up at the stop sign in confusion. A second man approached and looked up as well, to see a small bullet hole in the very center of the sign. He took a small step to his right to look the sign from the side and noticed that there were actually two signs close together that were now touching each other in the center, where the bullet had gone through. They looked at each other and simultaneously shrugged their shoulders. They looked up at the sign for a second or two and then turned back to the burning car to help clear the civilians away from the scene.

Sitting in the bed of the truck with his back to the cab, Luke watched the village get smaller as they sped away. Smoke from the burning SUV billowed up from the center of the village. He heard two knocks on the glass separating him from the cab and turned his head to see Frank giving him thumbs-up with a large grin. Smiling back, Luke nodded at Frank and grabbed the rails of the truck bed for stability as the trucks bounced down the dirt road.

With Shir-Wali now out of the picture and the Taliban back on their heels, it wouldn't be much longer before they were moving on Kabul. Fighting in an open battlefield like the Shomali Plains was different from advancing on a large city, and they would have to shift their focus to planning the operation. There was also the issue of the Shelter Me hostages' ransom exchange, which would have to be planned as well.

Little did Luke know that the men of the Northern Alliance had plans of their own.

# CHAPTER 22

*Venus favors the bold.*
-Ovid

"Luke, wake up," Frank whispered as he shook his commander's shoulder to arouse him from sleep.

"What is it? What's going on?"

"Get up. You have to come see this."

Frank got up from a kneeling position next to where Luke had been sleeping and headed to the doorway of their sleeping area. Luke unzipped his sleeping bag and got to his feet. Not bothering to put on pants, he pulled a pair of boots over his bare feet and walked to the door in his silky black running shorts and brown T-shirt.

As he reached the door, he did not have to ask anything, as it was easy to hear the noise of heavy machinery on the road one hundred meters below the Crow's Nest. Luke's eyes grew wide as they followed a large convoy of tanks, trucks, jeeps, and buses on the road below. There were hundreds of Northern Alliance soldiers walking in between the vehicles in the convoy and riding on the various vehicles. Men were sitting on any available space on the tanks and on top of the buses and trucks to avoid walking.

"What the hell are they doing?" Luke asked as he stepped out into the courtyard to get a better look.

"I think they're going to Kabul," Frank answered with a large smile on his face.

"Get the boys up. I'll find out what's going on," Luke dictated as he walked to the operations center to have a discussion with Jerry as to why he had not been informed.

Luke charged angrily into the far room of the compound with the large conference table and saw all three of the advisers talking into either a phone or a radio. He walked past Cliff and Jack and went right up to Jerry. Before he could say a word, Jerry held up his right hand for silence. He kept the phone against his ear but lowered the mouthpiece and said, "I know. I had no idea either."

Jerry held the phone back up to his mouth. "Yes, sir. We will do what we can. I'll call you when we hit the city."

He pulled the satellite phone away from his face and closed the antenna. He looked back at Luke. "All right, we don't have much time. They have a pretty good head start on us."

He walked over to the large table with the map laid on it. "They are consolidating as we speak down at the airfield. According to Babazheen, they will split into two assaulting forces," he said, pointing just north of the capital city on the map, "and enter the city here, and here."

Two main roads led into Kabul: one directly north and one northeast of the city. A large mountain was directly north of the city, and the Northern Alliance was going to head south to it and split up around either side, to enter the city from two directions.

"Cliff is going with this group," Jerry said, pointing to the north road, "and Jack is going with the other one. I am going to hang back at Bagram until I get word they are set up in the city somewhere safe. It's your call—you can come with me or go into the city. Either way, we must act quickly. Your men have done a good job with these guys. Tell them it's more about reacting to what they do and trying to limit their failures, rather than expecting them to be perfect." Jerry looked up at Luke with a smile. "It's kind of like when you suck at golf—you just try to play each hole without making a ten."

Luke laughed and calmed down some. "We'll split up and send half the team with each assaulting element," he responded calmly. "I take it we are not coming back here?"

"With what you have done with these guys lately, I find that highly unlikely," Jerry replied. "If you can have all your shit packed quickly, leave it outside, and I'll have it brought down on one of my trucks."

"All right. I'll brief the fellas," Luke said as he turned to walk out the door.

Jerry stopped him. "Wait, Luke. We have another issue." Luke turned back to Jerry, who now had a concerned look on his face. "We have to get those hostages."

"And just how do you propose we do that, now?" Luke asked with a slightly condescending tone.

"We know they are being held in a jail of some kind." Jerry again leaned forward to the map. "There are two on the north side of the city—here and here." He pointed to each location. "The way I see it, if you guys are splitting up and moving in fast with these guys, you might come across one of them." Jerry paused and looked at Luke with a smile. "So just go in and get them."

"Just go get 'em?" Luke asked angrily. "It's not like running in and grabbing a pizza, ya know."

Jerry smiled. "Come on. Buncha high-speed Green Berets? This should be easy for you guys."

"You watch too many movies," Luke said as he stormed out of the room.

Luke headed back to his room to get dressed and update Frank on the plan. On the way into his room, he saw most of the team up on the roof of one of the mud buildings, watching the convoy go by below. They were laughing at the scene and taking pictures. Luke changed direction and headed their way.

"Hey, nice outfit, Luke!" Steve yelled down.

"We're going to war, sir," Alan chimed in. "You might want to put some pants on."

"It looks like there's a big rock concert down in Kabul. Can we go?" Tony asked with a smile.

"Where's Frank?" Luke asked Shane, ignoring the adolescents on the roof.

"In your room, sir," Shane replied.

"Start packing up your shit. We're moving out in thirty," Luke said as he turned back to his room.

Hearing the news of their participation, the men began a series of celebratory high-fives and fist pounds. As the crew climbed down from their perch on the roof, Alan looked over at Tony with a smile.

"Maybe it's REO Speedwagon."

"Who the hell is that?" Shane asked as he climbed down the makeshift ladder.

"Only the greatest band ever," Alan replied as he dropped down from the roof without using the ladder.

"I doubt its REO," Steve replied from the roof. "I don't see anyone on the road with a walker." They all laughed as they headed to their respective areas to pack up their gear.

Even though they had been living in this area for more than two months, they had the gear packed rather quickly and were standing around their vehicles, ready to move to the airfield. They had most of their team gear separated and put off to the side to be put on trucks. Steve had put together small vehicle aid bags and was putting one into each vehicle that would accompany the team into the city, so they would have enough medical supplies in case of a catastrophic event. Each man was now wearing a tactical vest with plenty of ammunition, a radio, GPS, and other gear in various pockets. Each man had a tactical earpiece coiled around his right ear and wore ballistic eye protection, and several men wore the NYFD baseball caps they had brought with them. The mood was still jovial, with joking and smiling going on to help ease the tension from what they all knew was approaching rapidly.

Once they had gathered at Bagram, Luke gave them the plan of the Northern Alliance. The team would split into two smaller teams and accompany each element in an advisory role. They were to refrain from becoming active participants in the taking of the city, both for their own safety and to allow the Northern Alliance to know they were in the lead. They were going along to assist the local commanders, providing guidance when necessary, and to provide ground truth so the JSOTF would know what was happening.

They were also briefed on the Shelter Me hostage situation and the locations of the jails in each of their respective areas. They were to gather information only and relay the intelligence back to Jerry at the airfield for a follow-on mission. Under no circumstances were they to engage the hostiles or put the hostages in any danger, because if something were to happen to one of them, it would undermine everything the team had done up to this point. Everyone knew that if something went wrong with those civilians, there would always be a "yeah, but" associated with the mission.

Within an hour of arriving at Bagram, they were loading into their jeeps to accompany their respective Northern Alliance groups. They stayed in their normal split-teams, with Luke, Rusty, Tony, Steve, and Calvin going with Jack and the group approaching from the northeast. Frank, Shane, Alan, JT, and Blaine were joining Cliff and approaching the city from the north, down the main highway from Bagram.

Calvin had already coordinated for air support in the form of multiple flights of F-16s and B52 bombers that would be in play throughout the day. He was going to have to have his "A-game" to balance that many aircraft with two separate assault forces coming into a major populated area. And even though none of them would admit it for fear of elevating his ego, there wasn't a man on the team who wasn't confident that Calvin could handle such a daunting task. Having him control their air support on such an important operation gave them all confidence and relieved some of the anxiety.

They had coordinated their link-up in the city at a small military compound just north of the city center. With such short notice on their movement, Luke had to cover a lot of points in his brief, including the handling of prisoners of war and the wounded, and keeping their forces from getting too aggressive in the city.

With both groups trying to hit the city at the same time and from different directions, fratricide was always a concern. They had to know where the other elements were at all times to keep from engaging each other. It would be imperative to maintain good communications throughout, and JT made sure there were enough spare batteries for each man to keep them talking throughout the day and into the night if necessary.

Steve opened the passenger-side door of his jeep and looked at his close friend. "Hey, bro, be safe."

"Safety through violence," Alan replied with a large smile as he got into Akmal's jeep.

Each convoy headed off in a different direction to join the Northern Alliance, which had already begun its movement south. From the forces that were already well on their way to the city, there had been no reports of contact or resistance. The intelligence claimed that the Taliban forces were amassing at strategic positions north of the city to thwart any advance by the Northern Alliance. The area to the northeast was relatively flat, and the advancing forces spread out on the desert floor along both sides of the paved road leading into the city. This would make the assault easier to control and more difficult to repel by any enemy forces in the area.

The area directly to the north, however, was channelized by two small mountain ranges, making the task much more difficult, as the advancing element would be forced into a single-file approach with hills on both sides of the road.

The goal was to overwhelm the enemy with Northern Alliance by moving the entire force systematically through the city and leaving small, squad-sized elements strategically at major intersections to man checkpoints as the main effort continued. This would give the NA superior numbers and firepower should they meet any pockets of resistance. The difficulty would lie in the command and control of the assaulting force. They had to maintain an aggressive operational tempo to assault faster than the enemy could withstand, but not get too aggressive.

As they drove south along the main paved road leading into the city, Frank and Cliff discussed their plan to control their group once they reached the city itself. Their vehicle would remain in the center of their forces with the commander; the other two jeeps containing Americans would provide the left and right limits of the force. This would allow them to maintain control and keep the entire force online throughout the assault.

The more pressing problem would be getting into the city itself. Even from several miles away, they could make out the hills on both sides of the road beginning to come together, creating an easily defensible chokepoint ahead. A small group of Taliban on each hilltop would create enough resistance to easily hold off a superior force below. Calvin had told them prior to departing that he would have them covered with plenty of CAS before they hit the city, but with Calvin joining the other group, Frank had no way to predict what the priority of those birds would be.

As they moved farther south, they began to see the tail end of a large convoy of vehicles. Much like what they had witnessed earlier passing the Crow's Nest, it contained tanks, trucks, and buses loaded down with Northern Alliance. As their jeep began passing the convoy on the dirt shoulder to the right of the convoy, Frank grew concerned at the number of civilians that had joined the convoy.

"Where did all these people come from?" he asked Cliff.

"They want their homes back," Cliff responded as the two men continued past the large procession of both military and civilians on the main road.

"A large amount of civilian Afghan people were displaced when the Taliban seized control of Kabul years earlier, and they moved north, where there was a good source of water and fertile land," Cliff explained. "They were provided protection from the Taliban by the Northern Alliance and were making the best of their difficult situation by farming. With the word of the assault on Kabul spreading rapidly among the villages north of Bagram, we knew it wouldn't be long before they would join the movement to return to the city."

Frank radioed Luke to fill him in on the news of all the civilians that had joined his group, only to find out there was a similar situation on Luke's side.

They would have to do their best to get to the front of the convoy and assign a portion of their troops to keep the civilians out of the initial assault and allow the military vehicles to move in first. But as Frank soon found out, the convoy was larger than he had initially perceived, and getting to the front in time was rapidly becoming a source of concern.

\* \* \*

Ahead of both assaulting elements, large forces of Taliban were massing at strategic locations to repel the oncoming Northern Alliance forces. In the large flatlands to the northeast, there were several T-72 Russian tanks in a linear formation, surrounded by several large antiaircraft ZU-23 guns. Hundreds of men were gathering together on foot, along with a dozen or so pickup trucks with mounted automatic weapons in the beds.

On the hilly north side of the city, the tops of both hills guarding the entrance were buzzing with Taliban soldiers preparing for the oncoming forces, which they could now see in the distance. The convoy stretched over several miles, and from their position, it looked like an entire army was headed their way. This was much more than the supposed fifteen hundred troops the Northern Alliance was rumored to have. Having the civilians mixed in with their forces gave the Taliban the impression that the Northern Alliance was coming with a larger force than previously anticipated.

They were still too far away to begin firing the large anti-aircraft weapons, and the hills were too steep for any tanks to make the climb, leaving them vulnerable to a larger force. The troops on the hills were calling frantically to their Taliban leader for more reinforcements to be sent to the city limits.

Meanwhile in the main Taliban command center in Kabul, a sense of panic was overtaking the men inside the buildings. Senior leaders were packing up their desks, collecting everything they could carry, and moving to their vehicles in the parking lot. They were loading large trucks with as many troops carrying weapons as they could, to be pushed to the north. If the Northern Alliance broke through the main defenses at the city limits, they would be able to rip through Kabul with little resistance. The city was much too large to defend against any sizeable force, and the reports from the front lines were at least four times the numbers previously reported. This changed the Taliban's plan from defending to merely surviving.

The streets of the city cleared of civilian traffic with the increased movement of armed vehicles and troops. Rumor spread quickly that the Northern Alliance was moving into the city shortly, and the citizens began showing signs of anti-Taliban sentiment. There was yelling from windows and rooftops at the troops moving in the streets; young Afghan men threw rocks and fruit at passing trucks. The population had a rising hatred toward their oppressors, and it was building to a powerful force in anticipation of the return of freedom.

* * *

Luke was standing next to his vehicle in a large, open field several kilometers in front of the convoy approaching from the northeast. He had been able to maneuver his jeep alongside the massive influx of both military and civilians who chose to remain on the paved road. This allowed his small element to scurry past the entire line to get a picture of what they had to work with and what they might be facing. He had gotten well ahead of the convoy headed south, stopping several kilometers short of the Taliban defensive positions, and was now directly between the two opposing forces. He looked through his twenty-power spotting scope at the Taliban up ahead of them and grew concerned about the size of the enemy stronghold.

He radioed Frank, who was in a similar position on the opposite side of the large mountain that separated the two assaulting elements. Frank had pulled up short of the city as well and was directing his senior Northern Alliance leaders to bring forward some heavy firepower and troops to put in front of the civilians. This was becoming difficult, because the civilians were starting to outnumber the Northern Alliance forces, and they did not like being held up from entering the city. Much of the displaced populace had lived in Kabul and wanted to return to their homes, which were now occupied by Taliban forces. Should the Taliban be killed or captured or flee the city completely, the homes would be available to anyone who got there first. Needless to say, there was growing tension on the part of the civilians to continue south and reclaim their homes, but if they were allowed to get in front of the military forces, they would be cut down quickly by the Taliban guarding the city.

Discussing the situation with the commanders was becoming even more difficult, as they saw no problem in letting the civilian not only accompany them into the city but lead the way. Frank saw right through their counterfeit devotion to their people and assumed they were acting out of sheer safety of their forces. He stressed to Luke that they were about to be forced into making a decision, as the mob moving south could not be stopped by the six Americans at the front.

Luke was giving Frank guidance on his plans when a tank round hit several hundred meters south of his position, causing him to seek shelter behind his jeep. The Taliban was gauging the distance and attempting to inflict damage to the oncoming assault from as far off as it could manage.

Almost as if a starter pistol had been fired, signaling the beginning of a race, the convoy moving south began spreading out to both sides of the paved road, making a much wider signature. An enormous dust cloud began to fill the sky behind the approaching forces, which caused Luke and the others to pause as they took in the magnitude of the scene forming in front of them. They were still several kilometers away from the oncoming group, but it was spreading to almost a mile wide, with what appeared to be several thousand troops. The civilians in the line had moved to areas between the military vehicles to avoid the dust directly behind them, and from a distance they just looked like more troops.

The large dirt field separating the two forces exploded with several more rounds from more than a dozen enemy tanks, and the rounds were slowly getting closer to Luke's position. The Taliban was making elevation adjustments to gain more distance from its rounds, and even though the Northern Alliance was still well out of the maximum range, it was rapidly approaching it.

Luke was trying to stress to the several leaders he had gathered around him to slow down their forces until the close air support arrived, but they were quickly running out of time. Communication between the leaders and the oncoming forces was difficult, because the limited number of small radios were used to talk to the other leaders and not the mechanized vehicles.

Luke directed several jeeps of Northern Alliance leaders to get in front of the lead elements of the convoy and set a slower pace. If they had the perception that they were still advancing, they would be more apt to follow the slower pace to stay in some kind of formation. The civilians would also be hesitant to get in front of the military forces, as long as they were still toward the front of the pack.

* * *

More than a mile north of the entrance to the city, Frank and Alan were discussing their options. "I know there is going to be resistance in that choke point, and aside from climbing that hill," said Frank, pointing to a large hill roughly three hundred meters in elevation above their position, "how are we going to keep these guys from getting cut to pieces as they go through the pass?"

"If we leave now, Rusty and I can make it up there and pick some of them off, but I doubt we would make it before that Trail of Tears gets here," Alan replied, pointing back to the large, approaching procession.

"And if we bust right through the pass," Frank responded, "we lose a third of our control over these guys without you. And do you think you can catch up to us from the middle of that madness?" he asked, referring to the ever-growing mob heading their way. "And what happens if you guys get into contact on the way up? I can't accept that risk. We have to think of something else, and fast."

"We are running out of options, Frank," JT added to the conversation. "We might just have to roll the dice and let them shoot at the front of the convoy. When they expose themselves, we do our best to take them out. If we split our guys up into two files and have them concentrate their fire on their own side of the road, it may allow a large number to push on through, into the city."

"Let's get all the crew-served weapons and RPGs to the front, to maximize the damage," Frank directed. "And if there are any snipers you guys trained," Frank said, turning to Rusty, "we're going to need them up here too."

They split up into their two-man teams and drove back north to meet the front of the convoy. Cliff and Frank directed the convoy commander to stop the front of the motorcade and placed an armored vehicle sideways in the road to limit the vehicle traffic. They placed soldiers on both sides of the road to stop the civilians from passing them. Blaine and Rusty drove against traffic in the desert off the main road to find men holding RPGs and Dragunovs. Alan and JT were directing an armored personnel carrier with mounted machine guns to bypass the vehicles ahead, to provide some firepower once the madness began.

\* \* \*

Luke had the team gathered around the hood of his vehicle, which was now directly between the two opposing forces, as if they were on the fifty-yard line; he was giving last-minute instructions before assaulting the Taliban front lines. "Remember, no matter how chaotic this gets, we have to maintain control of these guys. Let's do our best to focus the chaos in a generally southern direction and keep them within the limits we established." Luke pointed to the small mountain to their west. "Cal," he said loudly and quickly, "go with Jack, and try to get as high as you can, to see what you are working with—and keep the CAS on the bad guys. Tony, you guys have the outside flank when we hit the city. They are going to try and move faster, because it will be less dense. We can't afford for them to get too far out in front, so try to slow them down by having them go through random houses and businesses as you go through each block. I want a heads-up every few blocks, so we can bounce our line of advance off each other and coordinate that with Frank on the other side."

Luke pointed to the city map he had laid out on the hood of the jeep. "Shane, you're with me on the inside flank. It will be our job to link up with Frank's inside element, to merge the two in the center quickly and continue south. Once that happens, it's all on them."

Luke looked around at each of his men. "I know none of us thought we would ever be here this fast, and there is no way we would be, had it not been for the things you guys have done so far. I am extremely proud of each one of you. Keep your focus and be safe. Remember our rules." Luke looked around and held up three fingers, one at a time. "Situational awareness, attention to detail, and a sense of urgency. You have the compound where we will do link-up marked on your maps. Keep on your radios, and if you need help, make the call."

Luke looked at Steve and Tony and said crossly, "And no hero shit."

He cracked a small smile, looked around at his men, and asked, "Since Alan isn't here, does anybody else have a good movie line to kick this off?"

"And the third one says, well, I'm gonna finish the game. I shall finish the game, Doc," Shane offered. He was resting both hands on the weapon slung in front of him, and his head was tilted down, but he was looking up with a slight grin.

Calvin made the catch with a sly smile, "Billy the Kid, Young Guns II. Nice."

"I like it," Luke announced as he looked around at his men. "So let's finish the game."

The group split up into different directions to assume their positions. Calvin and Jack headed to the hills on their west and drove up a small dirt trail. They stopped about one hundred meters up the trail and got out of their jeep. They walked around the rocky terrain to find a better view of the landscape below; using their binoculars, they scanned both the Taliban positions and the oncoming Northern Alliance. With the civilians intermixed with Northern Alliance troops, it appeared as if the Taliban were completely outnumbered by the advancing horde.

Calvin immediately set up his two radios to check on the status of the air support. Time was beginning to run out, and nobody cared how good he was at his job; without the aircraft, he was just a guy holding a radio, sitting on the hillside. He made a commo check with both Luke and Frank to make sure he could keep them informed of what he was working and tailor their support as the situation changed.

He had just finished getting Frank's status when he received the call he had been desperately waiting for. "Tiger-Zero-One, this is Phoenix-Six-Six," the calm voice echoed through his headset. "We are a flight of two F-16s entering your airspace from the south. We are carrying a full load of six five-hundred-pound bombs and both have five hundred rounds of 20mm guns. Request SITREP and employment directions."

"Roger, Phoenix. We are in an active assault on the city of Kabul from two directions, north and northeast," Calvin began. "I want to focus you first on the main effort to the northeast of the city. We have an assaulting force of roughly three thousand personnel with dozens of civilian, military, and armored vehicles mixed together. We have run into a large component of enemy defending the entrance to the city. Using the city as a clock, with north being twelve o'clock, they are dug in at the two o'clock position."

Calvin was now standing up, looking at the view from his elevated position and explaining exactly what he saw to the pilots.

"There are about ten tanks, sporadic armored vehicles, and hundreds of personnel in a linear formation from east to west, several hundred meters wide. We have taken several tank rounds short of our assaulting element but are quickly coming within range. I'd like you to begin a run on those tanks first, to allow us to get our guns in play. Approach from the east and move along the lines of advance. There are friendlies on the northern side of the large hill separating our two maneuver elements at the twelve o'clock position north of the city. The ground forward air controller will mark that position with VS-17 panel. Egress will be to the southwest and back around to keep the two elements separate."

"Roger, Tiger-Zero-One. We are flying north over the city and circling around to the east for the first run," Phoenix replied calmly.

"Contact on the northeast friendlies moving south, and tally enemy tanks south of that position. I will start with the far end and move east to west." The pilot uncharacteristically broke normal radio chatter to comment on what he was witnessing below. "You guys really have a pretty good fight on your hands down there. It looks like a damn video game from up here. We'll see what we can do to help you guys out."

"Roger that, Phoenix. We appreciate the help," Cal replied with appreciation. "Tiger-Zero-One has clearance on final. Standing by."

Calvin lowered the hand-mic from his face and pressed the talk switch connected to his earpiece cord "Lima-Whiskey, Charlie-Mike. I have two F-16s inbound, circling around to the east for their first run. Stay alert down there, break … Fox-Golf, Charlie-Mike. I need a SITREP

on your status and what it looks like, so I can divert these birds to your side after the first run."

Cal heard the hand-mic squelch in his right hand and held it back against his face. "This is Tiger-Zero-One. Say again. Over."

"Roger, Tiger-Zero-One," a different voice announced. "This is Dragon-Four-Four. We are a flight of two F-16s entering your AO from the south. We have a full payload of bombs and guns. Request SITREP and objective. Over."

Calvin looked up at Jack with a grin, knowing the timing couldn't be more perfect. "Roger, Dragon. We have friendly forces split into two elements heading south from both the due north and northeast directions onto Kabul. Be advised, Phoenix-Six-Six is slightly ahead of you, flying north and coming around to the east for an east-west attack heading," Calvin explained calmly. "I need you to continue your northern heading through the city of Kabul, and you will see a north-south- running road coming out of the city just west of the twelve o'clock position that is flanked by two hills on either side. North of that pass, there will be a large contingent of military forces moving south on the road to enter the city. Those are friendly forces.

"What I need from you is to focus on those two large hills at the entrance to the city," Calvin continued. "You might have to come down a bit and put eyes on the peaks, as we cannot see them from the ground below, and provide us some intel on what's up there. But be careful—they have ZU-23 anti-aircraft and may be looking for you," Cal warned.

"Then I need you to hang north until I have Phoenix make his run on the northeastern side, and I will guide you in to take out the enemy guarding that pass. There are also friendlies on the large hill, just north of the twelve o'clock position of the city, and their position is marked with VS-17 panel. To make this easier, I need you staying on the east half of the imaginary line coming due north of the center of the city, and I will give Phoenix the west side. How copy? Over."

"This is Dragon-Four-Four. Copy all. WILCO," the voice responded. "I'll give you an update on the pass as I move off to the north. Will contact Phoenix on my channel. Dragon standing by."

Calvin looked up at Jack, who had a large grin on his face and was just staring at Calvin, shaking his head. "What is it?" Cal asked.

"Dude, you're the fucking man!" Jack exclaimed. "That was some good shit right there," he continued, pointing up at the sky. Air traffic control was probably one of the most stressful occupations available, and that was with all the technology at their disposal. Doing this job in a combat environment and controlling several flights of multiple aircraft with weapon systems, in enemy territory with friendlies all over the place, was not only difficult, it was also impressive.

"I'm just happy to be here, Jack. This is the mission of a lifetime for me," Cal answered with a smile, holding up both hand-mics.

Before he could enjoy his moment for very long, another squelch came over the hand-mic in his left hand, and he quickly held it to his ear. He heard an extremely muffled voice, different from the previous two conversations, almost as if the person was talking with his hand over his mouth. "Tiger-Zero-One, this is Doom-One-Three, entering your AO."

Before the pilot even finished his check-in, Calvin's eyes became very wide, and he looked up at Jack with both surprise and excitement.

"What is it?" Jack asked.

Calvin held up the hand-mic and, with a large smile on his face, replied, "This shit just got real. Let's finish the game."

# CHAPTER 23

*I am the punishment of God. If you had not committed great
sins, God would not have sent a punishment like me upon you.*
-Genghis Khan

In the outskirts of the eastern entrance to Kabul, two Taliban soldiers bent
over and put both hands up to their ears for protection as the tank they were
standing next to fired another round at the oncoming Northern Alliance. The
ground trembled around them with the concussion of the tank firing. After
several seconds, they reached into a large pile of tank rounds on the ground
behind them and handed another round up to the man standing next to the
turret on top of the tank to reload into the large gun.

As the soldier handed down the round into the open hatch on top of the
Russian tank, he paused as a large whistling sound caught his attention. He
looked skyward to see where the loud noise was coming from but could not
determine the direction. The other men gathered around the tank all paused too
as the sound grew louder.

The tank exploded from the detonation of a five-hundred-pound MK 82
general-purpose bomb, sending bystanders hurling in several directions from
the overpressure. Chaos quickly ensued in every direction around the tank as
Taliban men tried to find cover of any kind. Several more fired their weapons
directly into the air as the sound of a jet engine tore through the sky above.

Thirty seconds later, a second tank two hundred meters west of the first
one exploded, with a similar outcome. The second pilot of the Phoenix flight
pulled up hard on his stick and maneuvered his jet off to the south to come

around for a second pass.

Several hundred meters to the north, hundreds of Northern Alliance soldiers and civilians cheered the destruction of the Taliban tanks on the front lines. They continued to advance slowly toward their objective and were quickly coming into range of the Taliban tank rounds hitting the large desert field in front of them. The rounds were still impacting the dirt in front of the oncoming assault, but in another few seconds, the Northern Alliance forces would be directly in the impact zone.

Luke looked skyward at the F-16 turning off to the south and knew it would be several minutes before it made another pass. By the time it came around again, he would be well within the range of the enemy tank fire. The only viable option at this point was to increase their speed and drive right through the impact area before the Taliban could make any adjustments. Luke drove across the desert in front of the large assaulting force and signaled the vehicles to increase their speed.

The Northern Alliance commander following Luke in his own jeep yelled into his radio for the entire force to pick up its speed across the desert and advance on the enemy. The force had now spread out over a kilometer wide and several hundred meters deep. The military vehicles and trucks had increased their speed and were now well in front of the civilians that had joined the horde.

Luke heard his radio squelch in his earpiece, but because of the ambient noise of his jeep and the armored vehicles passing by, he could not make out what was being said. He continued across the desert in front of the advancing Northern Alliance and pulled up next to Steve and Tony in their jeep. He made eye contact with Steve in the passenger seat of his jeep and pumped his fist in the air several times, signaling for them to pick up the pace. Steve acknowledged the hand and arm signal and relayed the information to his driver.

With his message received, Luke made his way back to his position at the west side of the formation. As he crossed the desert, several more tank rounds hit the earth around his jeep, and he grabbed a hold of the dashboard to stabilize himself as his driver lurched the vehicle back and forth in anticipation of the next round.

Across the desert to the west, Frank was leaning against his jeep, looking through his binoculars high and to the south at the two large anti-aircraft guns guarding the entrance to the city and pointing into the sky in Frank's direction.

The convoy was now only several hundred meters behind him and approaching fast.

Alan walked up to Frank with a concerned look on his face. "What's the plan, boss? There's no way we are going to be able to stop these guys."

Ignoring Alan, Frank continued to stare through his binoculars at the group of Taliban gathered on the hilltop ahead. "Come on, guys, we're only going to have one shot at this," he said to himself softly.

Without warning, a small black object entered from the top of his reticle and impacted the center of the manned gun position. A millisecond later, as if in slow motion, the handful of Taliban men surrounding the gun were ejected from view by the overpressure of the bomb. The gun position was obliterated, and a large dust cloud rose up from the hilltop, to the elation of the troops in the approaching convoy.

"One more, baby, one more," Frank said aloud as he stood erect and moved his view to the opposite hilltop. He watched a large group of men flee the hill at the sound of the first jet passing overhead. Several men begin shooting their rifles into the air at the sound of the F-16, never having actually seen the plane.

Seconds later, the second hilltop exploded with a thunderous blast, sending men and vehicles plummeting down the hillside.

Simultaneously, hundreds of troops passed Alan and Frank and made their way down the road toward the city. Frank lowered his binoculars with a smile and quickly moved to the passenger side of his jeep.

"Let's go, brother," he said to Alan as he quickly climbed into his seat. Alan turned and made his way through the oncoming crowd to his own vehicle, where JT was holding the door open for him, the front passenger seat bent forward to allow access to the rear. "God, I love those flyboys," Alan commented as he jumped into the back seat. JT threw the seat back into an upright position and got in the passenger seat, slamming the door closed behind him.

"Remind me to buy Cal a bottle of whiskey when we get back," JT replied, looking back at Alan as the jeep joined the mixed procession of military and civilian vehicles. "A blind shot with multiple flights of birds—friendlies closing in, and no optics or laser. That was a once-in-a-lifetime shot, and he fucking nailed it!"

As the convoy made its way through the entrance to the city, large groups of Northern Alliance men were exchanging gunfire with small pockets of

Taliban men, who were shooting down from rooftops and out of windows at the incoming vehicles. The now well-trained shooters in the Northern Alliance were quickly picking off the enemy while most of the convoy pushed past.

Now completely separated from both Frank's jeep and Blaine and Rusty, Alan and JT rode into the city with a mix of sheer excitement and fear racing through them. As the crowd began swarming through the city streets, there was no way of telling what might lie ahead. They made the first right turn they could and headed to the western flank of the city. JT had a map of the city on his lap and a notebook in his right hand. He began writing down times, streets, and landmarks he passed, to keep Frank informed of their position.

Likewise, Blaine and Rusty turned to the left and headed into the center of the city to watch the eastern flank of their element and try to conduct a link-up with the other half of the team. As they drove through the city streets, they made eye contact with men, women, and children who were lining the streets, taking in the scene unfolding before their eyes. Word of the Northern Alliance's arrival in the city had spread quickly, and the streets were lined with civilian onlookers observing the unfolding events. With large smiles on their faces, groups of men and children waved at the passing convoys of Northern Alliance.

The Americans took in the scene as they directed their forces throughout the eastern half of the city with little resistance from the fleeing Taliban forces. As they moved east, they looked to their south to see the Northern Alliance and hundreds of civilians moving quickly through the streets. They scanned every direction constantly as the sounds of sporadic gunfire and small explosions filled the air.

\* \* \*

"What the hell are they doing?" Calvin said aloud. Jack was now standing up, looking through binoculars at Luke's jeep driving south, right into the enemy defenses.

"Why won't he answer?" Jack asked.

"He can't hear the radio over the noise of that jeep. I've got to get his attention," Calvin said. He got up and ran back to their jeep.

He opened the back gate and unzipped his backpack. Reaching inside, he pulled out two M159 white star cluster signal flares and ran back to the edge of the hill. He removed both flares from their protective cases, pulled off the caps, and with one signal device in each hand, slammed them both onto the ground, striking the firing pins. This sent them flying from the edge of the hill, and Calvin watched as the five-star illumination clusters spread brightly against the sky.

Seeing the two white clusters in the sky in front of him, Luke held his hand up to his driver, signaling for him to stop. He put his right hand to his ear to insert the earpiece further. "Who just shot those star clusters?" he demanded.

"Luke, stop moving," Calvin ordered loudly. "Stop the assault, right now!"

"We're right in their range. We have to keep going," Luke replied. Another tank round impacted fifty meters to his right, sending dirt and dust into his jeep and causing his driver to steer quickly away.

"Goddammit, Luke, stop!" Calvin yelled into the hand-mic.

"Look up, look up!"

Hearing the direction, Luke leaned forward and looked at the sky through the windshield. Not seeing anything, he scanned both ways with angry eyes for anything that would let him know why Calvin would fire signal flares. His gaze fixed on the east, and his eyes grew wide with surprise. "Stop the jeep! Stop, stop!" he yelled to his driver as he pounded him on the right shoulder. "Go back! Turn around, now!"

The driver spun the steering wheel hard left and drove back toward the oncoming Northern Alliance forces. As he approached the front vehicles, Luke climbed out of the window and stood on the seat, holding onto the roof for support. As they drove by the lead vehicles, he held up a closed fist, signaling for them to stop their assault. He then pointed into the sky and continued to the next vehicle down the line.

He looked up to see Steve's jeep racing toward him, and he held up both hands to signal them. The two jeeps skidded to a halt next to each other, and Steve leaned out of his window and said, "Not a good idea to stop here, sir."

"Oh, yeah," Luke replied as he pointed into the sky to the east. "You want to keep driving, be my guest."

Steve looked to the east, and much like his team leader before him, his eyes grew wide, and his face turned white as he watched two sets of condensation trails track across the sky, directly over their position. He looked back at Tony in the back seat. "Give me those binos!" he yelled.

Tony handed him a pair of M-22 binoculars and asked, "What the hell is going on?"

* * *

"Doom this is Tiger-Zero-One," Calvin began. "We only have one shot at this, and I want you to error to the south, away from my friendlies."

"Roger, Tiger-Zero-One," came the muffled call of the radar navigator. "What are your spread parameters?"

"I want you to try to cover the entire length of that enemy front and keep the spread as narrow as possible—under three hundred meters if you can," Calvin ordered.

"WILCO," Doom responded. "Your friendlies are danger close. Ground FAC has authority to call the drop. Over."

"You are cleared hot, Doom," Calvin replied. "God help us," he said under his breath as he marked himself with the sign of the cross.

Thirty-five thousand feet above the earth, a Boeing B-52 Stratofortress tracked across the desert below. "Ten seconds," came the call over the headset of the bombardier sitting at a large computer module within the belly of the massive jet.

"Roger, ten seconds. Standing by," he echoed into the radio built into the mask he wore that delivered oxygen at high altitudes. He monitored a computer screen that showed the target area below. With directions from Calvin on the spread of the bombs, he had entered the calculations into his computer, which adjusted the openings on the bottom of the bomber, focused the bombs to create either a narrow or wide girth, and adjusted the speed of release to increase the length of the bombing run. Calvin had asked for a three-hundred-meter spread covering two kilometers that would blanket the Taliban front lines.

"Bombs away," echoed the voice over the headset within the bomber.

"Aye, bombs away," the bombardier replied and began flipping switches on his control panel.

Underneath the plane, the bomb doors opened and began releasing more than sixty five-hundred-pound bombs that would take more than thirty seconds to get to the earth below.

Hearing the call, Calvin ignited two red star clusters by pounding them together on the ground in front of him, sending them shooting across the desert sky in front of the Northern Alliance.

The four Americans, now standing outside their jeeps and looking skyward, saw the red signal flares come screaming across the sky from the hill Calvin was working from.

"Red is bad, right?" Tony asked sarcastically.

Steve held the binoculars to his eyes and looked up at the condensation trails almost directly above them. Unable to make out anything but the outline of a plane, he started to drop the optics, but something sparkled underneath the plane and caught his eye. He looked for a second longer and noticed that the sparkles seemed to be falling. The reflection of the sun off the falling bombs told him exactly what he feared. "Bombs away!" he yelled to the crowd.

The other three Americans looked at each other for less than a second before Steve pushed his way past them to get behind his jeep. The rest of the men followed suit and ran around to the far sides of their jeeps, diving to the earth behind them. Steve frantically started pushing dirt and dust to the side to create a small depression in which to lie.

Seconds later, the earth began to shake as if it were being torn in half. Each man clapped his hands over his head as the continuous cracking of the bombs striking the ground filled the air. Seconds later, dirt and dust began flowing over the men from the massive wave of overpressure created by so many bombs landing in such close proximity. Behind them in the halted tanks and vehicles, people's clothing began blowing as if a strong wind was passing over them, covering them with desert dust.

From the hilltop to the west, Jack and Calvin safely watched the scene unfold as the bombs impacted the far enemy positions and gradually moved west, covering the Taliban front lines. From his elevation, it sounded like a pack of firecrackers going off as the bombs landed in succession across the desert.

They watched the earth explode as a large curtain of dirt and dust rose across the desert floor, covering the entire enemy. They could not tell if anything was moving within the curtain, because the area it was covering was so massive. Neither man had ever seen anything so extraordinary, and they stood in awe of the scene below.

Jack and Calvin felt the earth begin to shake below their feet, and both looked down to make sure they were still standing on solid ground. They looked up at each other with large smiles; without having to say a word, they shared the excitement of such an amazing moment.

* * *

Inside the city, Frank was standing outside his jeep, directing several Northern Alliance men into a large building to search for Taliban when the ground shook below his feet. He looked down and around in several directions, as if he were waiting for the earth to open up in front of his eyes. When the rumbling stopped, many men around him were just standing still, looking around for what might have caused the small earthquake. Frank looked up to the sky; he saw the contrails of the B-52 overhead and knew exactly what had transpired.

"Proof through the night that our flag was still there. Alright, Calvin," he said, cracking a large smile, and returned to directing the men into the building.

* * *

Several seconds went by after the blast, and Steve looked up from his position behind the jeep. His face and hair were completely covered in desert sand, and he stood up slowly. Running his hand over his face and hair to rid himself of some dust, he stared in awe at the scene in front of him. The other men rose to their feet as well and stood silent as they observed the devastating impact of the bombing run.

The curtain of dust was several hundred feet high and covered an area almost two kilometers wide in front of them. There was no way of knowing whether the bombs had hit the enemy or just put up a wall of dust. Knowing he had little choice, Luke walked slowly around his jeep to get into the passenger side.

"Come on, guys, let's go," he told the other men, who were still staring at the large wall of smoke in front of them. Shane joined him immediately, jumping in the back seat of his jeep.

Tony walked past Steve and gave him a hard slap to the shoulder that sent a cloud of dust flying off him. "You got down pretty fast for a big fella," he joked.

Steve continued to brush himself off and looked up at Tony with a smile. "The only things keeping me from getting any lower were the buttons on my shirt."

Steve followed Tony into the jeep, and they returned to their position at the eastern flank of the Northern Alliance. The entire force was again moving toward the city at a steady speed.

Calvin and Jack were making their way down the hill to join the assault. Most of the smoke and dust from the B-52 strike had settled, and they saw very little movement in the Taliban front lines. Those who had survived were now moving south into the city, leaving the entrance unprotected. With the massive amount of people and vehicles that were converging on Kabul, there was little to stop them from entering the city now. They would have to catch up to Frank's group, which was already moving within the eastern half of the city.

* * *

Across the city to the west, Frank was putting several prisoners into a large transport truck. They had surrendered gladly when the Northern Alliance quickly overtook the first several blocks. Frank had given his troops handfuls of zip-ties to be used as handcuffs for any prisoners taken. They had several large, empty trucks following them as they moved through the streets to gather the prisoners.

Small pockets of resistance were easily engulfed by using a larger force than necessary to clear each block. They would leave two-man patrols on the corners of streets that were cleared and continue south with a force that could easily enter several houses at once and find any stragglers that had not run away. Whenever the troops became too aggressive moving through the streets, Frank would tell the group to check inside more buildings, keeping them slowed to a steady pace in a southern direction.

Several Northern Alliance troops approached Frank and looked very anxious. They began pointing down the street they were about to go through, and something was obviously bothering them. Frank had difficulty making out what they were trying to get across, and with Akmal in the truck with Alan and JT, all he could do was follow them as they cautiously moved down the street.

When he reached the end of the block, he didn't need any more information, as he now saw what they were so concerned about. Frank stopped the men from advancing any further and quickly went inside a small courtyard. He gathered some of the men together and began to get a head count of the troops he had to work with.

Halfway up the next block, there was a large building with several armed men on the roof; the roof had sandbags and barbed wire around the top, and several more armed men stood guard at the front of the building.

"What is it?" Cliff asked as he entered the courtyard.

Frank was trying to reach Alan on his radio and paused to answer, "See all those guys on that building down there?" He pointed to the heavily guarded building. "This is what we've been looking for. That's the jail."

# CHAPTER 24

*He who does not punish evil commands it to be done.*
-Leonardo da Vinci

"Do you think there's anyone still in there?" Alan inquired as he peeked from the courtyard at the building down the street.

"I have no idea, but why would they stay if it was empty?" Frank answered.

The other Americans joined Frank and Cliff in the courtyard to make a quick plan of action. JT made a small terrain model on the ground, showing the jailhouse and the several buildings around it and using small rocks as people. Frank made the call: they were going in,

because with the amount of Northern Alliance troops flooding the area, it would only be a matter of time before they were at the jail, and he just wasn't willing to assume that risk. Having the Northern Alliance make contact with the Taliban at the jail would spell almost certain doom for any prisoners inside.

"Rusty and I will take out the guys on the roof and try to get the ones at the door before you reach it but be ready to handle them yourselves if we take too long," Frank explained. "With the gunfire in the distance, they won't even realize what is happening until you're on them, but you have to cover that ground fast."

Frank continued. "As soon as you're through the door, I'll send a truck up to the door with security. Akmal, I need you to lead the truck in there and be ready for these guys when they come out."

Akmal nodded and continued to translate the plan to the Northern Alliance soldiers gathered around in the courtyard.

"Try not to let anyone shoot at me as we come out this time," Alan said to Akmal sarcastically.

"You should tell me when you come," Akmal replied with a smile.

"Oh, so it was my fault?" Alan asked.

"What are you going to tell Jerry?" JT asked Frank.

"The truth, of course," Frank replied with a sly grin. "They were just walking down the street, and we picked 'em up. All right, let's go. We're running out of time here," Frank said, and he walked to the large building within the courtyard.

"Tell me again why you're not going," JT asked Frank with a smile as he loaded a fresh magazine into his M-4.

"Because I'm too old and slow to keep up with you three," Frank replied, pointing to Alan and Blaine, who were doing last-minute checks on their weapons.

"I'll second that one!" Alan yelled as he holstered his pistol. He began cracking the knuckles of both hands in preparation.

"Hey, rock star!" Frank yelled at Alan. "Just be smart in there, please!" Alan looked up and blew Frank a kiss before following JT and Blaine out of the courtyard.

"Damn that guy," Frank mumbled to himself as he followed Rusty up the ladder to the rooftop.

Once atop the roof of the building, Rusty crawled forward on his hands and knees as far as he could without being seen from the street below, with Frank close behind him. The two men dropped into prone firing positions and aimed their rifles at the rooftop of the two-story building two hundred and fifty meters down the street.

There were five armed men in black clothes on the roof, behind several sandbags. Two more men were stationed outside the door below, behind a small wooden barrier, and there were two large, steel anti-vehicle barriers in front of the building.

Frank positioned his body in the familiar sniper position and pulled his rifle tight into his shoulder, slowly flipping the selector switch to fire. "Ready," he said softly to Rusty.

He heard a click as Rusty followed suit, making his weapon ready to fire. "Ready," said Rusty.

"I'll go left to right. Make sure they stay down," Frank directed.

"Not going to be a problem," Rusty said without changing his sight picture through the scope on his SR-25.

"In three … two … one …"

With simultaneous shots, two of the men on the rooftop were thrown back violently from the impact of rounds to the head. Before the other three knew what was happening, they too were quickly put down by the accurate fire of Frank and Rusty.

On the corner below, the three Americans took off at a dead sprint with the crack of the first shot. They stayed as close to the row of buildings as they could, so as not to attract the attention of the two armed men standing in front of the jail. Even loaded down with gear, they moved quickly down the sidewalk in front of the row of buildings, running between fruit stalls and sidewalk vendors and closing fast on their intended targets.

While they were still several buildings away, one of the armed men spotted the approaching Americans. He yelled to his partner and raised his rifle to shoot.

JT kept running at full speed directly toward the jail as he watched the first man raise his rifle and point it directly at him. Realizing he had been spotted, JT brought his weapon up to his face and aimed at the guard. Just as he was about to fire, Frank put a bullet right into the man's forehead; a nanosecond later, the man's partner fell to the ground from Rusty's shot.

"Let's go," Frank said calmly, and the two men got up quickly from their firing positions and moved across the roof. They climbed down the ladder and jumped onto the outside of the cab of the large truck preparing to move down the street. Standing on the running board and holding onto the side mirror for support, Frank directed the truck to move out. The gate of the courtyard opened, and the truck turned onto the street in the direction of the jail.

As the two armed men fell, JT continued running at full speed until he was next to the door of the jail. He paused calmly and covered the door with his weapon while the other two approached his position. Alan brought up his rifle and covered the door from the other side, while Blaine stepped between them and placed a small breaching charge onto the door handle.

Blaine unwound a long wire attached to the charge and stepped behind Alan. Once against the wall, he called off, "Three … two … one …"

Both JT and Alan kept their weapons on the door until they heard "one" and immediately turned their faces away from the blast of the small breaching charge.

JT reached in, grabbed the door by the hole left by the charge, and pulled it open violently. Alan and Blaine quickly flowed in through the open door, with JT following close behind them.

Staggered on each side of the hallway, the men maneuvered with illumination provided by the flashlights from their rifles, which shone through the smoke produced by the small explosion. Two men came around a corner from a small office and were immediately put down with two shots each, center mass. At the far end of the hallway there was a stairway that led to the cells in the basement.

Keeping up his speed down the hallway, Alan pushed right through the doorway and moved down the stairs, never lowering his weapon. As he rounded the corner at the bottom of the stairs, his rifle was grabbed and pulled down by a guard waiting for him. Feeling the pull, Alan pushed his weapon farther down, lowering the man's body to a slightly bent over position. Alan released the grip of his weapon with his hand and wrapped his arm around the man's body, driving him into the wall. Quickly the man pushed back hard from the wall, and instead of competing, Alan immediately fell backward to the ground, pulling the attacker into his guard. Lying on his back with his legs wrapped around the man's waist, Alan held one of the man's arms with his left hand and put his right hand under the attacker's chin, pushing his head up as high as he could.

Instinctively, Alan closed his eyes and turned his head to the left, just in time for JT to put a round into the face of the attacker, showering Alan with blood and skull pieces. Alan rolled to his right, dumping the convulsing body to the side, and Blaine helped him back to his feet. From the far end of the hallway, they heard several screams in response to the gunshot.

"You all right, man?" JT asked as he helped his teammate to his feet.

"Thanks, bro," Alan said as he raised his weapon, and the three continued down the hallway.

At the far end, there were two cells on each side of the hallway, with four people in each one. Seeing the three Americans dressed in local garb with beards, the prisoners were unsure who they were, and immediately they moved to the far wall, away from the doors of the cages, and began screaming.

"Shelter Me—are you with Shelter Me?" JT asked harshly as he lowered his weapon and went right to the door of the cage. "We're Americans. We're here to take you home."

Hearing spoken English, several men moved to the front of the cages and started reaching through the bars, touching JT and thanking him. Alan moved to the far cell and looked at the lock securing the door. He lowered his weapon to his side and pulled a tension wrench and lock rake from his shirt pocket.

As he began working on the padlock, another scream came from inside the cell, which startled him. Alan paused and looked up. "Lady, that's not helping the situation," he said firmly and continued working on the lock.

"Dude, seriously?" JT scolded Alan.

"What? I'm trying to work here," Alan said as he continued his work on the lock.

"I was talking about the lock," JT responded. Using the butt end of his rifle, he hammered the padlock on the door of the cage in front of him, freeing it from the hasp.

"Oh, sure, I could have done that," Alan said, smiling, "but this takes skill." He looked up to JT with a large smile and pulled hard on the lock, opening it.

"Show-off," Blaine said as he opened the cell door, allowing the prisoners to enter the hallway.

"Who is in charge? Is there anyone hurt? Can everyone walk?" JT asked the prisoners loudly.

"We have a couple men that were beaten pretty badly," answered a man with an Australian accent.

"You need to pair them up and assist them up the stairs. We have a truck waiting outside," JT directed.

Suddenly, two loud screams filled the basement hallway. The men turned around quickly and saw another guard near the staircase holding one of the Shelter Me prisoners around the neck. He had his left arm draped over the prisoner's left shoulder and throat, and in his right hand was an AK-47assault rifle, pointed at the prisoner's head. He was screaming in Dari and slowly backing toward the stairs. He was obviously trying to use the prisoner to make his escape.

Alan slowly approached the two men down the hallway with his weapon still slung behind his back and both hands in the air, palms facing forward to show he was not a threat.

"I don't understand what you are saying," Alan said calmly and cautiously. The man started to yell at Alan as he approached the stairs. He took his weapon away from the prisoner and began to point it in Alan's direction.

This small hesitation was all that Alan needed. Quickly he reached down to his thigh holster and drew his pistol. Bringing it up to chest level, he joined both hands together around the gun and extended his arms in the direction of the guard while simultaneously pulling the slack out of the trigger. Looking at the front sight of the weapon, Alan finished the trigger squeeze and put a round into the guard's forehead, causing his head to be thrown back violently. As the guard released his grip on the prisoner and dropped to the ground, Alan continued walking toward them and scanned the rest of the hallway before holstering his pistol. He grabbed the man, pulling him away from the dead body on the floor, and moved him back to the middle of the hallway.

"Sorry about that. Let's just keep this one between us," Alan said to the man with a smile and handed him the scarf from his own neck to wipe the blood off his face. The man visibly shaken from the scene that just transpired.

"Alan, lead us out. Blaine in the middle. I'll take the rear. Let's go. Let's go," JT directed the prisoners, who gathered into a group and made their way to the stairwell.

"Frank, we're coming out," JT announced into the microphone attached to his shirt collar as he went up the staircase behind the prisoners.

"You're clear," Frank responded. Outside, there was a large military cargo truck parked in the street with about a dozen Northern Alliance soldiers spread around it, pulling security. The truck was backed up to the door, with a small ladder leading into the back of it.

When Alan emerged from the door, he guided the hostages into the truck, helping them navigate the ladder. Each time another person passed, he would wrap his arms around Alan and thank him, which Alan enjoyed fully.

"Lima-Whiskey, this is Fox-Golf. Over," Frank announced over the radio.

"Go ahead, Frank," Luke answered.

"We have secured the Shelter Me personnel and are moving them back to Bagram. Over."

There was a long pause over the radio. Frank looked up at Alan and JT, who were in the back of the open truck, providing first aid to the injured hostages. "I don't think he believes us," he said jokingly.

"Did you just say you had the hostages?" Luke said over the radio with slight anger in his voice.

"Please let me take this one," Alan asked Frank, holding up one hand.

"Be my guest," Frank said, opening his hand in Alan's direction as if to say, Here ya go.

"Yes, sir, we have them right here. Want to say hello?" Alan looked around the back of the truck and directed the crowd, "Say hi to Luke, everybody." He held down the push-to-talk button on his microphone and presented it to the people in the back of the truck.

In unison, the crowd yelled, "Hi, Luke!"

"See, we got 'em," Alan said with a smile. "And, um … in your face!"

"What's the plan for exfil?" Luke came back over the radio, completely ignoring the remark.

"We have them on one of the NA five-tons, and Cliff is going to take them up to the airfield under guard," Frank responded. "He has already coordinated with Jerry for transport out of country once they get there."

Frank paused slightly and looked up at the truck of people. "We had no choice, sir. They were never in any danger."

"Good job," Luke responded. "Get the boys back to work, and let's get linked up."

"They're en route. See you soon." Frank walked up to the truck, where Cliff was in the passenger seat, and gave him a brief on the route back to the airfield. He shut the door and returned to where the other guys were standing by the doorway of the jail. He looked at the four men and smiled. "Do I even want to know what went down in there?"

"No problems. Went off without a hitch," JT replied with a grin as he lowered his Oakley M-Frame sunglasses to cover his eyes.

"I saw JT pick a lock faster than Alan," Blaine offered.

"I got some dude's skull all over me," Alan contributed, giving JT a slight nudge.

"All right, let's get back to work," Frank said. "We've got a city to take. Rusty, Blaine, get linked up with the other inside element. And be careful—they are going to be firing up anything coming their way." The two walked back to the end of the block, where their jeep was parked. Blaine began reenacting the scene from inside the jail for Rusty, with several slight exaggerations to make the story sound more interesting.

"Come on, JT," Alan said as he began walking away, "I think I saw a Hooters a few blocks over. Happy hour ends at five."

"Hey!" Frank yelled to the two men walking away. Alan turned around to see Frank just standing in the middle of the street. "Are you ever going to grow up?"

Alan smiled wide. He held both arms out to his sides with his palms up and replied, "God, I hope not."

Frank just shook his head and turned back to the courtyard where the jeep was parked.

* * *

Across the city, Luke had explained to the others that the search for the Shelter Me hostages was now over, and they could turn their focus on keeping the Northern Alliance under control as they maneuvered through the city. He also passed along Alan's response to them, to plenty of chagrin from the team, as they knew they would have to hear the overinflated stories for many years to come. Luke and Shane were following several SUVs with some Northern Alliance commanders south down a major street in central Kabul. There was a lot of activity as the curious children and young adults flooded the streets to get a look at the Northern Alliance. They wielded flags, waved their hands, and cheered loudly at the passing procession of cars; they would walk up to the men on foot to shake their hands. They were extremely happy that the Taliban was being removed from the city, and it showed on their faces.

As the small convoy entered a large traffic circle, Shane was continuously scanning the sidewalks and buildings out his window for signs of enemy activity. He saw little children staring at him as he rode by. He managed to elicit several waves from onlookers as he smiled from the back seat. He locked eyes with a little boy holding an Afghan flag and gave him thumbs-up for his patriotism. As his eyes moved off the little boy, they caught a glimpse of something along the wall the jeep was passing.

"Stop! Stop the jeep!" he yelled, his head turning to maintain the visual.

"What? What is it?" Luke turned and looked past Shane out the back window, trying to catch a glimpse of what had Shane so unusually excited.

"Look, right there," said Shane, pointing toward the sidewalk. "On the wall."

Luke again tried to adjust his view around the driver and Shane in the back seat, but he still could not see what Luke was seeing.

"I don't see anything. Where are you looking—?" Luke's eyes fixed on the same target as Shane, and they became wide too.

"Stop the jeep," he told the driver. "Turn around. Go back there," he directed, pointing back the way they had just come. He leaned over and started beeping the horn to get the other vehicle's attention. He watched the other vehicles make their way around the traffic circle and head back in his direction.

The jeep pulled off to the side of the road, and both Shane and Luke exited. Luke ran up to the approaching vehicles and signaled for the men to join him on the street. He directed two small groups to pull security on the far sides of their position, and he took a dozen men with him and Shane to a large iron gate.

It was about twelve feet high, and the bars were too close together for them to fit through. It was connected on both sides by a ten-foot-high brick wall that extended down the road on both sides of the gate. They all began looking through the bars of the gate as Luke tried the latch. The gate was unlocked, and it swung open freely. Luke and Shane entered, splitting up in both directions, with a small contingent of Northern Alliance men trailing. After an immediate sweep of the area, Luke picked up a position behind a small group of trees in the compound and went to a knee. He put his left hand to his ear to help support his earpiece and signaled Frank.

"Fox-Golf, Lima-Whiskey," he transmitted.

"Go ahead," Frank responded quickly.

"What is your status?" Luke asked. "Do your counterparts have things under control?"

"Yes, sir," Frank responded. "We're kind of just riding along at this point."

"Then I need your entire element at my location, right now," Luke said with a sense of urgency in his voice.

"Is everything okay?" Frank asked.

"I'll fill you in when you get here," Luke replied. "Just bring everyone to me now. Shane will send the grid in two mikes."

"Roger that, sir," Frank replied. "We're en route."

The entire team was privy to the conversation, and a sense of paranoia began to spread quickly. And as usual, speculation about who had messed up became the target of each jeep's conversation as they all converged on Luke's location.

"Way to go, man," JT criticized Alan.

"What did I do?" Alan asked angrily.

JT looked at Alan in the back seat and crinkled his nose while using a childlike accent. "In your face!"

"That's not it," Alan said, returning the look to his teammate.

"He's probably going to yell at you for not seeing that last guard that almost got a hostage killed. This one's on you, bro," he replied, and he stared back out the window.

After a few seconds, Alan leaned forward between the two front seats and looked at JT. "Do I really sound like that?"

JT looked back at Alan with raised eyebrows and gave several small nods.

Akmal sped the jeep through the city as JT directed the way to Luke's location. They had no idea why Luke wanted everyone there, and they definitely were not feeling good about it.

# CHAPTER 25

*The deed is everything, the glory naught.*
-Johann Wolfgang von Goethe

The three jeeps carrying Frank and his crew arrived at Luke's location about thirty minutes later. They saw a handful of Northern Alliance men standing guard outside the gated compound, who then directed them inside the gate. As they pulled in, they saw several trucks with dozens of Northern Alliance soldiers walking around within the compound.

There was a large three-story brick building in the center, with large steps going up the front. It looked like an office building or the residence of an affluent person. The windows and doors were covered with large pieces of plywood, like a Florida home before a hurricane. Inside the brick wall surrounding the property was a long row of rose bushes and other flowers that were neatly trimmed and obviously well cared for. And there was grass: real grass, neatly mowed and trimmed, with small sprinklers offering a fine mist of water.

There was a large circle drive in front of the building, and the Americans were gathered around a jeep parked there. As Frank and his men approached, they noticed that everyone was present except for Tony and Steve. The air was peaceful, as if they were completely removed from the conflict outside the gate. Everything seemed calm, and there were uncharacteristic smiles on both the Northern Alliance men and the Americans who had gathered. Luke, however, had a stoic look on his face, and Frank had a hard time gauging his mood as they approached him.

Something caught Frank's attention from the steps of the large building, and he looked up to see Steve and Tony coming down them, carrying a large duffle bag. Each was supporting an end of the bag, so whatever was in it, it was heavy.

The two men approached the jeep where the rest of the team was gathered and put the bag into the back.

"What's in the bag, Dad?" Blaine asked the two men.

"Mind your business," Tony fired back sarcastically.

"Just a little piece of Meditation Number 17, that's all," Steve offered with a smile as he closed the back gate of the jeep.

"What the hell does that mean?" Rusty inquired.

"Another fine product of the public-school system, everybody," Steve announced to the crowd, and he presented an open hand in Rusty's direction.

"Whatever, college boy," Rusty fired back.

"Settle down," Frank commanded. "What's up, sir? Why the important conference?"

"I'm glad you asked, Frank," Luke began. "I know we still have a lot of work to do, but I just wanted to get you guys here, on this historic day, and say thank you."

He looked around at his team members individually. "Thank you, and you, and you ... for not fucking this all up."

The group laughed at their leader showing his seldom-seen humorous side. "We haven't always done things by the book or as appropriately as I had hoped," he said, glancing at Alan and Steve, "but we have always gotten them done well.

"I had a long discussion with Frank, prior to this trip, about the importance of the mission and your responsibility in it. We agreed that we would not get in your way or try to stifle the antics of some of our personalities. Because for some crazy reason, this team operates better that way."

"I am extremely proud of all of our characters," Luke continued, "even you two." He pointed to Alan and Steve.

"Luckily, I learned early on that you guys were a lot more than just a bunch of clowns, and the things I have seen you do here go well beyond what I could have ever predicted. I am lucky to have been a part of this and to have worked with each one of you. This is a moment we will share for the rest of our lives, however long that may be.

"No one will know the true significance of this operation for years to come, but I can tell you it is extremely significant to me now. The motto of

221

Special Forces is to liberate the oppressed, and that is just what we have done here." He pointed outside the gate. "There are people out there who were being told they had no say, no choice, no freedom. And now they will, because of you men. And regardless of what comes next for this place, that is significant.

"So, I brought you guys here to say thank you." Luke turned around and held out both arms, as if to present the building to his men. "And to welcome you home."

The rest of the men followed Luke as he approached the steps, and Frank now noticed the reason for the gathering.

"Is that what I think it is?" Blaine asked out loud, to no one in particular.

"It sure is," Calvin replied with a large grin.

Above the doors at the top of the stairs hung a large silver plaque, maybe eight feet in diameter, with a large eagle carved onto the surface like a coin.

It was the Great Seal of the United States: a shield borne on the breast of an American eagle holding an olive branch and arrows. It was the most beautiful thing these men had seen in months, and it left the normally garrulous crowd speechless.

They were standing on the steps of the American embassy that had been closed since January 1989. They were all amazed at the pristine condition of the building and the compound itself. From the roses to the cut grass and the condition of the interior, it was remarkable how little it had been affected. From what they could gather from the Afghan men who were working the grounds when they arrived, the Taliban was under the assumption that the building had been booby-trapped before it was vacated and had just left it alone. The gardening crew had continued the upkeep of the grounds in anticipation of its reopening one day and with no intent of ever getting paid for their service.

Embedded in the wall of the building was a small metal plaque with raised letters establishing it as an EMBASSY OF THE UNITED STATES OF AMERICA, 1948. Calvin walked over to the plaque and rubbed his hand over the raised metal words. He took a deep breath to calm himself as his emotions and eyes began to swell.

JT walked over to his friend and put his arm around Calvin's shoulder. "Can you believe this?" he asked.

"It's amazing. I can't believe it's still here." Calvin looked at JT.

"I've got to get my camera. Stay here," he said, and he ran down the steps to his jeep and got his camera out of the pack sitting on the front seat.

"Akmal!" he yelled at their friend, who was talking with one of the gardeners. "Come take our picture, will ya?" Akmal smiled and walked up to the steps where the Americans were now gathered.

"Let's get everyone on the steps," Luke announced to the group. The men began getting into rows on the steps leading up to the front door for a team photo.

"Wait," Steve announced and ran down the steps to his jeep.

"Now what the hell?" Frank commented. Steve reached into his backpack in the jeep and grabbed a smaller bag within it. He ran back to the building and tossed the bag to Alan, who was on the first step. Alan unzipped the small bag and smiled wide. He reached inside, pulled out the team's American flag, and unfolded it.

Their team flag had been around the world with them as a daily reminder of what they were doing and who they actually worked for. Alan handed one end to JT, who stretched it out, taking great care not to let any part of it touch the ground below. The rest of the team gathered on the steps behind the large flag, and Akmal took the photograph.

Looking across the faces of the men on the steps, the overwhelming sense of the moment could be seen easily. It left them silent for some time as they thought of what had gotten them to this point. Some smiled; some didn't; the moment meant something different to each one.

Although they were thousands of miles from home, in a country that had offered nothing but the images and sounds of war for months, they felt satisfied standing again on American soil.

And for that one moment, they were no longer soldiers or airmen; they were just Americans......

… and proud of it.

# The End

30236162R00140

Made in the USA
Columbia, SC
01 November 2018